TWENTIETH CENTURY VIEWS

The aim of this series is to present the best in
contemporary critical opinion on major
authors, providing a twentieth century
perspective on their changing status in an era
of profound revaluation.

Maynard Mack, *Series Editor*
Yale University

JOHN DONNE

A COLLECTION OF CRITICAL ESSAYS

Edited by
Helen Gardner

Prentice Hall  **International**

Englewood Cliffs, New Jersey   London   Mexico   New Delhi
Rio de Janeiro   Singapore   Sydney   Tokyo   Toronto   Wellington

Prentice-Hall Inc., *Englewood Cliffs, New Jersey*
Prentice-Hall International (UK) Ltd, *London*
Prentice-Hall of Australia Pty Ltd, *Sydney*
Prentice-Hall Canada Inc., *Toronto*
Prentice-Hall Hispanoamericana S.A., *Mexico*
Prentice-Hall of India Private Ltd, *New Delhi*
Prentice-Hall of Japan Inc., *Tokyo*
Prentice-Hall of Southeast Asia Pte Ltd, *Singapore*
Editora Prentice-Hall do Brasil Ltda, *Rio de Janeiro*
Whitehall Books Ltd, *Wellington, New Zealand*

Printed and bound in Great Britain for
Prentice-Hall International (UK) Ltd,
66 Wood Lane End, Hemel Hempstead,
Hertfordshire, HP2 4RG
at the University Press, Cambridge

2 3 4 5   90 89 88 87

0-13-218768-X

Table of Contents

Introduction

by Helen Gardner

The essays collected here cover the years from 1896 to 1960 and include the years *entre deux guerres* during which Donne enjoyed a higher reputation and a greater popularity than at any time since the thirty years following the first publication of his poems. An older reader of these essays, aware of this as a fact of his own experience, may well feel puzzled at the absence of any essay in which the case for regarding Donne as providing a "norm" of excellence in English poetry is argued. He will find a certain number of essays in which this point of view is being contested and he may well ask who were the writers and critics whose extravagant praise J. E. V. Crofts and C. S. Lewis are attempting to correct, and where, if not here, can he find essays which will sum up the intense enthusiasm for Donne's poetry which the young of both sexes felt in the Twenties and Thirties of this century. I must own that I have been surprised at the difficulty of finding any essay in which this view is argued at length, rather than taken for granted or opposed. I had not realized, until I came to make this collection, that I should find little beyond scattered sentences and odd paragraphs to support the statement that from 1921, the year of Mr. T. S. Eliot's review of Grierson's anthology of metaphysical poetry, to the middle Forties it was largely taken for granted among literary persons, by many university teachers, and, I should say, by the majority of undergraduates that Donne was a more interesting and significant poet than Milton, and that in him English poetry reached a kind of high-water mark. To print a volume of twentieth century essays on Donne in which this view is not fully represented seems like presenting *Hamlet* without the Prince of Denmark. I can only assure my readers that it is not the result of a deliberate policy of exclusion, but of my failure to discover a worthy written monument of what memory tells me was a pervasive "orthodox" view.[1]

It was held equally strongly that Donne's greatness was a discovery of the twentieth century after over two hundred years of neglect. Here again, although scholarship can correct the view that Donne was unread in the

[1] For an extended discussion of changes in the reputation of Donne see Joseph E. Duncan, *The Revival of Metaphysical Poetry* (University of Minnesota Press, 1959).

nineteenth century[2] and push the Donne revival back to Johnson, there
is a measure of general truth. When I sat for an Oxford scholarship in
1926 I was told that I had won it by my answers on Donne and Milton.
I reported this to my grandfather, a retired schoolmaster well-read in
poetry classical and English. He was delighted by my passion for Milton,
but hesitated when I mentioned Donne. Then, with an effort of memory,
he went to his shelves, picked out an obviously unread book and handed
it to me with the comment "Queer stuff. If you like it you had better have
this." It was Tonson's edition of 1719, my first "Donne item." I cannot
believe that a septuagenarian of similar education twenty years later
would have been so unaware of Donne's poetry, and would not have had
on his shelves either Grierson's one-volume edition of the poems or Mr.
John Hayward's immensely popular "Nonesuch" Donne. The evidence
for Donne's sudden rise to wide popularity in the twentieth century is the
same as the evidence for his popularity in the thirty years after his death:
the number of editions of his poems.

There is little to suggest that Donne's poetry was at all widely known
before 1620. The few references that have been found are to the Satires
and "The Storm" and "The Calm." A few of his lyrics came into the
hands of musicians and were set; but they were neither quoted from nor
imitated. The dedication to the "Metempsychosis," dated August 1601,
suggests that Donne was planning a long poem and intending to publish
it; but he stopped after one canto and changed his mind. His only other
attempt to win fame as a poet was with the two *Anniversaries,* published
in 1611 and 1612. Here again he abandoned his plan, which was for an
annual tribute. With his ordination in 1615 it was out of the question
for him to publish his verse and Jonson in 1619 told Drummond that
Donne "since he was made Doctor" repented highly and wished to destroy
his poems. It was too late. The existence of a large number of manuscript
copies, mainly dating from the 1620's, shows that by then Donne's poems
had reached a wider circle than the friends of his youth, and as soon as
the Dean of St. Paul's was dead his poems were got into print. They
appeared in 1633 with an impressive collection of funeral elegies ap-
pended. The most famous of these is that by Thomas Carew, the most
accomplished of the Caroline poets. He spoke for his generation when he
wrote Donne's "epitaph":

> Here lies a King, that rul'd as hee thought fit
> The universall Monarchy of wit.

It was the "wit" of Donne, not his music or his passion, or his dramatic
force, that the Caroline poets tried to emulate, and it was because of a
change in the notion of what "true wit" was that Donne sank in repute.

---

[2] See Kathleen Tillotson, "Donne's Poetry in the Nineteenth Century," *Elizabethan
and Jacobean Studies Presented to F. P. Wilson* (Oxford, 1959).

There were further editions of his poems in 1635, 1639, 1649, 1650, 1654 and 1669. After this there was only one edition in over a hundred years: Tonson's of 1719. In his *Essay of Dramatick Poesy* (1668) Dryden compared Donne favorably as a satirist with his disciple Cleveland, praising him for giving us "deep thoughts in common language," but adding the reservation "though rough cadence." By 1693, in the dedication to his translation of Juvenal, Dryden had become more severe. Donne is blamed for not having sufficient care of his diction as well as of his versification, and faulted for affecting the metaphysics "not only in his satires but in his amorous verses where nature only should reign." But in summing up Dryden once more pays tribute to Donne's intellectual vigor: "If we are not so great wits as Donne yet certainly we are better poets," echoing his tribute in the preface to *Eleonora* the year before where he spoke of Donne as "the greatest Wit, though not the best Poet of our nation." Pope's rewriting of Donne's *Satires* was the result of a similar distinction, between Donne's intellectual vigor which was to be admired and his "roughness" which was to be deplored, and this with Pope's remark to Spence that "Donne had no imagination, but as much wit, I think, as any writer can possibly have" shows Pope, like Dryden, with Donne's earlier admirers in finding his distinctive quality to be "wit," and with seventeenth century tradition in regarding Donne as primarily a satirist.[3]

More than the change in the conception of the proper language and true harmony of English verse led to the neglect of Donne in the eighteenth century. He lost his standing as a "great Wit" when wit was reduced, in Johnson's phrase, "from strength of thought to happiness of language." Johnson's disquisition on the "race of writers that may be termed the metaphysical poets" in his *Life of Cowley* (1781) was in large measure a protest against this tame conception of wit, embodied in Addison's famous essay and in Pope's often-quoted definition:

> True Wit is Nature to advantage dress'd,
> What oft was thought, but ne'er so well express'd.

By his copious quotations from Donne, and his declaration that to write in the metaphysical manner "it was at least necessary to read and think," Johnson brought back into literary discussion a body of poetry that had largely sunk into oblivion.[4] He brought it back as illustrative of a certain

---

[3] See W. Milgate, *Notes and Queries*, 27 May, 10 June, 8 July, 2 September 1950 for lists of early references to Donne's poetry, the great majority being to his Satires and Epistles.

[4] Boswell said that Johnson had exhibited the metaphysical poets "at large, with such happy illustration from their writings, and in so luminous a manner, that indeed he may be allowed the full merit of novelty, and to have discovered to us, as it were, a new planet in the poetical hemisphere."

kind of "wit": not his own "more noble and more adequate conception" of wit as that which is "at once natural and new," but wit "more rigorously and philosophically considered as a kind of *discordia concors:* a combination of dissimilar images, or discovery of occult resemblances in things apparently unlike." In singling out this kind of wit as the chief mark of metaphysical poetry and illustrating it so effectively from Donne, Johnson opened a way that criticism in the twentieth century was to take. It was to accept Johnson's definitions but dispute the qualifications with which he tempered his praise of these poets' originality. What he regarded as perverse was to be exalted as the sign of a true individuality; and the more heterogeneous the ideas that the metaphysicals "yoked by violence together," the more praise was thought due to them for their capacity to fuse disparate experiences into a unity. The Donne revival begins with Johnson.

All the same, admiration for Donne and the Metaphysicals was essentially an individual not a general preference for most of the nineteenth century. Coleridge, Lamb, De Quincey praise Donne justly; but Hazlitt condemning metaphysical poetry as "dry matter-of-fact, decked out in a robe of glittering conceits, and clogged with the halting shackles of verse" and Byron who, if the index to his *Letters and Journals* can be taken as proof, would seem not to have read Donne at all, are perhaps better guides to general opinion. The great Romantics, however, strike a new note in Donne criticism. Coleridge's precious notes are mainly on the "Songs and Sonnets": Lamb and Leigh Hunt valued the "warmth of soul and generous feeling" that shone through the "conceits" and the "bewildering maze of tropes," and both admired particularly the Elegy "On his Mistress," which Hazlitt describes Lamb reading "with suffused features and a faltering tongue." Donne the love poet and, though to a less degree, Donne the religious poet replace Donne the satirist, and strength of personal feeling rather than wit is the quality for which he is praised. Some argue that this feeling shines through and glows *in spite of* the conceits; others find the secret of his power in the blend of feeling and wit, in the "union of opposite qualities." [5] From the time of the Romantics onward Donne is primarily, as he is today, the poet of the "Songs and Sonnets" and the Divine Poems, and inevitably, as these were increasingly valued for their warmth of feeling, the attempt was made to relate the poetry to Donne's life and to look in it for personal revelations. In the last quarter of the nineteenth century the conception of Donne as a mysterious and enigmatic personality began to take shape. As early as 1880 he was compared to Hamlet, and Donne the melancholic, Donne the skeptic, Donne the bitter and sardonic amorist saved from the "queasie pain of being belov'd and loving" by his "pure" love for his wife, Donne the myriad-minded man, replaced the simple picture that Walton had

[5] Notably Coleridge and the writer of an article in *The Retrospective Review* (1823) discussed at length by Mrs. Tillotson.

drawn of Donne the "second Augustine." The interest in Donne that
had been growing through the century culminated in the Nineties with
the publication of the Grolier Club edition in America, edited by James
Russell Lowell and Charles Eliot Norton, the Muses' Library edition in
England, edited by E. K. Chambers, and Gosse's two volume *Life and
Letters of John Donne* (1899). This last stamped on the public imagination the picture of Donne the fascinating personality, the enigma and
the rebel. The poems as well as the letters were pressed into the service
of a book whose charm and grace of manner and deceptive air of learning
lightly carried gave it wide influence. To the romantic story of Donne's
wooing of Anne More, Gosse added a story of his "criminal liaison" with
a married woman in his youth, and started criticism on the hopeless quest
of deciding which of Donne's poems were written to his wife.[6]

George Saintsbury's essay, which opens the present collection, represents
the criticism and scholarship of the late nineteenth century at its best and
touches lightly on many of the topics that were to engage the critics of
the twentieth century. It is written out of a personal passion for Donne
and displays in a mild form the "emotionally possessive attitude to
Donne" that Mrs. Tillotson has noted in writers of our century. But
Saintsbury is cool enough to realize that Donne is possibly not everyone's
meat. Briefly, by an anecdote, he sets Donne in the European context of
the late Renaissance. He gets quickly out of the way the notion of Donne's
"roughness," by pointing out that it is confined to the Satires and is there
deliberately cultivated. Except for *The Second Anniversary,* his greatest
love, he unequivocally sets the lyrics above all Donne's other poems,
excerpts several "wondrous phrases" and short passages, makes a glancing
comparison with Baudelaire, thus hinting at Donne's "modernity," and
ends by exalting Donne for the "variety and rapid changes of his thought
and feeling," though denying him "the praise of the highest poetical art."
The psychological veracity of Donne's love poetry, his power to render
"the infinite of passion," and the striking brilliance of isolated lines make
Donne, if not "an accomplished poetical artist," an "inspired poetical
creator."

Saintsbury's essay was written in the old tradition of the man of letters
writing to an educated but not specialist public. It was among men of
letters rather than academics that Donne first became the rage. At Cambridge, before the first World War, he was passionately admired by Rupert
Brooke and his circle and Brooke's two brief essays on Donne, inspired
by Grierson's edition, anticipated, as Professor Duncan has pointed out,

[6] The desire to connect Donne's poems with the romantic story of his marriage goes
back to the seventeenth century, when the scribe of one manuscript headed Lamb's
favorite Elegy "His wife would have gone as his Page"; and Walton in the fourth
(1675) edition of his *Life of Donne* reported that "A Valediction: forbidding Mourning" was handed by Donne to his wife when he left her for the Continent in 1611.
Interestingly, Gosse rejects this, thinking the poem belongs to an earlier period of
Donne's life.

ideas to which Eliot was to give wide currency. Brooke declared that with
Donne, unlike other men, "when passion shook him . . . expression
came through intellect," noted his "lack of solemnity that does but
heighten the sharpness of the seriousness," and said that "it must not
appear that his humor, or his wit, and his passion alternated." Brooke's
friend, Geoffrey Keynes, later a distinguished surgeon, became Donne's
bibliographer and the most notable private collector of his works; and
another Cambridge man of letters, Desmond McCarthy, projected for
years a life of Donne which, alas, came to nothing.[7] The greatest of the
converts to Donne was Yeats to whom Grierson sent his edition.

Grierson's classic edition in 1912, the first edition of an English poet in
old spelling, with its long introduction and full commentary, gave to
Donne a standing with Shakespeare, Milton, Dryden, and Pope as a poet
to engage the full powers of scholarship. The most influential section of
the introduction, which is included in this volume, was that which attempted to disengage from Donne's love poems their author's "philosophy
of love." The conception of Donne as a pioneer in developing "a justification of love as a natural passion in the human heart the meaning and
end of which is marriage" and of doing justice "to love as a passion in
which body and soul have their part" was very largely accepted. In the
Twenties and Thirties Donne came to be thought of popularly as a kind
of early D. H. Lawrence, boldly adumbrating a modern sexual ethic.

As Grierson's edition inspired Rupert Brooke, so his delightful anthology *Metaphysical Poetry, Donne to Butler* (1921) provided the occasion
for Mr. T. S. Eliot's famous essay "The Metaphysical Poets." This is not
strictly an essay on Donne and since it is easily available I have not included it here. The seminal ideas put forward, in an attempt to define
metaphysical poetry, were that "a degree of heterogeneity of material
compelled into unity by the operation of the poet's mind is omnipresent
in poetry"; that the language of the metaphysical poets was "simple and
pure" but the *"structure"* of their sentences was not simple because of
their "fidelity to thought and feeling"; and, most important, the suggestion that instead of, with Johnson, defining the metaphysical poets by
their faults, we should consider "whether their virtue was not something
permanently valuable, which subsequently disappeared, but ought not
to have disappeared." This virtue was defined as "a direct sensuous
apprehension of thought, or recreation of thought into feeling," and
to illustrate the loss of this valuable quality a feeble passage from
Tennyson was set against some lines from Lord Herbert of Cherbury's
Ode. It was allowed that Tennyson and Browning both thought and felt;
but it was declared that they did not "feel their thought," whereas "a

---

[7] It is one of the curiosities of twentieth century scholarship that Gosse's *Life of
Donne* has not been replaced by a more accurate and critically balanced biography.
Even that famous series "The English Men of Letters" contains no life of Donne.

thought to Donne was an experience; it modified his sensibility." The theory was then put forward that during the seventeenth century "a dissociation of sensibility set in," aggravated by the influence of Milton and Dryden, language becoming more refined but feeling more crude. Finally it was suggested that our complex civilization demanded "difficult poetry," that modern French poetry was nearer to Donne than modern English poetry was, with the implicit corollary that the latter ought to be closer, and that poets should look not only into their hearts but into *"the cerebral cortex, the nervous system, and the digestive tract." In conclusion Donne and his followers were firmly placed "in the direct current of English poetry."

This essay with its "brief exposition of a theory" which its author characteristically described as "too brief, perhaps, to carry conviction" had an immense effect. By 1931, Mr. Eliot had himself largely withdrawn from his position and in an essay he contributed to *A Garland for John Donne,* which he has never thought worth reprinting,[8] he declared that in Donne there is "a manifest fissure between thought and sensibility" and that there is in his poetry "hardly any attempt at organization." These withdrawals were hardly noticed by the more enthusiastic applauders of the first essay[9] and much thought was given to, and much ink spilt on, the twin topics of how exactly thought was "sensuously apprehended" by Donne and what was meant by thought modifying his sensibility, and of what it was that "went wrong" with English culture and consequently English poetry in the mid-seventeenth century. Most of these essays make curious reading today and I have not found any that I thought would stand reprinting.[10]

[8] Mr. Eliot had delivered the Clark Lectures at Cambridge in 1926 on "The School of Donne." These were never printed, and in the 1931 essay he says that "by now (i.e., by 1931) the subject has been so fully treated that there appears to me no possible justification for turning my lectures into a book."

[9] Classic expressions of the uncritical acceptance of Eliot's suggestions are the opening paragraphs of two essays in *Scrutiny* by Dr. F. R. Leavis: "Milton's dislodgement, in the past decade, after his two centuries of predominance, was effected with remarkably little fuss. The irresistible argument was, of course, Mr. Eliot's creative achievement; it gave his few critical asides—potent, it is true, by context,—their finality, and made it unnecessary to elaborate a case" (September 1933); and "The work has been done, the re-orientation effected: the heresies of ten years ago are orthodoxy. Mr. Eliot's achievement is matter for academic evaluation, his poetry is accepted, and his early observations on the Metaphysicals and Marvell provide currency for university lectures and undergraduate exercises" (December 1935).

Similarly in the United States, John Crowe Ransom in *The World's Body* (New York, 1948) takes it for granted that Donne's lyrics provide a standard of excellence and measures Shakespeare's sonnets by them.

[10] I considered an essay from *Scrutiny* (1933) which was much praised in its day: James Smith, "On Metaphysical Poetry." Mr. Smith suggested that we should confine the term to poetry "to which the impulse is given by an overwhelming concern with meta-physical problems; with problems either deriving from or closely resembling in the nature of their difficulty the problem of the Many and the One." At first sight this

One element in Mr. Eliot's change of front was his reading of a brief but impressive work by Pierre Legouis, *Donne the Craftsman* (Paris, 1928). This long essay drew attention first to Donne's extreme originality as a metrist, and secondly to the pervasiveness of the dramatic element in his poetry. Unfortunately criticism fastened on Professor Legouis' interpretation of "The Ecstasy" as a dramatic poem, and the striking merit of his book was so obscured by the violence of the reaction to his treatment of this one poem that M. Legouis is often referred to only as the critic who thought "The Ecstasy" was a dramatization of a seduction. The importance of *Donne the Craftsman* was that it directed attention away from Donne's tortured soul, his philosophy of love, or the supposed biographical interest of his poetry to his art. By defining that art as akin to the art of the dramatist, it challenged the notion of Donne as writing directly out of passionate personal experience.

Another continental critic, Mario Praz, also let in a breath of air from a wider world by relating Donne's poetry to European poetry. His *Secentismo e Marinismo in Inghilterra* (Florence, 1925) provided a much needed corrective to the conception of Donne as a lone rebel against Elizabethan prettiness and as the inventor of the "metaphysical conceit." Grierson's pioneer commentary, though it paid some attention to classical sources, concentrated, on the whole, on exegesis of Donne's conceits and gave primacy to elucidating the ideas he took from ancient medicine, scholastic philosophy, and law. In an essay contributed to *A Garland for John Donne* (1931), reprinted in its revised form in this volume, Professor Praz displayed Donne against his European background. The years of the great Donne vogue were years in which the study of English literature in universities expanded and became increasingly isolated from the study of other literatures and increasingly taught by those who had themselves studied only English literature. Many of those who praised and analyzed Donne's ingenuity and originality did so in ignorance of European poetry, mediaeval and renaissance, as well as of classical poetry. One has at times the impression that the critic has read almost nothing but Donne.

The Donne vogue also corresponded with the rise of what is called

would seem to rule out Donne; but Mr. Smith takes Donne very seriously as "an independent thinker," setting him in this above Dante who only "took over" Aquinas. It is perhaps worth adding here that another of Mr. Eliot's less fortunate bequests to critical discussion was a stereotyped view of Dante.

Scrutiny will also provide examples of critics wrestling with why "sensibility" became "dissociated." See L. C. Knights, "The Social Background of Metaphysical Poetry" (1945) and H. Wendell Smith, "The Dissociation of Sensibility" (1951-2). A book devoted to the topic is S. L. Bethell, *The Cultural Revolution of the Seventeenth Century* (London, 1951). The treatments of this subject divide into two categories, the Marxist or semi-Marxist and the Anglo-Catholic. In both cases the writers are hunting in the past for an ideal culture by comparison with which the culture of today can be found wanting or in which it may find a model.

the "new criticism," and Donne, whose poetry invited and repaid close analysis was a favorite among the "new critics." The term is a loose one, but it may be taken generally to distinguish critics who attempt to discuss a poem as an object *per se*, without reference to its historical or literary context. This was in many ways a healthy movement, in spite of its aberrations. It replaced the habit of quoting isolated lines and phrases and generalizing about a body of poems by the habit of attending to a poem as a whole, to the "texture" of its language, the organization of its argument and the relation of its images to each other. Two of the essays in this book, William Empson's (1930) and Cleanth Brooks's (1948), display the new critical technique of linguistic analysis in the service, in each case, of a general theory of the nature of poetry. Both theories may be said to derive partly from, or at least be related to, Mr. Eliot's declaration that "heterogeneity of material is omnipresent in poetry." Professor Empson, who was highly successful in obeying Mr. Eliot's injunction to modern poets to be difficult, displays Donne as meaning more than one thing at once; Professor Brooks's theory that the language of poetry is the "language of paradox," is, if we give "paradox" a very extended meaning, a theory of the same kind. Both writers are trying to distinguish the language of poetry from the language of prose. The attempt to define poetry as a special form of language is obviously related to twentieth century developments in philosophy. To move from Grierson to Empson and Brooks is to become aware of a change in the intellectual climate in which literature is discussed.

As early as 1931 Mr. Eliot had much modified his enthusiasm for Donne, and toward the end of the decade two academic writers provided notable "cooling cards." Professor Crofts's essay is a return to the Saintsbury tradition of the general essay. With great liveliness and shrewdness he paints his portrait of Donne the self-dramatizer, the coxcomb and egoist, denying that he has any right to be considered as a "philosophic poet," and finding his "brain-sick fancies, twaddle upon twaddle" effective only in "giving us a sense of difficulty overcome when at last we arrive at "a passionate outcry." The famous "thought" becomes here a form of cats-cradling. Mr. C. S. Lewis, fresh from the great success of his *Allegory of Love*, attacked at the center by presenting Donne as the reactionary and Spenser as the true revolutionary in their attitudes to love, and rejecting the notion that Donne had anything of value to say on this topic. Mrs. Bennett took up this last challenge and restated with grace and moderation Grierson's distinction between poems that may be called "cynical" and poems that are "serious." [11]

Side by side with the conception of Donne as being peculiarly "modern"

[11] See Joan Bennett, "The Love Poetry of John Donne: A Reply to Mr. C. S. Lewis," *Seventeenth-Century Studies Presented to Sir Herbert Grierson* (Oxford, 1938), pp. 85-104. Reprinted in *Seventeenth-Century English Poetry: Modern Essays in Criticism,* William R. Keast, ed. (New York: Galaxy Books, 1962).

in his poetic technique and in his "philosophy of love" went the conception of "Donne the skeptic." Donne's obvious interest in science had engaged scholars, as had his interest in philosophic relativism.[12] In popular treatments Donne's scientific curiosity, his notable advice "Doubt wisely," and his summary statement "The new Philosophy calls all in doubt" were seized upon to create a powerfully attractive image of Donne as the spiritual brother of modern agnostics, driven by the intellectual conflicts of the seventeenth century as they were by those of the twentieth into a purely relativist position. As exemplar of the "Baroque doubt"[13] Donne exerted as great a fascination as he did as the prophet of sane sexual relations.

As early as 1934 in a learned and witty essay Merritt Y. Hughes had protested against "Kidnapping Donne." The strong reaction against the conception of Donne as a "modern" came in the Forties. Rosemond Tuve argued convincingly that whatever the differences between Elizabethan and metaphysical imagery they were as nothing to the differences between Renaissance theory and practice and modern.[14] In both England and the United States it was clear that Donne was ceasing to be an inspiration to the younger poets and the way was open for a cooler look at his achievement. Also the excesses of the "new criticism" had led to a vigorous revival of historical scholarship which was able to profit by the virtues of its opponents while avoiding their extreme subjectivity.

The very title of J. B. Leishman's book, *The Monarch of Wit* (1951) indicates its rejection of the notion of "Donne the modern." I have excerpted its first chapter which sets Donne in his English context. In the remainder of the book Mr. Leishman argues against the term "metaphysical" as applied to Donne and stresses instead the dialectical cast of his verse and the expression in it of a "personal drama." Mr. Leishman remained to a great extent in the Grierson tradition. He attempted to separate poems purely witty from the "serious" poems, and he felt the fascination of the personality revealed in Donne's works, concluding "Donne has often appeared to me a character whom Shakespeare might have invented." His book, which was widely welcomed and has just entered its fifth edition, is a notable attempt to define Donne's peculiar genius as a man and a poet by setting him among writers of his own age and by studying his work as a whole.

The benefits of reading Donne's poetry in the light of his prose were withheld from most readers by the inaccessibility of his prose works except in extracts. The noble edition of his *Sermons* undertaken by the University of California Press, under the editorship of an American and an English scholar, has removed this difficulty. Professor Potter's untimely

---

[12] See, particularly, L. I. Bredvold, *Studies in Shakespeare, Milton and Donne* (New York, 1925), and C. M. Coffin, *John Donne and the New Philosophy* (New York, 1937).
[13] See Kathleen Raine, "John Donne and the Baroque Doubt," *Horizon,* xi, 1945.
[14] See R. Tuve, *Elizabethan and Metaphysical Imagery* (Chicago, 1947).

death after the publication of two volumes and the completion of others left his co-editor Evelyn Simpson to finish the enterprise alone.[15] Her essay is the only extended attempt I know of to discuss Donne as an artist in prose. The publication of Donne's Sermons coincided with a growing admiration for his religious poetry. In 1931, in his essay in *A Garland for John Donne,* Mr. Eliot had spoken of "a new interest in devotional verse." This was an obvious result of the marked revival of belief in dogmatic Christianity among intellectuals in the Thirties and Forties. Although most of those who felt this "new interest" agreed with Mr. Eliot in setting Donne below Herbert as a religious poet, interest shifted somewhat from Donne the love poet to Donne the divine poet,[16] and studies of his life become increasingly interested in his religious position. It was quite independently, in the first place, that Professor Martz and I began to explore the relation of Donne's religious poetry to the current devotional practices of his age. In doing so we were following the trend shown in Mr. Leishman's book: attempting to read Donne in the light of a knowledge of his age's habits of thought, and to define his originality by a study of the traditions that he turned to his own purposes. This is the road that seems to me still to offer the best hope of arriving at the secret of his power.

The last essay included in this book is by a young scholar who has taken up the very fruitful topic, handled by Professor Praz and touched on by Mr. Leishman as well, of Donne's knowledge of and use of Italian literature. It represents a blending of the scholarly and the "new critical" approach. Mr. Smith carries much further than Mr. Leishman the idea of Donne as "Monarch of Wit" by refusing to allow to the poem he discusses any biographical interest or serious intellectual content. His treatment can be compared with Mrs. Bennett's discussion of the same poem in her essay referred to above, and with my own discussion of it in my book *The Business of Criticism* (1959), published while Mr. Smith's article was in press.[17]

I cannot go as far as Mr. Smith. Although to try to connect particular lyrics with particular ladies and write a *Vie Amoureuse de John Donne*

[15] Mrs. Simpson's pioneer study, *The Prose Works of John Donne,* first published in 1924, extensively revised in 1948; her work on the *Paradoxes and Problems;* and her editions of *The Courtier's Library, or Catalogus Librorum Aulicorum* (1930) and of *Essays in Divinity* (1951), along with the edition of the Sermons, represent the greatest single contribution to our knowledge of Donne made by any scholar since Grierson.

[16] In the essay printed in this book, C. S. Lewis speaks of Donne's "best work" as lying outside his love-poetry and refers to the "dazzling sublimity" of his best religious poems. Dr. H. W. Garrod showed himself as rather old-fashioned when in his selection from Donne in the Clarendon English Series he owned to thinking Donne's "divine poems not his divinest poems."

[17] Mr. Smith's earlier article on Donne and neo-Platonism, "The Metaphysic of Love." *Review of English Studies,* November 1958, appeared when my essay "The Argument about 'The Ecstasy'" in *Elizabethan and Jacobean Studies* (Oxford, 1959) had just gone to press. Here again we were drawing attention to the same sources for Donne's love-poetry but coming to rather different conclusions.

out of the Elegies and "Songs and Sonnets" seem to me to be to chase a
will-of-the-wisp, I cannot believe that Donne's poetry had no relation
to the development of his moral, intellectual, and emotional life, and
that his readers in our century were wholly astray in finding in his poetry
the revelation of a very powerful individuality. If ideas were mere
counters and playthings to him, why did he so persistently recur to certain ideas and not to others? We may laugh at Gosse's fiction of the
"criminal liaison" and point to Ovid as the source of the Elegies Gosse
read autobiographically; but can we doubt that the author of these
Elegies, if not a rake, had a rake's imagination? We may allow Mr. Smith
that the question handled in "Air and Angels" is a commonplace among
the Italian love-casuists; but why did such "questions of love" so engage
Donne's imagination and why did he alone among the poets of his
age give them such memorable expression? He was not the only Englishman of his day able to read Italian. The scholars and source-hunters
(of whom I am one) have still to explain why a whole generation in
this century appropriated Donne and found in lines and phrases from
his poems words that echoed the feelings of their own hearts. We still
await a life of Donne, written out of a full knowledge of his age, the
circumstances of his life, and his works as a whole. When that has been
written, it will be time for a full critical study that will display the works
as the expression of the man and do justice to him both as the "Monarch
of Wit" and as the author of those verses on parted lovers of which Walton
said: "I have heard some Criticks, learned, both in Languages and Poetry,
say, that none of the Greek or Latine Poets did ever equal them."

NOTE ON THE TEXTS: I have attempted, as far as possible, to standardize
methods of reference in the essays that follow, and, in the interests of
consistency have used modern spelling for the titles of poems throughout.
Unless it is otherwise stated in the first note, the essays are printed without alteration or omissions, except that spelling and punctuation have
been adapted to American usage.

John Donne

by George Saintsbury

There is hardly any, perhaps indeed there is not any, English author on whom it is so hard to keep the just mixture of personal appreciation and critical measure as it is on John Donne. It is almost necessary that those who do not like him should not like him at all; should be scarcely able to see how any decent and intelligent human creature can like him. It is almost as necessary that those who do like him should either like him so much as to speak unadvisedly with their lips, or else curb and restrain the expression of their love for fear that it should seem on that side idolatry. But these are not the only dangers. Donne is eminently of that kind which lends itself to sham liking, to coterie worship, to a false enthusiasm; and here is another weapon in the hands of the infidels, and another stumbling-block for the feet of the true believers. Yet there is always something stimulating in a subject of this kind, and a sort of temptation to attempt it. . . .

The circumstances of his life do not greatly concern us here; nor does that part—an eminent and admirable part—of his work which is not in verse. But it does concern us that there is a strange, though by no means unexampled, division between the two periods of his life and the two classes of his work. Roughly speaking, almost the whole of at least the secular verse belongs to the first division of the life, almost the whole of the prose to the second. Again, by far the greater part of the verse is animated by what may be called a spiritualized worldliness and sensuality, the whole of the prose by a spiritualism which has left worldliness far behind. The conjunction is, I say, not unknown: it was specially prevalent in the age of Donne's birth and early life. It has even passed into some-

"John Donne." Preface by George Saintsbury to *The Poems of John Donne*, edited by E. K. Chambers, 2 vols. (London, 1896). Reprinted in G. Saintsbury, *Prefaces and Essays* (London, 1933). Reprinted by permission of Routledge and Kegan Paul Ltd. [A summary account of Donne's life, now seriously out-of-date, has been omitted between the first and second paragraphs. Saintsbury's quotations are from Chambers' text (*The Muses' Library*) which followed the second edition of Donne's poems (1635) and modernized the spelling. They differ, therefore, from quotations in the majority of the essays that follow which are taken from Grierson's text (1912), based on the first edition (1633) and preserving its spelling. *Ed.*]

thing of a commonplace in reference to that Renaissance of which, as it slowly passed from south to north, Donne was one of the latest and yet one of the most perfect exponents. The strange story which Brantôme tells of Margaret of Navarre summoning a lover to the church under whose flags his mistress lay buried, and talking with him of her, shows, a generation before Donne's birth, the influence which in his day had made its way across the narrow seas as it had earlier across the Alps, and had at each crossing gathered gloom and force if it had lost lightness and color. Always in him are the two conflicting forces of intense enjoyment of the present, and intense feeling of the contrast of that present with the future. He has at once the transcendentalism which saves sensuality and the passion which saves mysticism. Indeed the two currents run so full and strong in him, they clash and churn their waves so boisterously, that this is of itself sufficient to account for the obscurity, the extravagance, the undue quaintness which have been charged against him. He was "of the first order of poets"; but he was not of the first among the first. Only Dante perhaps among these greatest of all had such a conflict and ebullition of feeling to express. For, as far as we can judge, in Shakespeare, even in the Sonnets, the poetical power mastered to some extent at the very first the rough material of the poetic instinct, and prepared before expression the things to be expressed. In Dante we can trace something of the presence of slag and dross in the ore; and even in Dante we can perhaps trace faintly also the difficulty of smelting it. Donne, being a lesser poet than Dante, shows it everywhere. It is seldom that even for a few lines, seldomer that for a few stanzas, the power of the furnace is equal to the volumes of ore and fuel that are thrust into it. But the fire is always there—overtasked, overmastered for a time, but never choked or extinguished; and ever and anon from gaps in the smouldering mass there breaks forth such a sudden flow of pure molten metal, such a flower of incandescence, as not even in the very greatest poets of all can be ever surpassed or often rivalled.

For critical, and indeed for general purposes, the poetical works of Donne may be divided into three parts, separated from each other by a considerable difference of character and, in one case at least, of time. These are the Satires, which are beyond all doubt very early; the Elegies and other amatory poems, most of which are certainly, and all probably, early likewise; and the Divine and Miscellaneous Poems, some of which may not be late, but most of which certainly are. All three divisions have certain characteristics in common; but the best of these characteristics, and some which are not common to the three, belong to the second and third only.

It was the opinion of the late seventeenth and of the whole of the eighteenth century that Donne, though a clever man, had no ear. Chalmers, a very industrious student, and not such a bad critic, says so in so many words; Johnson undoubtedly thought so; Pope demonstrated his belief by his fresh "tagging" of the Satires. They all to some extent no doubt really believed what they said; their ears had fallen deaf to that particular concord. But they all also no doubt founded their belief to a certain extent on certain words of Dryden's which did not exactly import or comport what Mr. Pope and the rest took them to mean. Dryden had the knack—a knack of great value to a critic, but sometimes productive of sore misguiding to a critic's readers—of adjusting his comments solely to one point of view, to a single scheme in metric and other things. Now, from the point of view of the scheme which both his authority and his example made popular, Donne *was* rather formless. But nearly all the eighteenth century critics and criticasters concentrated their attention on the Satires; and in the Satires Donne certainly takes singular liberties, no matter what scheme be preferred. It is now, I believe, pretty well admitted by all competent judges that the astonishing roughness of the Satirists of the late sixteenth century was not due to any general ignoring of the principles of melodious English verse, but to a deliberate intention arising from the same sort of imperfect erudition which had in other ways so much effect on the men of the Renaissance generally. Satiric verse among the ancients allowed itself, and even went out of its way to take, licenses which no poet in other styles would have dreamt of taking. The Horace of the impeccable odes writes such a hideous hexameter as

Non ego, namque parabilem amo Venerem facilemque,

and one of the Roman satirists who was then very popular, Persius, though he could rise to splendid style on occasion, is habitually as harsh, as obscure, and as wooden as a Latin poet well can be. It is not probable, it is certain, that Donne and the rest imitated these licenses of *malice prepense.*

But it must be remembered that at the time when they assumed this greater license, the normal structure of English verse was anything but fixed. Horace had in his contemporaries, Persius and Juvenal had still more in their forerunners, examples of versification than which Mr. Pope himself could do nothing more "correct"; and their licenses could therefore be kept within measure, and still be licentious enough to suit any preconceived idea of the ungirt character of the Satiric muse. In Donne's time the very precisians took a good deal of license: the very Virgils and even Ovids were not apt to concern themselves very greatly about a short vowel before *s* with a consonant, or a trisyllable at the end of a pentameter. If therefore you meant to show that you were *sans gêne,* you had to make demonstrations of the most unequivocal character. Even with all this explanation and allowance it may still seem probable that Donne's Satires never received any formal preparation for the press, and are in the state of rough copy. Without this allowance, which the eighteenth cen-

tury either did not care or did not know how to give, it is not surprising
that they should have seemed mere monstrosities.

The satiric pieces in which these pecularities are chiefly shown, which
attracted the attention of Pope, and which, through his recension, became known to a much larger number of persons than the work of any
other Elizabethan satirist, have the least share of Donne's poetical interest. But they display to the full his manly strength and shrewd sense,
and they are especially noticeable in one point. They exhibit much less
of that extravagant exaggeration of contemporary vice and folly which
makes one of their chief contemporaries, Marston's *Scourge of Villainy*,
almost an absurd thing, while it is by no means absent from Hall's
Virgidemiarum. We cannot indeed suppose that Donne's satire was
wholly and entirely sincere, but a good deal in it clearly was. Thus his
handling of the perennial subjects of satire is far more fresh, serious, and
direct than is usual with satirists, and it was no doubt this judicious and
direct quality which commended it to Pope. Moreover, these poems
abound in fine touches. The Captain in the first Satire,

> Bright parcel-gilt with forty dead men's pay,

the ingenious evildoers in the second,

> for whose sinful sake
> Schoolmen new tenements in hell must make,

the charming touch at once so literary and so natural in the fifth,

> so controverted lands
> 'Scape, like Angelica, the striver's hands,

are only a few of the jewels five words long that might be produced as
specimens. But it is not here that we find the true Donne: it was not
this province of the universal monarchy of wit that he ruled with the
most unshackled sway. The provinces that he did so rule were quite
other: strange frontier regions, uttermost isles where sensuality, philosophy, and devotion meet, or where separately dwelling they rejoice or
mourn over the conquests of each other. I am not so sure of the *Progress
of the Soul* as some writers have been—interesting as it is, and curious as
is the comparison with Prior's *Alma,* which it of necessity suggests, and
probably suggested. As a whole it seems to me uncertain in aim, un-
accomplished in execution. But what things there are in it! What a line is

> Great Destiny, the Commissary of God!

What a lift and sweep in the fifth stanza

> To my six lustres almost now outwore!

What a thought, that

> This soul, to whom Luther and Mahomet were
> Prisons of flesh!

And the same miraculous pregnancy of thought and expression runs through the whole, even though it seems never to have found full and complete delivery in artistic form. How far this curious piece is connected with the still more famous *Anniversaries,* in which so different a stage of "progress" is reached, and which ostensibly connect themselves with the life and death of Mrs. Elizabeth Drury, is a question which it would be tedious to argue out in any case, and impossible to argue out here. But the successive stages of "The Anatomy of the World" present us with the most marvellous poetical exposition of a certain kind of devotional thought yet given. It is indeed possible that the union of the sensual, intellectual, poetical, and religious temperaments is not so very rare; but it is very rarely voiceful. That it existed in Donne preeminently, and that it found voice in him as it never has done before or since, no one who knows his life and works can doubt. That the greatest of this singular group of poems is *The Second Anniversary,* will hardly, I think, be contested. Here is the famous passage

> Her pure and eloquent blood
> Spoke in her cheeks and so distinctly wrought,
> That one might almost say her body thought,

which has been constantly quoted, praised, and imitated. Here, earlier, is what I should choose if I undertook the perilous task of singling out the finest line in English sacred poetry

> so long
> As till God's great *Venite* change the song—

a *Dies Irae* and a *Venite* itself combined in ten English syllables.

Here is that most vivid and original of Donne's many prose and verse meditations on death, as

> A groom
> That brings a taper to the outward room.

Here too is the singular undernote of "she" repeated constantly in different places of the verse, with the effect of a sort of musical accompaniment or refrain, which Dryden (a great student of Donne) afterwards imitated on the note "you" in *Astraea Redux,* and the *Coronation.* But these, and many other separate verbal or musical beauties, perhaps yield to the wonder of the strange, dreamy atmosphere of moonlight thought and feeling which is shed over the whole piece. Nowhere is Donne, one of the most full-blooded and yet one of the least earthly of English poets, quite so unearthly.

The Elegies, perhaps better known than any [other] of his poems, contain the least of this unearthliness. The famous "Refusal to allow his young wife to accompany him as his page," though a very charming poem, is, I think, one of the few pieces of his which have been praised enough, if not even a little overpraised. As a matter of taste it seems to me indeed more open to exception than the equally famous and much "fiefied" "To his mistress going to bed," a piece of frank naturalism redeemed from coarseness by passion and poetic completeness. The Elegies again are the most varied of the divisions of Donne's works, and contain next to the Satires his liveliest touches, such as

> The grim, eight-foot-high, iron-bound, serving-man,
> That oft names God in oaths, and only than [i.e., then]

or as the stroke

> Lank as an unthrift's purse.

In Epithalamia Donne was good, but not consummate, falling far short of his master, Spenser, in this branch. No part of his work was more famous in his own day than his Epistles which are headed by the "Storm" and "Calm," that so did please Ben Jonson. But in these and other pieces of the same division, the misplaced ingenuity which is the staple of the general indictment against Donne, appears, to my taste, less excusably than anywhere else. Great passion of love, of grief, of philosophic meditation, of religious awe, had the power to master the fantastic hippogriff of Donne's imagination, and make it wholly serviceable; but in his less intense works it was rather unmanageable. Yet there are very fine things here also; especially in the Epistle to Sir Henry Goodyere, and those to Lucy, Countess of Bedford, and Elizabeth, Countess of Huntingdon. The best of the Funeral Elegies are those of Mrs. Boulstred. In the Divine Poems there is nothing so really divine as the astonishing verse from *The Second Anniversary* quoted above. It must always however seem odd that such a poet as Donne should have taken the trouble to tag the Lamentations of Jeremiah into verse, which is sometimes much more lamentable in form than even in matter. The epigram as to Le Franc de Pompignan's

French version, and its connection, by dint of Jeremiah's prophetic power, with the fact of his having lamented, might almost, if any Englishman had had the wit to think of it, have been applied a century earlier to parts of this of Donne. The "Litany" is far better, though it naturally suggests Herrick's masterpiece in divine song-writing; and even the "Jeremiah" ought not perhaps to be indiscriminately disapproved. The opening stanzas especially have a fine melancholy clang not unknown, I think, as a model to Mr. Swinburne.

But to my fancy no division of Donne's poems—*The Second Anniversary* always excepted—shows him in his quiddity and essence as do the lyrics. Some of these are to a certain extent doubtful. One of the very finest of the whole, "Absence, hear thou my protestation," with its unapproached fourth stanza, appeared first in Davison's *Poetical Rhapsody* unsigned. But all the best authorities agree (and for my part I would almost go to the stake on it) that the piece is Donne's. In those which are undoubtedly genuine the peculiar quality of Donne flames through and perfumes the dusky air which is his native atmosphere in a way which, though I do not suppose that the French poet had ever heard of Donne, has always seemed to me the true antitype and fulfilment by anticipation of Baudelaire's

> Encensoir oublié qui fume
> En silence à travers la nuit.

Everybody knows the

> Bracelet of bright hair about the bone

of the late discovered skeleton, identifying the lover: everybody the perfect fancy and phrase of the exordium

> I long to talk with some old lover's ghost,
> Who died before the god of Love was born.

But similar touches are almost everywhere. The enshrining once for all in the simplest words of a universal thought

> I wonder by my troth what thou and I
> Did till we loved?

The selection of single adjectives to do the duty of a whole train of surplusage

> Where can we find two better hemispheres
> Without *sharp* north, without *declining* west?

meet us, and tell us what we have to expect in all but the earliest. In comparison with these things, such a poem as "Go and catch a falling star," delightful as it is, is perhaps only a delightful quaintness, and "The Indifferent" only a pleasant quip consummately turned. In these perversities Donne is but playing *tours de force*. His natural and genuine work reappears in such poems as "Canonization," or as "The Legacy." It is the fashion sometimes, and that not always with the worst critics, to dismiss this kind of heroic rapture as an agreeable but conscious exaggeration, partly betrayed and partly condoned by flouting-pieces like those just mentioned. The gloss does not do the critic's knowledge of human nature or his honesty in acknowledging his knowledge much credit. Both moods and both expressions are true; but the rapture is the truer. No one who sees in these mere literary or fashionable exercises, can ever appreciate such an *aubade* as "Stay, O Sweet, and do not rise," or such a midnight piece as "The Dream," with its never-to-be-forgotten couplet

> I must confess, it could not choose but be
> Profane to think thee anything but thee.

If there is less quintessence in "The Message," for all its beauty, it is only because no one can stay long at the point of rapture which characterizes Donne at his most characteristic, and the relaxation is natural —as natural as is the pretty fancy about St. Lucy

> Who but seven hours herself unmasks,

the day under her invocation being in the depths of December. But the passionate mood, or that of mystical reflection, soon returns, and in the one Donne shall sing with another of the wondrous phrases where simplicity and perfection meet

> So to engraft our hands as yet
>   Was all our means to make us one,
> And pictures in our eyes to get
>   Was all our propagation.

Or in the other dwell on the hope of buried lovers

> To make their souls at the last busy day,
> Meet at this grave, and make a little stay.

I am not without some apprehension that I shall be judged to have fallen a victim to my own distinction, drawn at the beginning of this paper, and shown myself an unreasonable lover of this astonishing poet. Yet I think I could make good my appeal in any competent critical court. For in Donne's case the yea-nay fashion of censorship which is necessary and desirable in the case of others is quite superfluous. His faults are so gross, so open, so palpable, that they hardly require the usual amount of critical comment and condemnation. But this very peculiarity of theirs constantly obscures his beauties even to not unfit readers. They open him; they are shocked, or bored, or irritated, or puzzled by his occasional nastiness (for he is now and then simply and inexcusably nasty), his frequent involution and eccentricity, his not quite rare indulgence in extravagances which go near to silliness; and so they lose the extraordinary beauties which lie beyond or among these faults. It is true that, as was said above, there are those, and many of them, who can never and will never like Donne. No one who thinks *Don Quixote* a merely funny book, no one who sees in Aristophanes a dirty-minded fellow with a knack of Greek versification, no one who thinks it impossible not to wish that Shakespeare had not written the Sonnets, no one who wonders what on earth Giordano Bruno meant by *Gli eroici Furori,* need trouble himself even to attempt to like Donne. "He will never *have done* with that attempt," as our Dean himself would have unblushingly observed, for he was never weary of punning on his name.

But for those who have experienced, or who at least understand, the ups-and-downs, the ins-and-outs of human temperament, the alternations not merely of passion and satiety, but of passion and laughter, of passion and melancholy reflection, of passion earthly enough and spiritual rapture almost heavenly, there is no poet and hardly any writer like Donne. They may even be tempted to see in the strangely mixed and flawed character of his style, an index and reflection of the variety and the rapid changes of his thought and feeling. To the praise of the highest poetical art he cannot indeed lay claim. He is of course entitled to the benefit of the pleas that it is uncertain whether he ever prepared definitely for the press a single poetical work of his; that it is certain that his age regarded his youth with too much disapproval to bestow any critical care on his youthful poems. But it may be retorted that no one with the finest sense of poetry as an art, could have left things so formless as he has left, that it would have been intolerable pain and grief to any such till he had got them, even in MS., into shape. The retort is valid. But if Donne cannot receive the praise due to the accomplished poetical artist, he has that not perhaps higher but certainly rarer, of the inspired poetical creator. No study could have bettered—I hardly know whether any study could have produced—such touches as the best of those which have been quoted, and as many which perforce have been left out. And no study could have given him the idiosyncrasy which he has. *"Nos passions,"* says

Bossuet, *"ont quelque chose d'infini."* To express infinity no doubt is a contradiction in terms. But no poet has gone nearer to the hinting and adumbration of this infinite quality of passion, and of the relapses and reactions from passion, than the author of *The Second Anniversary* and "The Dream," of "The Relic" and "The Ecstasy."

Donne's Love-Poetry

by Herbert J. C. Grierson

* * *

Donne's love-poetry is a very complex phenomenon. The two dominant strains in it are these: the strain of dialectic, subtle play of argument and wit, erudite and fantastic; and the strain of vivid realism, the record of a passion which is not ideal nor conventional, neither recollected in tranquillity nor a pure product of literary fashion, but love as an actual, immediate experience in all its moods, gay and angry, scornful and rapturous with joy, touched with tenderness and darkened with sorrow—though these last two moods, the commonest in love-poetry, are with Donne the rarest. The first of these strains comes to Donne from the Middle Ages, the dialectic of the Schools, which passed into mediaeval love-poetry almost from its inception; the second is the expression of the new temper of the Renaissance as Donne had assimilated it in Latin countries. Donne uses the method, the dialectic of the mediaeval love-poets, the poets of the *dolce stil nuovo,* Guinicelli, Cavalcanti, Dante, and their successors, the intellectual, argumentative evolution of their *canzoni,* but he uses it to express a temper of mind and a conception of love which are at the opposite pole from their lofty idealism. The result, however, is not so entirely disintegrating as Mr. Courthope seems to think: "This fine Platonic edifice is ruthlessly demolished in the poetry of Donne. To him love, in its infinite variety and inconsistency, represented the principle of perpetual flux in nature." [1] The truth is rather that, owing to the fullness of Donne's experience as a lover, the accident that made of the earlier libertine a devoted lover and husband, and from the play of his restless and subtle mind on the phenomenon of love conceived and realized in this less ideal fashion, there emerged in his poetry the suggestion of a new philosophy of love which, if less transcendental than

"Donne's Love-Poetry." From an Introductory Essay on "The Poetry of Donne" in *The Poems of John Donne,* edited by Herbert J. C. Grierson, 2 vols. (London, 1912) , vol. ii, pp. xxxiv-xlix. Reprinted by permission of The Clarendon Press.

[1] *History of English Poetry* (London, 1903), iii. 54. Mr. Courthope qualifies this statement somewhat on the next page: "From this spirit of cynical lawlessness he was perhaps reclaimed by genuine love," and so on. But he has, I think, insufficiently analyzed the diverse strains in Donne's love-poetry.

that of Dante, rests on a juster, because a less dualistic and ascetic, conception of the nature of the love of man and woman.

The fundamental weakness of the mediaeval doctrine of love, despite
its refining influence and its exaltation of woman, was that it proved
unable to justify love ethically against the claims of the counter-ideal
of asceticism. Taking its rise in a relationship which excluded the thought
of marriage as the end and justification of love, which presumed in theory
that the relation of the "servant" to his lady must always be one of
reverent and unrewarded service, this poetry found itself involved from
the beginning in a dualism from which there was no escape. On the one
hand the love of woman is the great ennobler of the human heart, the
influence which elicits its latent virtue as the sun converts clay to gold
and precious stones. On the other hand, love is a passion which in the
end is to be repented of in sackcloth and ashes. Lancelot is the knight
whom love has made perfect in all the virtues of manhood and chivalry;
but the vision of the Holy Grail is not for him, but for the virgin and
stainless Sir Galahad.

In the high philosophy of the Tuscan poets of the "sweet new style"
that dualism was apparently transcended, but it was by making love
identical with religion, by emptying it of earthly passion, making woman
an Angel, a pure Intelligence, love of whom is the first awakening of the
love of God. "For Dante and the poets of the learned school love and
virtue were one and the same thing; love *was* religion, the lady beloved
the way to heaven, symbol of philosophy and finally of theology." [2]
The culminating moment in Dante's love for Beatrice arrives when he
has overcome even the desire that she should return his salutation and
he finds his full beatitude in "those words that do praise my lady." The
love that begins in the *Vita Nuova* is completed in the *Paradiso*.

The dualism thus in appearance transcended by Dante reappears
sharply and distinctly in Petrarch. "Petrarch," says Gaspary, "adores not
the idea but the person of his lady; he feels that in his affections there is
an earthly element, he cannot separate it from the desire of the senses;
this is the earthly tegument which draws us down. If not as, according to
the ascetic doctrine, sin, if he could not be ashamed of his passion, yet he
could repent of it as a vain and frivolous thing, regret his wasted hopes
and griefs." [3] Laura is for Petrarch the flower of all perfection herself and
the source of every virtue in her lover. Yet his love for Laura is a long
and weary aberration of the soul from her true goal, which is the love
of God. This is the contradiction from which flow some of the most

---

[2] Gaspary: *History of Italian Literature* (Oelsner's translation) (London, 1904). Con-
sult also Karl Vossler: *Die philosophischen Grundlagen des "süssen neuen Stils"*
(Heidelberg, 1904), and *La Poesia giovanile &c. di Guido Cavalcanti: Studi di Giulio
Salvadori* (Rome, 1895).

[3] Gaspary, *op. cit.*

lyrical strains in Petrarch's poetry, as the fine canzone "I'vo pensando," where he cries:

> E sento ad ora ad or venirmi in core
> Un leggiadro disdegno, aspro e severo,
> Ch'ogni occulto pensero
> Tira in mezzo la fronte, ov' altri'l vede;
> Che mortal cosa amar con tanta fede,
> Quanta a Dio sol per debito convensi,
> Più si disdice a chi più pregio brama.

Elizabethan love-poetry is descended from Petrarch by way of Cardinal Bembo and the French poets of the *Pléiade,* notably Ronsard and Desportes. Of all the Elizabethan sonneteers the most finely Petrarchan are Sidney and Spenser, especially the former. For Sidney, Stella is the school of virtue and nobility. He too writes at times in the impatient strain of Petrarch:

> But ah! Desire still cries, give me some food.

And in the end both Sidney and Spenser turn from earthly to heavenly love:

> Leave me, O love, which reachest but to dust,
> And thou, my mind, aspire to higher things:
> Grow rich in that which never taketh rust,
> Whatever fades but fading pleasure brings.

And so Spenser:

> Many lewd lays (Ah! woe is me the more)
> In praise of that mad fit, which fools call love,
> I have in the heat of youth made heretofore;
> That in light wits affection loose did move,
> But all these follies now I do reprove.

But two things had come over this idealist and courtly love-poetry by the end of the sixteenth century. It had become a literary artifice, a refining upon outworn and extravagant conceits, losing itself at times in the fantastic and absurd. A more important fact was that this poetry had begun to absorb a new warmth and spirit, not from Petrarch and mediaeval chivalry, but from classical love-poetry with its simpler, less metaphysical strain, its equally intense but more realistic description of passion, its radically different conception of the relation between the lovers and of the influence of love in a man's life. The courtly, idealistic strain was crossed by an Epicurean and sensuous one that tends to treat with scorn the worship of woman, and echoes again and again the Pagan cry, never heard in Dante or Petrarch, of the fleetingness of beauty and love:

> Vivamus, mea Lesbia, atque amemus!
> Soles occidere et redire possunt:
> Nobis quum semel occidit brevis lux
> Nox est perpetua una dormienda.

> Vivez si m'en croyez, n'attendez à demain;
> Cueillez dès aujourd'hui les roses de la vie.

> Since brass, nor stone, nor earth, nor boundless sea,
> But sad mortality o'er-sways their power,
> How with this rage shall beauty hold a plea
> Whose action is no stronger than a flower?

Now if we turn from Elizabethan love-poetry to the "Songs and Sonnets" and the Elegies of Donne, we find at once two distinguishing features. In the first place his poetry is in one respect less classical than theirs. There is far less in it of the superficial evidence of classical learning with which the poetry of the "University Wits" abounds, pastoral and mythological imagery. The texture of his poetry is more mediaeval than theirs in as far as it is more dialectical, though a dialectical evolution is not infrequent in the Elizabethan sonnet, and the imagery is less picturesque, more scientific, philosophic, realistic, and homely. The place of the

> goodly exiled train
> Of gods and goddesses

is taken by images drawn from all the sciences of the day, from the definitions and distinctions of the Schoolmen, from the travels and speculations of the new age, and (as in Shakespeare's tragedies or Browning's poems) from the experiences of everyday life. Maps and sea discoveries, latitude and longitude, the phoenix and the mandrake's root, the Scholastic theories of Angelic bodies and Angelic knowledge, Alchemy and Astrology, legal contracts and *non obstantes,* "late schoolboys and sour prentices," "the King's real and his stamped face"—these are the kind of images, erudite, fanciful, and homely, which give to Donne's poems a texture so different at a first glance from the florid and diffuse Elizabethan poetry, whether romantic epic, mythological idyll, sonnet, or song; while by their presence and their abundance they distinguish it equally (as Mr. Gosse has justly insisted) from the studiously moderate and plain style of "well-languaged Daniel."

But if the imagery of Donne's poetry be less classical than that of Marlowe or the younger Shakespeare there is no poet the spirit of whose love-poetry is so classical, so penetrated with the sensual, realistic, scornful tone of the Latin lyric and elegiac poets. If one reads rapidly through the three books of Ovid's *Amores,* and then in the same continuous rapid fashion the Songs and the Elegies of Donne, one will note striking differences of style and treatment. Ovid develops his theme simply and concretely, Donne dialectically and abstractly. There is little of the ease and grace of Ovid's verses in the rough and vehement lines of Donne's Elegies. Compare the song,

> Busie old foole, unruly Sunne,

with the famous thirteenth Elegy of the first book,

> Iam super oceanum venit a seniore marito,
> Flava pruinoso quae vehit axe diem.

Ovid passes from one natural and simple thought to another, from one aspect of dawn to another equally objective. Donne just touches one or two of the same features, borrowing them doubtless from Ovid, but the greater part of the song is devoted to the subtle and extravagant if you like, but not the less passionate development of the thought that for him the woman he loves is the whole world.

But if the difference between Donne's metaphysical conceits and Ovid's naturalness and simplicity is palpable it is not less clear that the emotions which they express, with some important exceptions to which I shall recur, are identical. The love which is the main burden of their song is something very different from the ideal passion of Dante or of Petrarch, of Sidney or Spenser. It is a more sensual passion. The same tone of witty depravity runs through the work of the two poets. There is in Donne a purer strain which, we shall see directly, is of the greatest importance, but such a rapid reader as I am contemplating might be forgiven if for the moment he overlooked it, and declared that the modern poet was as sensual and depraved as the ancient, that there was little to choose between the social morality reflected in the Elizabethan and in the Augustan poet.

And yet even in these more cynical and sensual poems a careful reader will soon detect a difference between Donne and Ovid. He will begin to suspect that the English poet is imitating the Roman, and that the depravity is in part a reflected depravity. In revolt from one convention the young poet is cultivating another, a cynicism and sensuality which is just as little to be taken *au pied de la lettre* as the idealizing worship, the anguish and adoration of the sonneteers. There is, as has been said already, a gaiety in the poems elaborating the thesis that love is a perpetual flux, fickleness the law of its being, which warns us against taking them too seriously; and even those Elegies which seem to our taste most reprehensible are aerated by a wit which makes us almost forget their indecency. In the last resort there is all the difference in the world between the untroubled, heartless sensuality of the Roman poet and the gay wit, the paradoxical and passionate audacities and sensualities of the young Elizabethan law-student impatient of an unreal convention, and eager to startle and delight his fellow students by the fertility and audacity of his wit.

It is not of course my intention to represent Donne's love-poetry as purely an "evaporation" of wit, to suggest that there is in it no reflection either of his own life as a young man or the moral atmosphere of Elizabethan London. It would be a much less interesting poetry if this were so. Donne has pleaded guilty to a careless and passionate youth:

> In mine Idolatry what showres of raine
> Mine eyes did waste? what griefs my heart did rent?
> That sufferance was my sinne; now I repent;
> Cause I did suffer I must suffer pain.

From what we know of the lives of Essex, Raleigh, Southampton, Pembroke, and others it is probable that Donne's Elegies come quite as close to the truth of life as Sidney's Petrarchanism or Spenser's Platonism. The later cantos of *The Faerie Queene* reflect vividly the unchaste loves and troubled friendships of Elizabeth's Court. Whether we can accept in its entirety the history of Donne's early amours which Mr. Gosse has gathered from the poems or not, there can be no doubt that actual experiences do lie behind these poems as behind Shakespeare's sonnets. In the one case as in the other, to recognize a literary model is not to exclude the probability of a source in actual experience.

But however we may explain or palliate the tone of these poems it is impossible to deny their power, the vivid and packed force with which they portray a variously mooded passion working through a swift and subtle brain. If there is little of the elegant and accomplished art which Milton admired in the Latin Elegists while he "deplored" their immorality, there is more strength and sincerity both of thought and imagination. The brutal cynicism of

> Fond woman which would have thy husband die,

the witty anger of "The Apparition," the mordant and paradoxical wit of "The Perfume" and "The Bracelet," the passionate dignity and strength of "His Picture,"

> My body a sack of bones broken within,
> And powders blew stains scatter'd on my skin,

the passion that rises superior to sensuality and wit, and takes wing into a more spiritual and ideal atmosphere, of "His parting from her,"

> I will not look upon the quick'ning Sun,
> But straight her beauty to my sense shall run;
> The ayre shall note her soft, the fire most pure;
> Water suggest her clear, and the earth sure—

compare these with Ovid and the difference is apparent between an artistic, witty voluptuary and a poet whose passionate force redeems many errors of taste and art. Compare them with the sonnets and mythological idylls and "Heroicall Epistles" of the Elizabethans and it is they, not Donne, who are revealed as witty and "fantastic" poets content to adorn a conventional sentiment with mythological fancies and verbal conceits. Donne's interest is his theme, love and woman, and he uses words not for their own sake but to communicate his consciousness of these surprising phenomena in all their varying and conflicting aspects. The only contemporary poems that have the same dramatic quality are Shakespeare's sonnets and some of Drayton's later sonnets. In Shakespeare this dramatic intensity and variety is of course united with a rarer poetic charm. Charm is a quality which Donne's poetry possesses in a few single lines. But to the passion which animates these sensual, witty, troubled poems the closest parallel is to be sought in Shakespeare's sonnets to a dark lady and in some of the verses written by Catullus to or of Lesbia:

> The expense of spirit in a waste of shame.

But neither sensual passion, nor gay and cynical wit, nor scorn and anger, is the dominant note in Donne's love-poetry. Of the last quality there is, despite the sardonic emphasis of some of the poems, less than in either Shakespeare or Catullus. There is nothing in his poetry which speaks so poignantly of an outraged heart, a love lavished upon one who was worthless, as some of Shakespeare's sonnets and of Catullus' poems. The finest note in Donne's love-poetry is the note of joy, the joy of mutual and contented passion. His heart might be subtle to plague itself; its capacity for joy is even more obvious. Other poets have done many things which Donne could not do. They have invested their feelings with a garb of richer and sweeter poetry. They have felt more deeply and finely the reverence which is in the heart of love. But it is only in the fragments of Sappho, the lyrics of Catullus, and the songs of Burns that one will find the sheer joy of loving and being loved expressed in the

same direct and simple language as in some of Donne's songs, only in
Browning that one will find the same simplicity of feeling combined with
a like swift and subtle dialectic.

> I wonder by my troth what thou and I
> Did till we loved.

> For Godsake hold your tongue and let me love.

> If yet I have not all thy love,
> Deare, I shall never have it all.

Lines like these have the same direct, passionate quality as

> Φαίνεταί μοι κῆνος ἴσος θέοισιν
> ἔμμεν ὤνηρ

> [Like to the heavenly Gods to my sight seems
> That man. . . .]

or

> O my love's like a red, red rose
> That's newly sprung in June.

The joy is as intense though it is of a more spiritual and intellectual
quality. And in the other notes of this simple passionate love-poetry,
sorrow which is the shadow of joy, and tenderness, Donne does not fall
far short of Burns in intensity of feeling and directness of expression.
These notes are not so often heard in Donne, but

> So, so break off this last lamenting kiss

is of the same quality as

> Had we never lov'd sae kindly

or

> Take, O take those lips away.

And strangest of all perhaps is the tenderness which came into Donne's
poetry when a sincere passion quickened in his heart, for tenderness, the
note of

O wert thou in the cauld blast,

is the last quality one would look for in the poetry of a nature at once so intellectual and with such a capacity for caustic satire. But the beautiful if not flawless "Elegy XVI,"

By our first strange and fatal interview,

and the Valedictions which he wrote on different occasions of parting from his wife, combine with the peculiar *élan* of all Donne's passionate poetry and its intellectual content a tenderness as perfect as anything in Burns or in Browning:

> O more than Moone,
> Draw not up seas to drowne me in thy spheare,
> Weepe me not dead in thine armes, but forbeare
> To teach the sea, what it may doe too soone.

> Let not thy divining heart
> Forethink me any ill,
> Destiny may take thy part
> And may thy feares fulfill;
> But thinke that we
> Are but turn'd aside to sleep;
> They who one another keepe
> Alive, ne'er parted be.

> Such wilt thou be to mee, who must
> Like th'other foot, obliquely runne;
> Thy firmnes makes my circle just,
> And makes me end, where I begunne.

The poet who wrote such verses as these did not believe any longer that "love . . . represents the principle of perpetual flux in nature."

But Donne's poetry is not so simple a thing of the heart and of the senses as that of Burns and Catullus. Even his purer poetry has more complex moods—consider "The Prohibition"—and it is metaphysical, not only in the sense of being erudite and witty, but in the proper sense of being reflective and philosophical. Donne is always conscious of the import of his moods; and so it is that there emerges from his poems a philosophy or a suggested philosophy of love to take the place of the idealism which he rejects. Set a song of the joy of love by Burns or by Catullus such as I have cited beside Donne's "Anniversary,"

> All Kings, and all their favorites,
> All glory of honors, beauties, wits,
> The Sun itselfe, which makes times, as they passe,
> Is elder by a year, now, than it was
> When thou and I first one another saw,

and the difference is at once apparent. Burns gets no further than the experience, Catullus than the obvious and hedonistic reflection that time is flying, the moment of pleasure short. In Donne's poem one feels the quickening of the brain, the vision extending its range, the passion gathering sweep with the expanding rhythms, and from the mind thus heated and inspired emerges, not a cry that time might stay its course,

> Lente, lente currite noctis equi,

but a clearer consciousness of the eternal significance of love, not the love that aspires after the unattainable, but the love that unites contented hearts. The method of the poet is, I suppose, too dialectical to be popular, for the poem is in few anthologies. It may be that the pagan and Christian strains which the poet unites are not perfectly blended—if it is possible to do so—but to me it seems that the joy of love has never been expressed at once with such intensity and such elevation.

And it is with sorrow as with joy. There is the same difference of manner in the expression between Donne and these poets, and the deepest thought is the same. The "Nocturnal on St. Lucy's Day" is at the opposite pole of Donne's thought from the "Anniversary," and compared with

> Had we never lov'd sae kindly

or

> Take, O take those lips away,

both the feeling and its expression are metaphysical. But the passion is felt through the subtle and fantastic web of dialectic; and the thought from which the whole springs is the emptiness of life without love.

What, then, is the philosophy which disengages itself from Donne's love-poetry studied in its whole compass? It seems to me that it is more than a purely negative one, that consciously or unconsciously he sets over against the abstract idealism, the sharp dualism of the Middle Ages, a justification of love as a natural passion in the human heart the meaning and end of which is marriage. The sensuality and exaggerated cynicism of so much of the poetry of the Renaissance was a reaction from courtly idealism and mediaeval asceticism. But a mere reaction could lead no-whither. There are no steps which lead only backward in the history of human thought and feeling. Poems like Donne's Elegies, like Shakespeare's *Venus and Adonis*, like Marlowe's *Hero and Leander* could only end in penitent outcries like those of Sidney and Spenser and of Donne himself. The true escape from courtly or ascetic idealism was a poetry which should do justice to love as a passion in which body and soul alike have their part, and of which there is no reason to repent.

And this with all its imperfections Donne's love-poetry is. It was not for nothing that Sir Thomas Egerton's secretary made a runaway match for love. For Dante the poet, his wife did not exist. In love of his wife Donne found the meaning and the infinite value of love. In later days he might bewail his "idolatry of profane mistresses"; he never repented of having loved. Between his most sensual and his most spiritual love-songs there is no cleavage such as separates natural love from Dante's love of Beatrice, who is in the end Theology. The passion that burns in Donne's most outspoken elegies, and wantons in the Epithalamia, is not cast out in "The Anniversary" or "The Canonization," but absorbed. It is purified and enriched by being brought into harmony with his whole nature, spiritual as well as physical. It has lost the exclusive consciousness of itself which is lust, and become merged in an entire affection, as a turbid and discolored stream is lost in the sea.

This justification of natural love as fullness of joy and life is the deepest thought in Donne's love-poems, far deeper and sincerer than the Platonic conceptions of the affinity and identity of souls with which he plays in some of the verses addressed to Mrs. Herbert. The nearest approach that he makes to anything like a reasoned statement of the thought latent rather than expressed in "The Anniversary" is in "The Ecstasy," a poem which, like the "Nocturnal," only Donne could have written. Here with the same intensity of feeling, and in the same abstract, dialectical, erudite strain he emphasizes the interdependence of soul and body:

> As our blood labours to beget
>   Spirits, as like soules as it can,
> Because such fingers need to knit
>   That subtile knot, which makes us man:
> So must pure lovers soules descend
>   T'affections, and to faculties,
> Which sense may reach and apprehend,
>   *Else a great Prince in prison lies.*

It may be that Donne has not entirely succeeded in what he here attempts. There hangs about the poem just a suspicion of the conventional and unreal Platonism of the seventeenth century. In attempting to state and vindicate the relation of soul and body he falls perhaps inevitably into the appearance, at any rate, of the dualism which he is trying to transcend. He places them over against each other as separate entities and the lower bulks unduly. In love, says Pascal, the body disappears from sight in the intellectual and spiritual passion which it has kindled. That is what happens in "The Anniversary," not altogether in "The Ecstasy." Yet no poem makes one realize more fully what Jonson meant by calling Donne "the first poet in the world for some things." "I should never find any fault with metaphysical poems," is Coleridge's judgment, "if they were all like this or but half as excellent."

It was only the force of Donne's personality that could achieve even an approximate harmony of elements so divergent as are united in his love-verses, that could master the lower-natured steed that drew the chariot of his troubled and passionate soul and make it subservient to his yoke-fellow of purer strain who is a lover of honor, and modesty, and temperance, and the follower of true glory. In the work of his followers, who were many, though they owed allegiance to Jonson also, the lower elements predominated. The strain of metaphysical love-poetry in the seventeenth century with its splendid *élan* and sonorous cadence is in general Epicurean and witty. It is only now and again—in Marvell, perhaps in Herrick's

> Bid me to live, and I will live,
> Thy Protestant to be,

certainly in Rochester's songs, in

> An age in her embraces past
> Would seem a winter's day,

or the unequalled:

> When wearied with a world of woe
>   To thy safe bosom I retire,
> Where love, and peace, and truth does flow,
>   May I contented there expire,—

that the accents of the *heart* are clearly audible, that passion prevails over Epicurean fancy or cynical wit. On the other hand, the idealism of seventeenth century poetry and romances, the Platonism of the Hôtel de Rambouillet that one finds in Habington's *Castara*, in Kenelm Digby's *Private Memoirs*, in the French romances of chivalry and their imitations in English is the silliest, because the emptiest, that ever masqueraded as such in any literature, at any period. A sensual and cynical flippancy on the one hand, a passionless, mannered idealism on the other, led directly to that thinly veiled contempt of women which is so obvious in the satirical essays of Addison and Pope's *Rape of the Lock.*

But there was one poet who meditated on the same problem as Donne, who felt like him the power and greatness of love, and like him could not accept a doctrine of love which seemed to exclude or depreciate marriage. In 1640, just before his marriage, as rash in its way as Donne's but less happy in the issue, Milton, defending his character against accusations of immorality, traced the development of his thought about love. The passage, in *An Apology against a Pamphlet called "A Modest Confutation,"* &c., has been taken as having a reference to the *Paradise Lost.* But Milton rather seems at the time to have been meditating a work like the *Vita Nuova* or a romance like that of Tasso in which love was to be a motive as well as religion, for the whole theme of his thought is love, true love and its mysterious link with chastity, of which, however, "marriage is no defilement." In the arrogance of his youthful purity Milton would doubtless have looked with scorn or loathing on the Elegies and the more careless of Donne's songs. But perhaps pride is a greater enemy of love than such faults of sense as Donne in his passionate youth was guilty of, and from which Dante by his own evidence was not exempt. Whatever be the cause—pride, and the disappointment of his marriage, and political polemic—Milton never wrote any English love-poetry, except it be the one sonnet on the death of the wife who might have opened the sealed wells of his heart: and some want of the experience which love brought to Dante has dimmed the splendor of the great poem in which he undertook to justify the ways of God to men. Donne is not a Milton, but he sounded some notes which touch the soul and quicken the intellect in a way that Milton's magnificent and intense but somewhat hard and objective art fails to achieve.

The Dramatic Element in Donne's Poetry

by Pierre Legouis

That Donne possessed dramatic power has generally been acknowledged.[1] Indeed, one of the generation that came to manhood in the last decade of the sixteenth century might be credited with some measure of the instinct at work in Shakespeare and so many lesser playwrights, even before he had given evidence of it. In his fervid youth Donne was "a great Frequenter of Plays," [2] though the theaters probably found in him

---

"The Dramatic Element in Donne's Poetry." From *Donne the Craftsman*, by Pierre Legouis (Paris, 1928). Reprinted by permission of the author. [The pages reprinted (pp. 47-61 and 71-9) form the third section of Professor Legouis' defence of Donne as an artist. They omit his interpretation of "The Ecstasy" as a dramatic poem. This has given rise to so much controversy that to reprint it would have necessitated printing rebuttals. For a summary of the debate, see my article "The Argument about 'The Ecstasy,'" *Elizabethan and Jacobean Studies*, edited by Herbert Davis and Helen Gardner (Oxford, 1959). Professor Legouis approves this omission and has also kindly supplied me with some corrections and minor alterations of the text for this reprint. Ed.]

[1] Edward Dowden, *New Studies in Literature* (London, 1895), p. 103, goes near to denying it: "Touches of dramatic power are rare in Donne, whose genius was lyrical and meditative, not that of a dramatist; but in this Elegy ["By our first strange and fatall interview . . ."] there is one touch which might seem of triumphant power even if it had occurred in a tragedy of Webster." The remark applies to ll. 50-54; when I am gone on my continental journey, the lover says to his mistress, do not

> in bed fright thy Nurse
> With midnight startings, crying out, oh oh,
> Nurse, ô my love is slaine, I saw him goe
> O'r the white Alps alone; I saw him I,
> Assail'd, fight, taken, stabb'd, bleed, fall and die.

The passage is very beautiful and moving but it is not strictly dramatic since the lover merely conjures up a vision of the future as in "The Apparition" (see *infra*).

[2] Sir Richard Baker, *Chronicle of the Kings of England* (1730), p. 424, quoted in Grierson, *Poems*, ii. 172. Grierson also quotes a verse letter, addressed to Donne c. 1600 by "William Cornwaleys," which contains the lines:

> If then for change of howers you seem careles,
> Agree with me to lose them at the playes.

a hard patron to please; and even in his sermons he will not boggle at comparisons drawn from play-acting.[3]

Still that general agreement upon the epithet "dramatic" rather tends to confusion than enlightenment because no two critics seem to understand it in the same sense, and it may well be applied in Donne's poetry in more than one. If by "dramatic" you mean what stirs the emotions through the sight, especially, of attitudes and gestures, "The Apparition" will answer that definition best of all the "Songs and Sonnets." Here we have a sordid but striking *mise-en-scène:* the lovers in bed, the man pretending to sleep, the woman pinching him in vain, the "sicke taper" that begins "to winke" at the entrance of the ghost. Yet there is no touch of the melodrama in "The Apparition," as there is in those pictures of Greuze that Diderot admired so much for their emotional intensity and that we cannot help smiling at to-day, *"La Malédiction paternelle"* and *"Le fils puni."* But, with a difference in quality, there is the same method, the same composition. Such art is less akin to the drama than to the *tableau vivant,* be it said without a sneer. Action there is none; the poet even refuses to tell his false mistress now what his ghost will say to her then, an artifice that reminds us of Timanthes hiding Agamemnon's face

---

[3] ". . . those transitory and interlocutory prayers, which out of custome and fashion we make and still proceed in our sins; when we pretend to speake to God, but like Comedians upon a stage, turne over our shoulder, and whisper to the Devill . . ." (*Donne's Sermons: Selected Passages* . . . , by Logan Pearsall Smith, Oxford, 1920, p. 123).

There are several theatrical metaphors or comparisons in the poems:

> Men of France . . . .
> . . . . the rightest company
> Of Players, which upon the worlds stage be,
> > (Elegy XVI, "On his Mistris," 33-36).

> And Courts are Theaters, where some men play
> Princes, some slaves . . . .
> > ("To Sᴿ Henry Wotton" [Grierson, *Poems,* i. 181], 23-24).

> Beleeve me Sir, in my youths giddiest dayes,
> When to be like the Court, was a playes praise,
> Playes were not so like Courts, as Courts' are like playes.
> > ("To Sᴿ Henry Wotton" [Grierson, *Poems,* i. 188], 19-21).

> This is my playes last scene, here heavens appoint
> My pilgrimages last mile . . . .
> > ("Holy Sonnets," VI [Grierson, *Poems,* i. 324], 1-2).

Evelyn M. Simpson, in *A Study of the Prose Works of John Donne* (Oxford, 1924), pp. 61-62, says that in later life "he denounced comedies, wine, and women as 'Job's miserable comforters' to the down-cast soul." Yet, she adds, "his friendship with Ben Jonson shows that he did not dislike the serious drama, while in his sermon he took up the position, in contrast to the Puritans, of a champion of all innocent amusements."

in his picture of Iphigenia's sacrifice. As the extreme of pity, so the extreme of terror is produced by suppression rather than expression.

Directly opposed to this pictorial conception of the dramatic is the purely psychological one. Mr. Massingham, for instance, thus praises, apropos of "The Relic," the fitness of the style in the "Songs and Sonnets": "It is impossible to conceive those tremendous adventures of soul, mind, and sense expressed by dainty, tripping lines, by smooth, ambling lines or even by the majestic sounding-board line of Milton, which expresses the reposeful sweep of the mind rather than its dramatic stress and conflict." [4] This amounts to saying that the soul of Donne in his lyrics divides against itself as, for instance, that of Othello in Shakespeare's play. But owing to the assumed identity of author and character, this is just a roundabout way of stating the theory of the poet's unqualified earnestness. Art, if it exists at all in the eyes of such criticism, is strictly subordinate to thought and feeling, feeling instinct with thought, or thought quickened by feeling.

I shall take the word dramatic in a third sense:[5] in many of the "Songs and Sonnets" there are two characters; the second is indeed a mute; or rather his words are not written down; but we are enabled to guess how he acts and what he would say if he were granted utterance. The way in which Donne gives us those hints is both very clever and very modern. More important still for us here is the effect produced on the speaking character by the presence of a listening one, whom he tries to persuade and win over. What seemed at first disinterested dialectics, indulged in for truth's sake, or at least as "evaporations" of wit, sounds quite differently when the reader realizes this dumb presence.

Of downright dialogue I find no instance in Donne, unless it be the "eclogue" which serves as a prelude (and also a postlude) to the Somerset epithalamium: it is chiefly a device for heaping additional flattery upon the bride and bridegroom, and a courtly apology for absence at the wedding. In his Satires Donne sometimes gives the words of his victims in the direct style, not without liveliness. But in the "Songs and Sonnets" we have no such *carmen amoebaeum* as, say, Horace's with Lydia: "*Donec gratus eram tibi. . . .*" Donne's manner is at once more refined

---

[4] H. J. Massingham, *A Treasury of Seventeenth-Century English Verse* (London, 1919), p. 335.

[5] Perhaps this is the sense adopted by Professor Grierson (*Poems*, vol. ii, pp. xxxiv and xlii), but he does not explicitly distinguish it from the other senses; he seems to use "passionate" and "vivid" as equivalents to "dramatic"; yet the comparisons between Donne and Browning in the first passage, between Donne and Drayton in the second, lead directly to a definition of the dramatic lyric. The famous sonnet:

Since there's no help, come let us kiss and part . . .

is indeed the dramatic lyric *par excellence*. (See Emile Legouis, *Dans les sentiers de la Renaissance anglaise. Les Belles-Lettres* [Paris, 1925], pp. 43-45.) It was published only in the 1619 edition of *Idea*.

and more abrupt: it taxes the reader's imagination more severely; it lacks the ease of the Latin poet's dramatic lyric and has not such a wide appeal; but it grows upon the imagination and repays minute study.

The four pieces that go by the common title of "Valediction" are dramas of the simplest kind. In one of them at least, possibly in others, the mistress from whom the poet-lover parts is weeping. But the interest centers on the symbol that provides three of the pieces with their sub-titles: "of my Name, in the Window," "of the Book," "of Weeping"; and though Donne called the fourth "A Valediction: forbidding Mourning," the reader will be sure to remember it as the piece in which the parted lovers are compared to "stiffe twin compasses."—The song "Sweetest love, I do not goe" is to all intents and purposes a valediction, though Donne did not choose to entitle it so, perhaps because there was no symbol in it to emphasize its difference in sameness; but it is all the more touching for the directness of its appeal, since attention is not withdrawn from the characters and the scene to a mere term of comparison. "Break of day" also is a valediction, more precisely a descendant of the medieval *aube* as Professor Grierson points out. Here, for once in the "Songs and Sonnets," the woman speaks, and so well that this piece alone would suffice to prove Donne's ability to express the feelings of others, and allow us to surmise that even when the speaker is a man he need not be the poet's own self. "Break of day" stands not unworthy of comparison with the parting scene in *Romeo and Juliet*. True we hear in it no lark's song, which the lovers would persuade themselves to be the nightingale's; no "jocund day/Stands tiptoe on the misty mountain tops." The language is as naked as can be, but its very nakedness speaks passion:

> 'Tis true, 'tis day; what though it be?
> O wilt thou therefore rise from me?
> Why should we rise, because 'tis light?
> Did we lie downe, because 'twas night?
> Love which in spight of darknesse brought us hether,
> Should in despight of light keepe us together.

This is the reading of the editions; some of the manuscripts, Professor Grierson tells us, heighten the dialogue suggestion by punctuating line 3 thus:

> Why should we rise? Because 'tis light?

The first note of interrogation makes the symmetry with the next line less perfect, which may turn the scale in favor of the comma substituted for it by the editions; yet I cannot help preferring the more impassioned address, the short, panting questions, eagerly gasped out. The man's excuse, though unexpressed, is anticipated by the woman. Similarly, in the last stanza he pleads, or is supposed to be ready to plead, the call of his professional duties:

> Must businesse thee from hence remove?

The woman's anger against that bloodless rival sounds natural and sincere in its exaggeration:

> Oh, that's the worst disease of love,
> The poore, the foule, the false, love can
> Admit, but not the busied man.

Yet the final couplet smacks of epigrammatic wit:

> He which hath businesse, and makes love, doth doe
> Such wrong, as when a maryed man doth wooe.

The piece ends less dramatically than it began. But in Shakespeare also, at least in the earlier plays, do not the characters often parade their (or rather the playwright's) ingenuity after crying out what their hearts feel? The mixture is distinctly Elizabethan.

In "The Sun Rising" we find the same situation and a similar feeling; but here the lover addresses the sun, and his railings sound more rhetorical than dramatic. Yet the scenery, sketched in a few skilful strokes, redeems the piece from the fault of ranting in cold blood: the sunrays peer through windows and drawn curtains into the bed, a property only alluded to in "Break of day" but here brazenly mentioned in the concluding lines of the last two stanzas, so as to leave us in no doubt of its paramount importance:

> Aske for those Kings whom thou saw'st yesterday,
> And thou shalt heare, All here in one bed lay.
>
> Shine here to us, and thou art every where;
> This bed thy center is, these walls, thy spheare.

"The Good-morrow" seems related to the foregoing group of poems, but the connexion is merely metaphorical. The lovers are not parting, neither does the sun remind them it were time to part. Their souls, not their bodies, have just awakened. Their happiness is for the nonce unalloyed; they wonder how they lived before they loved. Therefore the dramatic element appears less vividly than in those pieces where there is fear, or at least a sense that joy is ephemeral. Yet "The Good-morrow" is no madrigal indited in the closet to a distant mistress; it is the report of an impassioned dialogue in that "little room" where the lovers have met and which has become to them "an every where." The woman remains silent, or rather her words are not given; but her presence is felt: "*her* face in *his* eye, *his* in *hers* appears."—Let no one misunderstand me: this piece *was* written by Donne in his closet, and with much care; it was revised by him (see Professor Grierson's note on the various readings of the manuscripts and editions) at leisure: what I mean is that it succeeds in creating a voluptuous atmosphere and calling up in it two flesh-and-blood human beings who act in relation to each other. The impression of passionate reality made upon the reader results partly from the poet's artfully concealed art, an art that is nothing if not dramatic.

However, against the applying of this epithet to "The Good-morrow," as indeed to almost every one of the pieces we have considered so far, it might be objected that they lack progression; the situation and even the feelings are at the end what they were at the beginning. But there remain for study a few of the "Songs and Sonnets" in which Donne's technique shows itself more complex: the initial situation evolves more or less, there are episodes and vicissitudes, or at least development.

The song "Sweetest Love, I do not goe . . ." differs, as we have noted, from the "Valedictions" in that it appeals to the heart, not through the medium of a symbol, but directly. It also gives more importance to the woman's part. The poet really speaks to her, not above her head, and he alters his tone according to the effect produced upon her by what he has just said. In the first stanza he tries to make her smile; but we see that he fails, since the second stanza more seriously attempts to comfort her by promising a speedy return. Yet this also proves unavailing, and he, feeling helpless at the sight of her redoubling grief, gives vent in the third stanza to his own despondency. Man, he generalizes, "cannot add another houre" to his good fortune, "nor a lost houre recall"; but we know how to assist misery when it comes and "teach it art and length,/It selfe o'er us to'advance." Such somber wisdom rather justifies the woman's grief as being consonant to human nature. So in the fourth stanza he returns to their own sad plight and entreats her to spare him; her grief is his death:

> When thou sigh'st, thou sigh'st not winde,
>> But sigh'st my soule away,
> When thou weep'st, unkindly kinde,
>> My lifes blood doth decay.

Besides, adds the first half of the fifth stanza, foreseeing of evil will bring it to pass. Pity, with a touch of superstition in it, succeeds where wit, sense, philosophy, have been of no avail. And now she listens, outwardly quieter, to his renewed invitation to make light of his absence, and to his assurance that no separation ever takes place between those "who one another keepe/Alive." Thus interpreted dramatically, this beautiful piece achieves a unity that was not apparent when one considered it as a lyric of the ordinary kind. The reader must fill the logical gaps with kisses and embraces, sighs and sobs, weeping and the wiping away of tears, and gazings into the woman's eyes to read her thoughts; he must also realize the failure of the lover's first efforts in order to understand the crescendo of pathos, and the relative success that ensues so as to appreciate the more subdued and pacified tone of the conclusion.

"The Canonization" stands alone among the "Songs and Sonnets" because the person addressed in it is a male friend, but love is still the theme. The character who is speaking rejects the worldly-wise advice offered to him and vindicates his own abandonment to passion. The *motif* had been treated a few years before by Sir Philip Sidney in sonnet XIV of *Astrophel and Stella:*

> Alas, have I not paine enough my friend,
> . . . .
> But with your rubarbe wordes you must contend,
> To greeve me worse in saying, that desier
> Doth plunge my well form'd soule, even in the mier
> Of sinfull thoughtes, which doe in ruine end?

The sestet defiantly repudiates the charge:

> If that be sinne which doth the manners frame,
> Well stayed with trueth in worde and faith of deede,
> Readie of wit, and fearing nought but shame;
> If that be sin which in fixt hartes doth breede,
> A loathing of all loose unchastitie;
> Then love is sin, and let me sinfull bee.

Sidney resumes the debate in sonnet XXI:

> Your words my friend (right healthful causticks) blame
> My young minde marde whom Love doth windlase so:
> That my owne writings like bad servants shew
> My wits, quick in vaine thoughts, in vertue lame; . . .

And after repeating the arguments of his well-meaning critics he concludes:

> Sure you say well, your wisedomes golden myne
> Dig deepe with learnings spade: now tell me this,
> Hath this world ought so faire as *Stella is?*

The difference between the two sonnets appears at once: in the former the poet glories in his love as an incitement to virtue; in the latter he

pleads guilty[6] and merely excuses himself on the strength of the temptation (though we may suspect his acknowledgement of "decline" from
youthful promise to be ironical). But either sonnet expresses one mood
only, as it should do, while "The Canonization" appears almost inco-
herent at the first reading, so much does the tone (not the theme) change
in the course of its five stanzas. Of these the title fits only the last two:
the first three having nothing to do with the admitting of the lovers to the
calendar of saints. To discover the essential unity of the piece one must
analyze it in detail.

The famous opening line:

> For Godsake hold your tongue, and let me love,

shows us Donne at his best in the brusque familiar style. In the rest of
the stanza he makes fun of himself:

> Or chide my palsie, or my gout,
> My five gray haires, or ruin'd fortune flout,

and then of his friend:

> Observe his honour, or his grace,
> Or the Kings reall, or his stamped face
> Contemplate, what you will, approve,

but shows all the strength of his passion in the appeal: do anything

> So you will let me love.

The satirical note reappears in the second stanza, where it sounds still
more clearly. The first line states the simple thought in simple terms:

[6] At least in the text of 1598, which I have adopted in the quotations. The first
edition (1591) not unfrequently prints downright nonsense (as in l. 13 of sonnet XIV),
but its reading in l. 1 of sonnet XXI is not impossible:

> Your words my freende me causelessly doe blame.

If Sidney wrote that, he no more pleaded guilty in this sonnet than in the preceding
one; but without the initial admission the final tercet loses much of its point:

> Well said, your wit in vertues golden myne
> Digs deepe. . . .

(the rest as in the 1598 text quoted above). Apart from that, the dramatic movement
appears as clearly in the earlier edition, published when Donne was eighteen, as in
the later, published when he had written most of his "Songs and Sonnets," if Ben
Jonson is to be trusted.

> Alas, alas, who's injur'd by my love?

The next lines are a rhetorical amplification of that thought. The poet here parodies the hyperbolical metaphors of the Petrarchists, used elsewhere by himself more seriously:

> What merchants ships have my sighs drown'd?
> Who saies my teares have overflow'd his ground?
> When did my colds a forward spring remove?
> When did the heats which my veines fill
> Adde one more to the plaguie Bill?

In the last three lines satire becomes more stinging; it still hits the love-poets who have exaggerated the influence of their heartbeats upon the world at large, but it also exposes the selfishness of the professional man:

> Soldiers finde warres, and Lawyers finde out still
> Litigious men, which quarrels move,
> Though she and I do love.

Among the accusations from which the lover pretends to be particularly anxious to clear himself, he places last, as the most heinous, that of having stopped all wars and law-suits, which would have brought upon him the just anger of two dangerous and vindictive kinds of men.

After this ironical outburst the lover pauses awhile to catch his breath, and the friend tries to get a word in. He upbraids the passionate couple with lack of sense: they are night-moths dazzled by a light. This speech, which takes place, if we may coin the word, in the interstanza, turns the lover's ardor from satire to self-glorification. So far he has told others to mind their own business and proved the harmlessness of his own all-engrossing pursuit; that strain recurs in the third stanza:

> Call her one, mee another flye,
> We'are Tapers too, and at our owne cost die,

which means: nobody suffers a loss by our death. But the main idea now is that of justification by love:

> Call us what you will, wee are made such by love,

—nay, more than justification, ennoblement:

> And wee in us finde the Eagle and the Dove.

Probably the metaphor of the birds was suggested by that of the insects, and corrects it; in the erotic-mystical language of the time "eagle" stands for "strength" and "dove" for "tenderness and purity"; let us remember Crashaw's rapturous appeal to Saint Theresa:

> By all the eagle in thee, all the dove.[7]

But the metaphor of the Phoenix, which comes up in the next line and proceeds from that of the self-burning night-moth, makes it likely that the eagle and the dove also arise from fire. When Joan of Arc died, a dove was seen ascending to Heaven (the same miracle probably happened at many another martyr's burning); and the Romans would let fly an eagle from near the pyre of their emperors: Dryden, at that time very much a disciple of Donne, recalls that rite in the first of his "Heroic Stanzas" on the death of Oliver Cromwell.[8] Anyhow, with the Phoenix Donne openly reverts to the type of traditional hyperbole he has just ridiculed, but he wears the hackneyed symbol with a difference:

> The Phoenix ridle hath more wit
> By us, we two being one, are it.

The fabulous bird, being unique of its kind, united in himself both sexes; the two lovers, having combined into one "neutrall" (not a very happy substitute for "hermaphrodite") thing, have also acquired this other property of the phoenix: they "dye and rise the same" as before.

Here the friend once more gets a chance and must be understood prosaically to object that, unless the poet means the metaphorical deaths and resurrections of parting and meeting again, he is straying very far from the truth: their love may well destroy the lovers, but not call them back to this nether world, not even provide them with a living while they are in it. The fourth stanza admits the hard fact, but answers defiantly:

> Wee can dye by it, if not live by love.

It then proceeds to improve upon a hint given in the last line of the third stanza: the love of the pair is a mystery; therefore they will have a

---

[7] "The Flaming Heart," *ad finem.*
[8]
> And now 'tis time, for their officious haste,
> Who would before have borne him to the sky,
> Like eager Romans, ere all rites were past,
> Did let too soon the sacred eagle fly.

The Stanzas were written after the funeral.

"legend," i.e., their marvellous but true story will be written for the edification of the faithful in after ages; their fame will rest safely, if not in a "Chronicle," at least in "hymns." This last word, with its religious import, leads up naturally to the announcement that the poet and his mistress will be *"Canoniz'd* for love," on which the fourth stanza ends. The friend this time probably opens his mouth to remonstrate against pride amounting to blasphemy, if he is a Roman Catholic, or idolatry if he is a Protestant; but no word of his can be even overheard, for the fourth stanza runs into the fifth, without a period. The new-made saints are already "invoked" by lovers who come after them; their intercession is prayed for in the most approved papistical style; the repetition of the words "You whom," "You to whom . . . ; who . . ." suggests a litany. Here Donne the lover turns to good account the learning of Donne the schoolman, and, in the impassioned subtleties of that imaginary address, the reader may well forget the friend who was the occasion of the piece. Yet without him, and unless we fill in his interruptions, we do not thoroughly realize why the lover-poet gradually warms himself up and passes from jesting impatience to an almost ecstatic vision. . . .*

Signor Mario Praz has excellently shown that the scholastic propositions in Donne's verse are but a barrister's special pleadings; mediaeval philosophy he regards not as a complete explanation of the universe but as "an arsenal" of arguments; his reason for choosing some and neglecting others is "practical rather than speculative." The Italian critic adds: "And the practical reason of Donne is an intellectual diversion," which consists in "the exercise of wit"; in other words the poet aims at using and showing his dialectical skill.[9] This last statement requires correction: in not a few of the "Songs and Sonnets" the barrister pleads, disingenuously indeed, but earnestly enough, because he pleads for himself, not before an academic jury of literary connoisseurs, but with the one woman whom he loves for the nonce. Persuading her to yield is the practical reason that decides upon the lover's choice of arguments and manner of presenting them. Seen in this light, even such a symmetrical piece of work as "The Prohibition" reveals a dramatic aspect that had so far escaped us. We took it for granted that the lover twice changed his mind: between the first and the second stanzas, then between the second and the third; if we read the piece again we begin to suspect that, here as in "The Ecstasy," he knew from the start where he wanted to go: he tacked twice in the road the more surely to enter the haven of his mistress's love when he put about the third time. We disbelieve the abnegation with which he pretends to regard only his mistress's interest, not his own. And in the final line:

> To let mee live, O love and hate mee too,

* [An interpretation of "The Ecstasy" as a dramatic poem has been omitted here. *Ed.*]
* *Secentismo e Marinismo in Inghilterra* (Florence, 1925), p. 100.

we surmise that the admixture of hate is intended only to salve the woman's conscience. The tone differs much, but the object little, from those of "The Damp," where the lover tells her who kills him with the help of "th'enormous Gyant, *her* Disdaine," and "th'enchantress Honor":

> Kill mee as Woman, let mee die
> As a meere man; doe you but try
> Your passive valor, and you shall finde than [i.e., then],
> In that you have odds enough of any man.

And one finds the same suit again in the two pieces that exhibit Donne's dramatic art in its most complex form, and which therefore I have kept for the end of this study, "The Flea" and "The Dream."

Extravagantly admired in the seventeenth century, not only by the erratic English but by the staid Dutch, "The Flea" has been pilloried again and again since good taste set in, as Donne's worst offense against literary, if not against moral, propriety. But it seems that both those who praised and those who censured the piece thought only of the hyperbolical conceits: in the second stanza the mingling of the lovers' blood in the flea's belly is said to be almost a marriage, yea more than that; the insect becomes at once woman, man, nuptial bed, and wedding church; in killing it the poet's mistress would commit, not only murder on him, a crime she is inured to, but suicide and sacrilege. Yet there is cleverness of another, and less obsolete, kind in "The Flea"; the scene it describes has the liveliness of the animal that plays there such a prominent part. So far Donne has given us scenes with two characters in them; here we have a third, much more real and active than the imaginary spectator in "The Ecstasy." And while a painter might represent "The Apparition" all on one canvas, it would take a suite of three pictures to reproduce the attitudes in "The Flea." Number one, the man is pointing to the insect that jumped from him on to her:

> Marke but this flea, ...
> It suck'd me first, and now sucks thee.

Number two, the woman is hunting the flea, perhaps she has already caught it, and the man tries to dissuade her from putting it to death:

> Oh stay, three lives in one flea spare.

Number three, the woman has disregarded the man's petition and crushed the once "living walls of Jet"; a vivid contrast of colors ensues:

> Cruell and sodaine, hast thou since
> Purpled thy naile, in blood of innocence?

Whatever pity he may feel for the victim, the man does not forget his own plea. Indeed the woman seems to have killed the insect less out of revenge than to vindicate the moral law questioned by the man on the strength of the insect's practice. He had told her:

>   marke in this,
> How little that which thou deny'st me is;
> ....
> And in this flea, our two bloods mingled bee;
> Thou know'st that this cannot be said
> A sinne, nor shame, nor losse of maidenhead,
>   Yet this enjoyes before it wooe,
>   And pamper'd swells with one blood made of two,
>   And this, alas, is more than wee would doe.

By punishing the brute offender against her chastity the woman has answered the man's sophism; but the latter does not accept his defeat and undertakes to clear the memory of the insect he has failed to save:

> Wherein could this flea guilty bee,
> Except in that drop which it suckt from thee?
> Yet thou triumph'st, and saist that thou
> Find'st not thy selfe, nor mee the weaker now;

the conclusion is so obvious that the logician scorns to complete his syllogism; from the flea's innocency, so well established, he passes at once to the harmlessness of his own design upon the woman:

> 'Tis true, then learne how false, feares be;
> Just so much honor, when thou yeeld'st to mee,
> Will wast, as this flea's death tooke life from thee.

This conclusion closely resembles that of "The Ecstasy," "just so much honor" in the one corresponding to "small change" in the other. Technically exception might be taken to the reporting of the woman's boast in the indirect style; that is undoubtedly a little awkward and, if the rule of the game forbids our hearing her, we would rather guess her retort than be told of it so bluntly. But apart from this fault, a small one in material extent, "The Flea" is good comedy, or, if one demurs to that word, good farce; its humor may appear rather low to the fastidious modern mind, but it did not transgress the rules of good breeding under Queen Elizabeth, of maiden fame.

Not less skilful in its technique, "The Dream" expresses, if not purer, at least more poetical feelings. The scene is a room, which we guess to be but dimly lit; the man is lying, if not in bed, at least, it seems, on a couch. The woman comes in while he is dreaming of her, and sits by him. Her entrance wakes him and he thanks her for doing so: the dream was happy, but its theme suited reason, the capacity of a waking soul, better than fantasy, that of a sleeping soul.[10] Yet he goes on, this visit does not interrupt his dream, but continues it; and he seizes upon the opportunity to pay a highly metaphysical compliment to his mistress: in God being and intelligence are one; similarly

> Thou art so truth, that thoughts of thee suffice,
> To make dreames truths; and fables histories;[11]

But the sensuous lover reappears at once, and we feel the kind of truth he prizes so much might be called more clearly by the name of reality:

> Enter these armes, for since thou thoughtst it best,
> Not to dreame all my dreame, let's act the rest.

The first stanza ends on this gesture of the man, one of gentle entreaty, arms held out, a fond smile on the lips and in the eyes.

The woman, it seems, remains seated, and out of reach. So the man tries to lure her forward; if he is not Donne himself, at least he resembles him like a twin brother in his use of scholastic theology. Here occurs the already-mentioned apology to the woman for thinking her at first sight to be an angel, and no more. But now we realize that the hyperbolical wit does not aim at pleasing any circle of fine gentlemen and ladies, except indirectly, as part of a dramatic action: while we read the second stanza we keep on seeing the stretched arms, and the couch; and the metaphysical subtleties reveal themselves as amorous blandishments.

Now comes the *peripeteia:* the woman rises, not to draw nearer but to go away. Is she afraid of her own boldness? Does she feel remorse already for jeopardizing her virtue? the lover asks himself; more likely she is a coquette and likes to play with fire. Perhaps, we may add, she thinks

---

[10]
> It was a theame
> For reason, much too strong for phantasie.

Cf. "Elegy X," 9-10:

> When you are gone, and *Reason* gone with you,
> Then *Fantasie* is Queene and Soule, and all.

The elegy, which had no title in the 1633 edition, received that of *The Dreame* in the 1635 edition, wrongly, Professor Grierson suggests. Yet the similarities between it and the piece in the *Songs and Sonnets* which bears the same title are curious; the elegy also might be interpreted dramatically.

[11] See in Grierson's note the quotation from Aquinas. One also remembers in this connection Saint Anselm's ontological proof of God's existence.

the man rather tame, and laughs in her sleeve at his too intellectual
method of seduction:

> Comming and staying show'd thee, thee,
>   But rising makes me doubt, that now,
>   That art not thou.
> That love is weake, where feare's as strong as hee;
>   'Tis not all spirit, pure, and brave,
> If mixture it of *Feare, Shame, Honor,* have.
> Perchance as torches, which must ready bee,
> Men light and put out, so thou deal'st with mee,
> Thou cam'st to kindle, goest to come; Then I
> Will dreame that hope againe, but else would die.

The invective against honor recalls that in "The Damp," but the tone is
far more subdued. The lover's morality has not improved, but the dreamy
atmosphere pervades his speech; his fierceness has left him, at least temporarily; even the woman's maneuver fails to rouse him. Yet, whatever
estimate she may form of his softness, we see in it the proof of his genuine
attachment, voluptuous indeed and not respectful, but tender and harmonizing well with the setting of the scene. In "The Dream" Donne's
dramatic art achieves its most delicate success.

Browning's admiration for his metaphysical predecessor has often been
noticed and commented upon. Yet no English critic, to my knowledge,
has ever pointed out exactly this resemblance between them, due either
to identity of temperament or conscious imitation on Browning's part.
Professor Grierson indeed puts into the same class of poetry "The Last
Ride Together" or "Too Late" and "The Ecstasy"; but he adds to this
"The Anniversary," which is not at all dramatic, though very passionate,
and he defines each of these pieces as "a record of intense, rapid thinking,
expressed in the simplest, most appropriate language," contrasting them
with a poem like "Come into the garden, Maude" by which thought is
suspended and the mind filled "with a succession of picturesque and
voluptuous images in harmony with the dominant mood." However true
in itself, the remark seems to miss the chief point that "The Ecstasy" and
"The Last Ride Together," for instance, have in common: their being
impassioned addresses spoken to interlocutors whose reactions we may
guess. "Too Late" is more of a soliloquy pure and simple, the lover
addressing only the memory of his beloved. But "My Last Duchess," not
mentioned by Professor Grierson, seems to me as good an instance as
any of Browning's likeness and unlikeness to Donne. Let us compare it
with "The Canonization": in both pieces we find a man telling his love-
story to another man whose questions or answers we are not allowed to
know directly, but whose suppressed words, or gestures, or looks, we
cannot leave out of account without misunderstanding the movement of

the scene entirely. On the other hand we see no touch in "The Canonization" of the local color that is so conspicuous in "My Last Duchess": Donne's lover might be himself, or one of his contemporaries; the Italian despot of the Renaissance, somber, jealous, and cruel, has nothing in common with the Mr. Browning who proved such a good husband to Miss Elizabeth Barrett. The older poet is modern, the later poet is historical. Or, if one objects that most of the Victorian's *dramatis personae* stand for permanent characters and that we must look through their temporary trappings, let us say he makes the Elizabethan's dramatic lyric more dramatic and less lyrical (I here take this last word in its meaning of "personal": that expresses the author's own thoughts and feelings).[12] The artistic imagination that could create some fifty *Men and Women* in one collection of verse certainly played a small part as yet in the "Songs and Sonnets," where it seldom, if ever, appeared unmixed with sentimental or intellectual self-expression. Nevertheless the technique Donne used to such effect remained substantially unaltered when it was resumed, after a lapse of over two centuries, by Browning: the latter's going out of himself only enabled him to apply it more variously.[13]

[12] One remembers that Browning's comment upon Wordsworth's famous definition of Shakespeare's sonnets as the key with which the dramatist opened his heart: "If so the less Shakespeare he!" called forth Swinburne's retort: "No whit the less like Shakespeare, but undoubtedly the less like Browning."

[13] Among the poets of today Paul Géraldy has used the dramatic lyric with great alertness in his verse-story, *Toi et moi* (Paris: Stock, 1913). The short pieces of which it is composed are linked together as the "Songs and Sonnets" are not, but each piece may be read as a whole and compared to individual lyrics of Donne's. In both poets we find the same emotional intensity (which, unlike Browning's, is or seems to be the result of personal experience) and clever dramatic suggestion. The "Finale" of *Toi et moi* treats in a very modern and disillusioned way the theme of Drayton's sixty-first sonnet.

"A Valediction: of Weeping"

by William Empson

"A Valediction: of Weeping" weeps for two reasons, which may not at first sight seem very different; because their love when they are together, which they must lose, is so valuable, and because they are "nothing" when they are apart. There is none of the Platonic pretense Donne keeps up elsewhere, that their love is independent of being together; he can find no satisfaction in his hopelessness but to make as much of the actual situation of parting as possible; and the language of the poem is shot through with a suspicion which for once he is too delicate or too preoccupied to state unambiguously, that when he is gone she will be unfaithful to him. Those critics who say the poem is sincere, by the way, and therefore must have been written to poor Anne,* know not what they do.

> Let me powre forth
> My teares before thy face, whil'st I stay here,
> For thy face coins them, and thy stampe they beare,
> And by this Mintage they are something worth,
> For thus they be
> Pregnant of thee,
> Fruits of much grief they are, emblemes of more,
> When a tear falls, that thou falst which it bore,
> So thou and I are nothing then, when on a divers shore.[1]

Allow me this foolishness; let me cry thoroughly while I can yet see your face, because my tears will be worth nothing, may, in fact, not flow at all,

" 'A Valediction: of Weeping.' " From *Seven Types of Ambiguity*, by William Empson. 3rd edition, revised (London, 1953: reprinted 1956), pp. 139-148. Copyright 1930 by Chatto and Windus, Ltd. Reprinted by permission of the author, Chatto and Windus, and New Directions. [The chapter from which this passage is excerpted deals with "a fourth type" of ambiguity which "occurs when two or more meanings of a statement do not agree among themselves, but combine to make clear a more complicated state of mind in the author." *Ed.*]

* [Professor Empson asks me to add here that he now thinks that "the poem may have been written to Donne's wife, because the ironies are not against the woman addressed but against his own previous uses of the fantastic argument." He wishes readers to be referred to his article "Donne the Spaceman," *Kenyon Review*, 1957. *Ed.*]

[1] The three verses of the poem are quoted and examined separately.

when once I have lost sight of you." "Let me plunge, at this dramatic moment, into my despair, so that by its completeness I may be freed from it, and my tears may be coined into something more valuable."

The metaphor of coining is suitable at first sight only "because your worth and your beauty are both royal," but other deductions from it can be made. In that his *tears* will not reflect her *face* unless he *stays here*, it may imply "because it is only when I am seeing your beauty that it matters so much to me; I only shed valuable tears about you when I am at your side." There is a shift of the metaphor in this, brought out by line 3, from the *tears* as molten metal which must be *stamped* with her value to the *tears* themselves as the completed *coin;* "because," then, "you are so fruitful of unhappiness"; and in either case, far in the background in so far as she is not really such a queenly figure, "because you are public, mercenary, and illegal." [2]

In each of the three verses of the poem the two short middle lines are separated only by commas from the lines before and after them; Professor Grierson on the two occasions that he has corrected this has accurately chosen the more important meaning, and unnecessarily cut off the less. In this verse, *for thus they be* may be a note to give the reasons why the tears are *something worth,* or may be parallel to *for thy face coins them,* so that it leads on to the rest of the stanza. Going backwards, "Let me pour out at once the tears I shall have to shed sooner or later, because if I do it now they will reflect your face and become valuable because they contain you"; going forwards, "Let me pour forth my tears before your face, because they are epitomes of you in this way, that they are born in sorrow, and are signs that there is more sorrow to come after." *Pregnant* because they are like her, in that they *fall* and are *emblems of grief,* and give true information about her (as in "a pregnant sentence"), because they are round and large like a pregnancy, because they hold a reflection of her inside them, and because, if they are wept in her presence, they will carry her more completely with them, and so do him more good. It is this last obscure sense, that he is getting rid of her, or satisfying her, or getting his feeling for her into a more manageable form, by a storm of emotion in her presence, that gives energy to the metaphor of *pregnancy,* and logic to the second alternative—the idea that she normally causes sorrow.

Corresponding to these alternative meanings of *for thus, that thou* means "the fact that you" and "that particular case of you." "The tears are emblems of more grief by foreshowing, when they fall, that you will fall who were the cause of them" (if *which* refers to a person it should

---

[2] I doubt now whether Donne would have minded leaving these conceivable implications lying about, even if the poem were in fact written for his wife. He might well have feared that she would throw up her reckless marriage. [The footnotes to this essay were added in the second edition of 1947, when the original footnotes were taken into the text and "second thoughts" were added as footnotes. *Ed.*]

be the subject of *bore*), or, beginning a new sentence at *when*, "when a tear falls, that reflection of you which it carries in it falls too" (*which* now refers to a thing and so can be the object).

And corresponding to these again, there is a slight variation in the meaning of *so*, according as the last line stands alone or follows on from the one before. "These tears by falling show that you will fall who were the cause of them. And therefore, because you will fall when we are separated, when we are separated we shall both become nothing," or "When the reflection of you is detached from my eye and put on a separate tear it falls; in the same way we shall ourselves fall and be nothing when we are separated by water."

All these versions imply that their love was bound to lead to unhappiness; the word *fall* expects unfaithfulness, as well as negation, from her absence; *then* means both "when you fall" and "when we are separated," as if they were much the same thing; and *nothing* (never name her, child, if she be nought, advised Mrs. Quickly) says the same of himself also, when a channel divides them deeper, but no less salt, than their pool of tears.

> On a round ball,
> A workeman that hath copies by, can lay
> An Europe, Afrique, and an Asia,
> And quickly make that, which was nothing, *All,*
> So doth each teare
> Which thee doth weare,
> A globe, yea world by that impression grow
> Till my tears mixed with thine do overflow
> This world, by waters sent from thee, my heaven dissolved so.

The first four lines are defining the new theme, and their grammar is straightforward. Then the *teare* may be active or passive, like the *workeman* or like the *ball*; on the face of it, it is like the *ball*, but *so doth* may treat it as like the *workeman*. For *doth* may be a separate verb as well as an auxiliary of *grow*; while, in any case, *grow* may either mean "turn into" or "grow larger." The *globe* and the *world* may be either the *teare* or *thee*. The other meanings of impression would be possible here. Either, then, "In the same way each tear that wears you, who are a whole world yourself or at least the copy of one, grows into a world," or "And so does every tear that wears you; each tear, that is, grows, so as to include everything, or to produce a great deal more water"; it is only this second, vaguer meaning which gives a precise meaning to *till*, and suggests, instead of a mere heap of world-tears, such a flood as descended upon the wickedness of the antediluvians.

Which thee doth weare suggests by the order of the words a more normal meaning, that her *tears* are jewels and she is *wearing* them; this is inverted by the grammar, so as to leave an impression that she is uniquely and unnaturally under the control of her tears, or even has no existence independent of them.

The last line but one may stand alone, with *overflow* meaning simply "flow excessively," or "flow into each other," so as to spoil each other's shape, and then the last line, by itself, means, "In the same way, the necessities of this, the real, world have dissolved my precarious heaven by means of, or into, tears." Or making *world* the object of *overflow*, it may mean, according as *this world* is the real world or the *tear*, either "we produce more and more tears till we drown the world altogether, and can no longer see things like ordinary people," or "my tear reflects you and so is a world till one of your tears falls on it, spoils its shape and leaves only a splash"; it is she who has made the *world* which is his *heaven*, and she who destroys it. The rest of the line then says, "in the same way my happiness in our love has been dissolved, by this meeting with your tears," making *heaven* the subject of the intransitive verb *dissolved*. But *my heaven* may be in apposition to *thee*; *dissolved* may be a participle; and *so* may be not "in the same way" but "so completely, so terribly"; it is not merely his memory and idea and understanding of her, it is the actual woman herself, as she was when they were happy together, who is *dissolving* under his eyes into the *tears* of this separation; *dissolved*, it has already happened. The waters are falling that were above the firmament; the heaven and crystalline spheres, which were she, are broken; she is no longer the person he made her, and will soon be made into a different person by another lover. These broken pieces of grammar which may be fitted together in so many ways are lost phrases jerked out whilst sobbing, and in the reading, "so my heaven dissolved this world," which though far in the background is developed in the following stanza, there is a final echo of unexplained reproach.

> O more than Moone,
> Draw not up seas to drowne me in thy spheare,
> Weep me not dead, in thine armes, but forbeare
> To teach the sea, what it may doe too soone,
> Let not the winde
> Example finde,
> To do me more harm, then it purposeth,
> Since thou and I sigh one another's breath,
> Whoe'er sighs most, is cruellest, and hasts the other's death.

She is *Moone*, with a unifying reference to the first line of the poem, because she draws up the tides of weeping both from him and from herself, a power not necessarily to her credit, but at any rate deserving adoration; the moon, too, is female, inconstant, chaste because though bright cold, and has *armes* in which the new moon holds the old one.

Some of the lyrical release in the line may be explained as because it is deifying her, and remembering the Sidney tradition, even now after so many faults in her have been implied, and are still being implied. She is *more than Moone* because she is more valuable to him than anything in the real world to which he is being recalled; because she has just been called either the earth or the heavens and they are larger than the moon; as controlling tides more important or more dangerous than those of the sea; as making the world more hushed and glamorous than does moon-light; as being more inconstant, or as being more constant, than the moon; as being able to draw tides right up to her own sphere; as shining by her own light; and as being more powerful because closer.

In thy spheare may be taken with *me,* "don't drown me, whether with my tears or your own, now that I am still fairly happy and up in your sphere beside you; don't trouble to draw up the seas so high, or be so cruel as to draw up the seas so high, that they drown me now, since tomorrow they will drown me easily, when I am thrown down into the world"; may be taken alone, as "your sphere of influence," your sort of drowning, "don't *you* go drowning me; I have the whole sea to drown me when I take ship to-morrow"; or may be taken with *Moone,* "you, far in your sphere, high and safe from sorrow in your permanence and your power to change, do not drown a poor mortal who is not in your sphere, to whom these things matter more deeply."

The machinery of interpretation is becoming too cumbrous here, in that I cannot see how these meanings come to convey tenderness rather than the passion of grief which has preceded them, how they come to mark a particular change of tone, a return towards control over the situation, which makes them seem more vividly words actually spoken. It is a question of the proportions in which these meanings are accepted, and their interactions; it is not surprising that the effect should be what it is, but I do not know that it could have been foreseen. Perhaps it is enough to say that the request, in its fantastic way, is more practical, and draws its point from the immediate situation.

Weep me not dead means: "do not make me cry myself to death; do not kill me with the sight of your tears; do not cry for me as for a man already dead, when, in fact, I am in your arms," and, with a different sort of feeling, "do not exert your power over the sea so as to make it drown me by sympathetic magic"; there is a conscious neatness in the ingenuity of the phrasing, perhaps because the same idea is being repeated, which brings out the change of tone in this verse. *What it may doe too soone,* since the middle lines may as usual go forward or backward, may be said of the *sea* or of the *winde;* if of the *winde* the earlier syntax may be "forbeare in order to teach the sea to be calm"; this gives point to the crude logic, which has in any case a sort of lyrical ease, of "do not weep, but forbeare to weep." The *sea* is going to separate them; it *may* be going to drown him; and so it *may* drown him, for all he cares, when he has lost her. The *winde purposeth* to blow him from her, and if she doesn't stop sighing she will *teach* it to do *more harm,* and upset the boat. One may notice the contrast between the danger and discomfort of this prospect, also the playfulness or brutality of the request, and the cooing assured seductive murmur of the sound *doe too soone;* by this time he is trying to soothe her.

I always think of this poem as written before Donne's first voyage with Essex, which he said he undertook to escape from "the queasy pain of loving and being loved"; the fancy is trivial but brings out the change of tone in the last two lines. In itself the notion is a beautiful one, "our sympathy is so perfect that any expression of sorrow will give more pain to the other party than relief to its owner, so we ought to be trying to cheer each other up," but to say this is to abandon the honest luxuriance of sorrow with which they have been enlivening their parting, to try to forget feeling in a bright, argumentative, hearty quaintness (the good characters in Dickens make the orphan girl smile through her tears in this way); the language itself has become flattened and explanatory: so that he almost seems to be feeling for his hat. But perhaps I am libelling this masterpiece; all one can say is that its passion exhausts itself; it achieves at the end the sense of reality he was looking for, and some calm of mind.[8]

This poem is ambiguous because his feelings were painfully mixed, and because he felt that at such a time it would be ungenerous to spread them out clearly in his mind; to express sorrow at the obvious fact of parting gave an adequate relief to his disturbance, and the variety of irrelevant, incompatible ways of feeling about the affair that were lying about in his mind were able so to modify, enrich, leave their mark upon this plain lyrical relief as to make it something more memorable.

I hope I have now made clear what the fourth type [of ambiguity] is like when it really gets under way; I shall add some much slighter cases which seemed illuminating.

> What if this present were the world's last night?
> Mark in my heart, O Soule, where thou dost dwell,
> The picture of Christ crucified, and tell
> Whether that countenance can thee affright,
> Teares in his eyes quench the amasing light,
> Blood fills his frownes, which from his pierc'd head fell.
> And can that tongue adjudge thee unto hell,
> Which prayed forgivenesse for his foes fierce spight?
> No, no; but as in my idolatrie
> I said to all my profane mistresses,

---

[8] It seems at least possible that they may choose to do each other less harm than they could; he seems therefore to have cured himself of some of the earlier suspicions. I still think that all this analysis is correct.

> Beauty, of pitty, foulness onely **is**
> A sign of rigour; so I say to thee,
> To wicked spirits are horrid shapes assign'd,
> This beauteous form assures a piteous mind.
>   (Donne, "Holy Sonnets," XIII.)

In one's first reading of the first line, the dramatic idea is of Donne pausing in the very act of sin, stricken and swaddled by a black unexpected terror: suppose the end of the world came *now?* The preacher proceeds to comfort us after this shock has secured our attention. But looking back, and taking for granted the end's general impression of security, the first line no longer conflicts with it. "Why, this *may* be the last night, but God is loving. What if it were?" In the first notion one must collect one's mind to answer the Lord suddenly, and Donne, in fact, shuffles up an old sophistry from Plato, belonging to the lyrical tradition he rather despised, and here even more absurdly flattering to the person addressed and doubtful as to its general truth than on the previous occasions he has found it handy. Is a man in the last stages of torture so beautiful, even if blood hides his frowns? Never mind about that, he is pleased, we have carried it off all right; the great thing on these occasions is to have a ready tongue.[4]

A similar doubt as to emphasis runs through "The Apparition," and almost leaves one in doubt between two moods; an amused part and fanciful contempt, written up with more elaboration than it deserves, so as to give him an air of being detached from her and interested in literature; and the scream of agony and hatred by which this is blown aside.

> *Then* thy *sicke taper* will begin to *winke*

is a bumping line full of guttering and oddity, but brisk with a sense of power over her. This has reached a certain intensity by the time we get to

> thinke
> Thou call'st for more,
> And *in false sleepe* will from thee *shrinke.*

with the stresses in the line almost equal; Crashaw uses a similar rhythm to convey a chanting and mystical certainty,

> And in her *first ranks* make thee *room.*

---

[4] I leave in my expression of distaste for the poem, but it has little to do with the ambiguity in question.

Donne's version conveys: "I am speaking quite seriously, with conviction, but with personal indifference, to this toad."

> And *then* poore Aspen *wretch, neglected* thou
> All* in a cold quicksilver sweat wilt lye
> A veryer ghost than I.

The stress is on *neglected:* "you would be glad to get me back now if you could." But

> since my love is spent
> I had *rather* thou shouldst *pain*fully re*pent*
> Than by my threatenings rest still innocent.

What a placid epigrammatical way of stopping, we are to think, and how trivial the affair is made by this final admission that she is innocent! He would not say that if he cared for her any more.

But, after all, the first line calls her a *murderess,* and the way most people read the poem makes the poet more seriously involved:

> Then *thy* sicke taper will begin to winke

("As does mine now; you have left me ill and exhausted," and the last part of the line gabbles with fury.)

> And in false sleepe will from *thee* shrinke

("As you, if I can credit it, as you have shrunk from *me;* with a disgust which I shall yet turn to terror.")

> And *then* poore Aspen wretch, neglected *thou*

(It is almost a childish cry; "I find it *intolerable* to be so neglected.")

> A veryer ghost than *I*

("Than I am now," not "than I shall be then"); that his *love* is *spent* has become pathetically unbelievable;

> I had rather *thou* shouldst painfully repent

* [The text actually reads "Bath'd. . . ." *Ed.*]

("As I am repenting, in agony"); and *innocent* has become a scream of jealous hatred at her hypocrisy, of an impotent desire to give any pain he can find.

The meaning of an English sentence is largely decided by the accent, and yet one learns in conversation to put the accent in several places at once; it may be possible to read the poem so as to combine these two ways of underlining it. But these last two cases are curious in that the alternative versions seem particularly hard to unite into a single vocal effect. You may be intended, while reading a line one way, to be conscious that it could be read in another; so that if it is to be read aloud it must be read twice; or you may be intended to read it in some way different from the colloquial speech-movement so as to imply both ways at once. Different styles of reading poetry aloud use these methods in different proportions, but perhaps these two last examples from Donne respectively demand the two methods in isolation.

Donne's Relation to
the Poetry of His Time

by Mario Praz

There are few themes more harped on by sixteenth century poets than the time-honored one of the love-dream. Its formula, as it was broadcast throughout Europe by the Italian sonneteers, amounted to this: the poet dreams that his cruel beloved has relented and comes to solace him, but just when he is about to enjoy this godsend, sleep forsakes him. This being the bare outline, one was left an extensive choice of trimmings. You could start with a brief and elegant description of night, or with a complaint addressed to Sleep, or with a cry of joy: "Is this the fair hair . . . ?" combined with the usual Petrarchan description of the lady; if you were at pains how to fill up the quatrains, mythology came to your rescue, with Morpheus, Endymion and Diana, Ixion, and similar pleasant purple patches; or you could quibble on the disappearance of the sun, and the rise of that other sun, the beloved, in the dead of night. When, in the eighties of the sixteenth century, Thomas Watson picked up (from the Latin poems of Hercules Strozza) "this kinde of invention . . . usuall among those that have excelled in the sweetest vaine of Poetrie," he set out with a mythological embroidery on the circumstances of his dream:

> In *Thetis* lappe, while Titan tooke his rest,
> I slumbring lay within my restless bedde,
> Till *Morpheus* us'd a falsed soary jest,
> Presenting her, by whom I still am ledde:
> > For then I thought she came to ende my wo,
> > But when I wakt (alas) t'was nothing so.

Alas, vain hope! Like Ixion's

"Donne's Relation to the Poetry of His Time." Originally contributed by Mário Praz to *A Garland for John Donne,* edited by Theodore Spencer (Cambridge, Mass.: Harvard University Press, 1931); revised and enlarged for inclusion in *The Flaming Heart,* by Mario Praz (New York: Doubleday Anchor Books, 1958). Copyright © 1958 by Mario Praz. Reprinted by permission of the author and the Harvard University Press.

Embracing ayre in steed of my delight,
I blamed *Love* as author of the guile,
Who with a second sleepe clozd up my sight,
And said (me thought) that I must bide a while
     Ixions paines, whose armes did oft embrace
     False darkned clouds, in steed of Junoes grace.

But now another lady appears to the lover: she is a *prosopopoeia* of Hope:

When I had laine and slumbred thus a while,
Rewing the dolefull doome that *Love* assign'd,
A woman *Saint*, which bare an Angels face,
Bad me awake and ease my troubled minde:
     With that I wakt, forgetting what was past,
     And sawe 'twas *Hope*, which helped thus at last.

About the same time, another minor poet, Sir Arthur Gorges, whom Spenser celebrated as Alcyon "fit to frame an everlasting dittie" in *Colin Clout's Come Home Again*, gave this less pompous, but equally commonplace, treatment of the theme, in imitation of Desportes ("Songs," in *Diane*, Livre II: "Celle que j'aime tant, lasse d'estre cruelle"):[1]

She whome I holde so deare
     too cruell thoughe She bee
Did in my sleepe appeare
     this other night to me
Sweet were the lookes shee lente
     and with such cheare Shee spake
As who shoulde say shee ment
     remorce on me to take
I pressed with my payne
     sayd unto her withall
Faire one doo not disdaine
     the harte that is your thrall
And with a vapored Eye
     this onely dyd I crave
That I the death might dye
     yf grace I might nott have
Wherwith she dyd disclose
     those faire sweet Coralls twaine
And sayde receave repose
     doo thow no more Complaine

[1] *The Poems of Sir Arthur Gorges*, ed. Helen Estabrook Sandison (Oxford, 1953), pp. 11-12.

Nor from thy wastede Eyes
  drawe not such dropps of griefe
From whence thy woes dyd ryse
  from thence receave releeffe
Oh sweet Elusion straunge
  o marvell of delighte
But oh how sone did chaunge
  the pleasure off this nighte
For loe this soddayne Joye
  so strake me to the harte
As that to myn annoye
  out of this sleepe I starte
And yett dyd doubtfull stande
  tyll lyftinge upp my heade
To kisse her comelye hande
  the shape awaye was fledd
But then I did devyse
  a slumber new to fayne
And closede kept myne Eyes
  althoughe it were in vaine
Att laste awakte I sayde
  oh dreame that didst surpasse
By thee I am betrayde
  as Bradamanta was
Yett that which lyked me beste
  my Mistres here shall fynde
That thoughe my Bodye reste
  I have her styll in mynde.

Of course, you will find a better treatment of the theme of the love-dream in Sydney ("Thus night while sleepe begins, with heavie wings . . ."), but, if the workmanship is superior, the spirit is much the same as in Watson's poor mythological concoction, or Sir Arthur Gorges' imitation of Desportes' "Songe."

Let us now read side by side with these poems, which faithfully reproduce a traditional formula, Donne's "Dream":

Deare love, for nothing lesse then thee
Would I have broke this happy dreame,
  It was a theame
For reason, much too strong for phantasie,
  Therefore thou wakd'st me wisely; yet
My Dreame thou brok'st not, but continued'st it,
Thou art so truth, that thoughts of thee suffice,
To make dreames truths; and fables histories;

> Enter these armes, for since thou thoughtst it best,
> Not to dreame all my dreame, let's act the rest.

One has only to think that even poets like Sidney and Shakespeare paid
tribute to that time-hallowed recipe of the love-dream, to realize to what
extent Donne's poem meant a new departure. The poet, on his waking
up, is no longer addressing a rhetorical complaint to an absent beauty.
It is not the sun which awakes him, as in Sannazaro ("Quando apersi,
ohimè, gli occhi, e vidi il Sole . . ."): the beloved has actually come to
his room, and the brightness of her eyes rouses the poet from sleep:

> As lightning, or a Tapers light,
>   Thine eyes, and not thy noise wak'd me;
>   Yet I thought thee
> (For thou lovest truth) an Angell, at first sight,
>   But when I saw thou sawest my heart,
> And knew'st my thoughts, beyond an Angel's art,
> When thou knew'st what I dreamt, when thou knew'st when
> Excesse of joy would wake me, and cam'st then,
> I must confesse, it could not chuse but bee
> Prophane, to thinke thee any thing but thee.

The last stanza concludes with a note of hope, as in Watson, but the
tone of the two poets could hardly be more different:

> Comming and staying show'd thee, thee,
>   But rising makes me doubt, that now,
>   Thou art not thou,
> That love is weake, where feare's as strong as hee;
>   'Tis not all spirit, pure, and brave,
> If mixture it of *Feare, Shame, Honor,* have.
> Perchance as torches which must ready bee,
> Men light and put out, so thou deal'st with mee,
> Thou cam'st to kindle, goest to come; Then I
> Will dreame that hope again, but else would die.

A comparison like the one I have suggested (which could be repeated
for most of Donne's songs) brings out very well the peculiarities of
Donne's poetry: its dramatic character,[2] its metrical originality, its
crabbed and prosaic imagery. The poem is not sung, but spoken; the
poet does not sit in state in his singing robes, with Apollo and the Muses
whispering into his ears; he has come down from the golden clouds of

---

[2] An analysis of this poem from a dramatic point of view will be found in Pierre
Legouis' study, *Donne the Craftsman* (Paris, 1928), pp. 75-77.

abstraction, and argues with his beloved. She is not the distant figure seen in a glimpse against the sky, hardly more human than the sun and the evening star to which she is compared. Such was the lady of the sonneteers, but Donne's lady is so much of a flesh-and-blood presence that she can be invited to "act the rest." The poet's passionate argument does not allow for those stately, self-contained lines whose perfection redeems many a lifeless sonnet. There is hardly a line in Donne's poem which makes sense by itself, or can claim the power of emblazoning in a musical cadence a whole state of mind. The sense is rounded off only at the end of the stanza, or rather at the end of the poem: the unit is not the line, as in many sonneteers, and not even the stanza, but the entire poem in its serpentine swerving from one excitement to another.[3] Donne's technique stands in the same relation to the average technique of Renaissance poetry, as that of mannerist to that of Renaissance painting. His main preoccupation is with the whole effect.

Seen from this angle, Donne's songs present a marked contrast to such poetry of *concetti* as was written by Marino and by Donne himself in the *Anniversaries*. True, one finds *concetti*, even the same kind of *concetti*, both in Marino and in Donne. Marino openly confessed that the poet's aim should be to produce wonder and surprise in the reader. Donne is not so deliberate. When that surprise is brought about by him, this is due to the way his mind is working rather than to the deliberate choice of a startling simile. Marino's aim being the *concetto* for its own sake, his poems are either epigrams or fall into loose sequels of epigrams, of decorative puns. A capital instance of this kind of poetry in England is given in Crashaw's "The Weeper." But the chief thing with Donne is not the *concetti*, no matter how quaint they seem to us and how apt, in consequence, to engross our whole attention. The chief thing with him is the dialectical slant of his mind.

Of the various elements Sir Herbert Grierson distinguished[4] in the notion of "metaphysical" poetry, the "argumentative, subtle evolution" of the lyric strain is the thing Donne shares only with such mediaeval poets as Guido Guinizelli, Guido Cavalcanti, and Dante in his minor mood; the other metaphysical characteristic, the "peculiar blend of passion and thought, feeling and ratiocination," of which "learned imagery" is the consequence, is by no means such a rare thing in poetry, that traces of it may not be found in many Elizabethan writers, chiefly in the dramatists, as Miss Elizabeth Holmes has shown in a penetrating study.[5] Indeed the definition T. S. Eliot gave in his Clark Lectures: "I take as metaphysical poetry that in which what is ordinarily apprehensible only

---

[3] See on the mannerist character of Donne's poetry, Wylie Sypher, *Four Stages of Renaissance Style* (Anchor Books, New York, 1955) especially, p. 151.

[4] *Metaphysical Lyrics and Poems of the Seventeenth Century* (Oxford, 1921), pp. xv-xvi.

[5] *Aspects of Elizabethan Imagery* (Oxford, 1929).

by thought is brought within the grasp of feeling, or that in which what
is ordinarily only felt is transformed into thought without ceasing to be
feeling," is singularly akin to a definition Professor Martino gave[6] of
Baudelaire's inspiration:

> L'idée n'est jamais absente des *Fleurs du mal:* il n'y a guère de livres qui
> soient plus philosophiquement pensés, au sens large du mot; mais l'idée ne
> cherche que bien rarement à s'abstraire; elle arrive portée par la sensation,
> et encore enveloppée en elle. C'est bien là le "frisson" dont parlait Victor
> Hugo.

My bringing together of the two definitions would be welcomed, I think,
by Mr. Eliot, who, in the lectures referred to above, spoke of three
metaphysical periods in European poetry: a mediaeval period, a seventeenth-century period, and a modern one with Jules Laforgue as its chief
representative.

The quality of "sensuous thought," prominent as it is in Donne, is
insufficient alone to describe his poetry. A passage like the following one:

> my love
> In whom the learned Rabbis of this age
> Might find as many wondrous miracles
> As in the theorie of the world,

might be read as Donne's,[7] if we did not know that it is Marlowe's
(2 *Tamb.,* IV. ii). Or take:

> We too, that with so many thousand sighs
> Did buy each other, must poorly sell ourselves
> With the rude brevity and discharge of one.

Were it not for the last line, this passage could be sought for in the
works of Donne, instead of Shakespeare (*Troilus and Cressida,* IV. iv).
Still nearer to Donne are the lines:

> Terms, tongs, reading, all
> That can within a man, cald learned, fall;
> Whose life is led yet like an ignorant mans:
> Are but as tooles to goutie Artizans
> That cannot use them; or like childrens arts,
> That out of habite, and by rootes of hearts,

---

[6] *Parnasse et symbolisme* (Paris, 1925), p. 100.
[7] Cf. "A Valediction: Of the book,"

> in this our universe
> Schooles might learne Sciences . . . .

> Construe and perce their lessons, yet discerne
> Nought of the matter, whose good words they learn:
> Or, like our Chimicke Magi, that can call
> All termes of Art out, but no gold at all.

Here we seem to listen to "a less swift and passionate Donne," as Miss Holmes calls Chapman, to whose pen the passage just quoted is due.[8] Like Donne's, Chapman's imagination is powerfully stimulated by this or that passage in the books he is reading, very often by a barren gloss, or such pieces of pedantic information as he could find in Natale Conti's mythological yarns. The poet boasts, every now and then, of the aptness and novelty of the figures and similes his own ingenuity has elicited from the sources: the thrill other poets receive from direct experience of life, he, with Donne, gets very often from either theological or ethical disquisitions, pedantic commentaries, and learned dictionaries. No doubt the "striking affinity" Chapman has to Donne[9] is partly due to the fact that his poetry, as Mr. Schoell noticed,[10] "plonge d'aussi profondes racines dans la métaphysique du moyen âge que celle de Donne." But, if I may be allowed another quotation, in order to show how that affinity has been concordantly emphasized from various quarters in the last few years,

such links are not accidental. They appear as results of a mental kinship. Donne's "Songs and Sonnets" were perhaps finding wide private circulation before Chapman wrote his tragedies or his "Tears of Peace," and "An Anatomy of the World" appeared a few years earlier than Chapman's elegiac poem "Eugenia." The two poets might well be acquainted, being both known to Ben Jonson, and both admitted to the literary circle of the Countess of Bedford. In any case Chapman must have read Donne sooner or later, but in several cases he anticipates him, for the metaphysical infection was in the air, and he was a likely subject.[11]

Whether Chapman had anything to learn from Donne, is matter of speculation; but in the case of another dramatist, Webster, we have positive proofs of imitation,[12] though, of course, imitation here presupposes an analogous frame of mind. In Tourneur's *Transformed Metamorphosis* we see reflected the same chaos of a changing world which forms the background of Donne's verse.

Much of the quaintness later ages have detected in metaphysical poetry can be accounted for if we try to realize what must have been the position

---

[8] See *The Poems of George Chapman*, ed. Phyllis Brooks Bartlett (New York, 1941), pp. 245-246 ("To yong imaginaries in knowledge").

[9] T. S. Eliot, *The Sacred Wood* (London, 1920), p. 20.

[10] F. L. Schoell, *Études sur l'Humanisme continental en Angleterre* (Paris, 1926), p. 19.

[11] Holmes, *op. cit.*, p. 99.

[12] See passages referred to in the Index to *The Complete Works of John Webster*, ed. F. L. Lucas (London, 1927).

of those poets living between two worlds, two cultures, in an age of scientific revolution. The best illustration of this peculiar position is offered by Donne. His cultural equipment was in many ways that of a Scholastic thinker; hence the curious affinity some of his poetry shows to that of Dante's circle. With the difference that, whereas those mediaeval poets believed in the scientific and philosophical theories they accepted as the background of their verse, Donne, living in an age of scientific revolution, could not help surveying with a skeptic's eye the state of confusion presented by the changing world. On the one side he had the Holy Fathers and a curious body of mediaeval lore, on the other Copernicus and Brahe, Galileo, Kepler, and Paracelsus. Though interested in thought, he was no original thinker himself. He aimed at artistic self-expression; therefore both the tentative creed of a new age, and the superannuated lore of centuries of old, merely supplied him indiscriminately with illustrations for his own poems and homilies. He was like a lawyer choosing the fittest arguments for a case in hand; not like a searcher after a universally valid truth. The scientific theories having only a value of conjectures or plausible speculations in his curious mind, do not belong to a world entirely distinct from the world of fancy, as they would in an era of settled convictions. Rather, there is a continuous interchange of suggestions from fancy to scientific thought and vice versa; and Donne is enabled to mix, in the same kaleidoscope, broken pieces of lore either old or new, and images properly belonging to the world of poetry. This state of mental osmosis, so to speak, is very likely responsible for the quality of "sensuous thought" we detect in many Elizabethan writers.

Also of the argumentative, dramatic mood, which we find so peculiar to Donne, instances are not lacking, every now and then, among his predecessors. Miss Holmes calls our attention to a sonnet in *Astrophel and Stella* which "plays with ideas in Donne's fashion, subtly and passionately at once." It is the sonnet concluding with the well-known line:

> Deare, love me not, that thou may love me more.

It is not difficult to see where the taste for this and similar quibbles originated. When we read that line of Sidney, or this one of Drayton:

> You're not alone when you are still alone;

or Panfilo Sasso's:

> Tu non sei tua, ma mia, son tuo, non mio;

or Ronsard's:

> En toy je suis et tu es dedans moy,
> En moy tu vis et je vis dedans toy;
> Ains noz toutz ne font qu'un petit monde

we are sent back to that fondness for scholastic subtleties which Petrarch retained from his predecessors. As a matter of fact a counterpart to Sidney's quibble can be found in an Italian poet of the thirteenth century, Guittone d'Arezzo:

> . . . poi che per amar m'odiate a morte
> Per disamar mi sarete amorosa.

And a rhymer of Guittone's school might well have written Donne's "Prohibition":

> If thou Love mee, take heed of loving mee;

or his "Lovers' infiniteness":

> If yet I have not all thy love,
> Deare, I shall never have it all
> . . . .
> Or if then thou gavest mee all,
> All was but All, which thou hadst then. . . .

The first of English poets to write in this dialectical style was, I suppose, the first Petrarchist, Sir Thomas Wyatt. Do we not see an anticipation of Donne's argumentative strain in the following poem?

> To cause accord or to aggre
> . . . .
> That man that hath his hert away,
> If lyff lyveth there as men do say,
> That he, hertles, should last on day
> Alyve, and not to torn to clay,
>   It is impossible!
> . . . .
> Yet Love, that all things doeth subdue,
> Whose power there may no liff eschew,
> Hath wrought in me, that I may rew
> These miracles to be so true,
>   That are impossible.

If Wyatt is seen here anticipating Donne, it is because he harks back to Petrarch:

> Talor m'assale in mezzo a'tristi pianti
>   Un dubbio, come posson queste membra

Dallo spirito lor viver lontane.
Ma rispondemi Amor: Non ti rimembra
Che questo è privilegio degli amanti,
Sciolti da tutte qualitadi umane? [13]

Yes, "harmlesse lovers" wrought such "miracles" already in Petrarch's time. And it would be difficult to find a better instance of metaphysical subtlety, of that subtlety which is a distinctive feature of "The Ecstasy," [14] than Petrarch's sixty-third sonnet *in vita*:

[29] Sonnet 11 *in vita*:

Sometimes a doubt assails my deep distress:
How can these limbs go on living at all,
So far away from their soul's happiness?
But then Love answers me:—Don't you recall
That lovers have the privilege to be
Rid of each human trait and quality? *

* Reprinted from *Petrarch: Sonnets and Songs*, translated by Anna Maria Armi, by permission of Pantheon Books. Copyright 1946 by Pantheon Books, Inc.

[14] The theory which is at the basis of Donne's "Ecstasy" occurs also in Giordano Bruno's *Candelaio*, I, x. Cf.:

Our hands were firmly cemented . . .

Our eye-beams twisted, and did thread
   Our eyes upon one double string:

So to entergraft our hands, as yet
   Was all the means to make us one,
And pictures in our eyes to get
   Was all our propagation. . . .

When love with one another so
   Interinanimates two souls,
That abler soul, which thence does flow,
   Defects of loneliness controls, etc. . . .

Bruno:

L'esser fascinato d'amore adviene, quando con frequentissimo over, benché istantaneo, intenso sguardo, un occhio con l'altro, e reciprocamente un raggio visual con l'altro si riscontra, e lume con lume si accopula. Allora si gionge spirto a spirto; ed il lume superiore, inculcando l'inferiore, vangono a scintillar per gli occhi, correndo e penetrando al spirito interno che sta radicato al cuore; e cossi commuoveno amatorio incendio. [Fascination by love takes place when owing to very frequent looking or to an intense, though instantaneous, look, one eye meets another, and two eye-beams reciprocally encounter, and light couples together with light. Then spirit joins with spirit; and the superior light informing the inferior one, they come to sparkle through the eyes, rushing to, and penetrating, the inner spirit which is rooted in the heart; and in this manner they kindle erotic fire.]

Merritt Y. Hughes, in "The Lineage of 'The Ecstasy,'" in *The Modern Language Review*, xxvii (January 1932) has conclusively shown how Donne's poem links up with the tradition of Italian Platonism as embodied in Castiglione's *Cortegiano*, and chiefly in Benedetto Varchi's *Lezioni sopra alcune quistioni d'amore* (the question whether in honest love one feels passions).

Quando giunge per gli occhi al cor profondo
L'immagin donna, ogni altra indi si parte;
E le virtù che l'anima comparte
Lascian le membra quasi immobil pondo.
E dal primo miracolo il secondo
Nasce talor; che la scacciata parte,
Da se stessa fuggendo, arriva in parte
Che fa vendetta, e 'l suo esilio giocondo.
Quinci in due volti un color morto appare:
Perché 'l vigor che vivi gli mostrava,
Da nessun lato è più là dove stava.
E di questo in quel dì mi ricordava,
Ch'i' vidi duo amanti trasformare
E far qual io mi soglio in vista fare.[15]

As we survey Donne's poetry after such a distance of time, we can hardly fail to notice how much this poet who in a sense led the reaction against Petrarchism in England was himself a Petrarchist, thanks to his mediaevally trained mind. Not a Petrarchist to the extent Sidney was, who, notwithstanding his protests of independent inspiration, was rehearsing most of the hackneyed tropes of the Continental sonneteers, nay, at the very moment he claimed to be no pickpurse of another's brain, was deriving from Du Bellay's ode "Contre les Pétrarquistes." No, Donne must have actually felt in opposition to the poetry of his day, and if he still remained a Petrarchist to some extent, this is due to the fact that, no matter how strong one's personal reaction is, one cannot avoid belonging to a definite historical climate.

One can find Donne's quality of sensuous thought in many other poets, and yet, if we restore the Donne-like passages of others to their context, we shall easily persuade ourselves that neither Marlowe, nor

[15] When through the eyes reaches the secret heart
A high image, the others dissipate,
And the virtues that are our soul's best part
Desert the members, leaving a dead weight.
And from this wonder a second sometimes
Derives its birth, and the excluded thing
Fleeing itself arrives in other climes
That revenge it and make its exile sing.
Hence in two faces comes a look of death;
Because the vigor that gave them life's breath
In neither place can stay where it had been.
And I remembered this a certain day
When I beheld two lovers' cheeks decay
And suddenly assume my usual mien.*

* Reprinted from *Petrarch: Sonnets and Songs*, translated by Anna Maria Armi, by permission of Pantheon Books. Copyright 1946 by Pantheon Books, Inc.

Shakespeare, not even Chapman, is like Donne, because, though metaphysical elements are to be found in them all, it is their frequency that
gives to poetry that peculiar flavor we recognize as Donne's. Again,
scholastic subtlety of thought is every now and then affected by many,
but nowhere do we find it enhanced by a dramatic technique like that
used by Donne. From this point of view, a comparison of *The First Anniversary* with "A Fever" is very telling. *The First Anniversary,* with its
central idea that the world has come to an end with the death of that
young girl, Elizabeth Drury, may be considered as a mere embroidery on
a theme which, in its simplest form, may be found in this sonnet by
Sannazaro, also inspired by the death of a girl:

> Una nova Angioletta a' giorni nostri
>   Nel viver basso apparve altera e schiva;
>   E così bella poi, lucente e viva
>   Tornò volando a li superni chiostri.
> Felice ciel, tu chiaro or ti dimostri
>   Del lume, onde la terra è oscura e priva;
>   Spirti ben nati, e voi l'alma mia diva
>   Lieti vedete ogn'or con gli occhi vostri.
> Ma tu ben puoi dolerti, o cieco mondo:
>   Tua gloria è spenta, il tuo valore è morto;
>   Tua divina eccellenzia è gita al fondo.
> Un sol rimedio veggio al viver corto,
>   Che avendo a navigar mar sì profondo,
>   Uom raccolga la vela, e mora in porto.[16]

The world is worth nothing, after such a death, says Sannazaro (and God
knows how many times the same thing had been said before!). "Sicke
World, yea, dead, yea putrified . . ." says Donne, bent on improving and
amplifying an old *concetto*. Had Donne always written in the style of the
Anniversaries, he would not rank much higher than Marino or Góngora.
But when we come across the same *concetto* in "A Fever," the impression
we receive is quite different:

> But yet thou canst not die, I know;
>   To leave this world behinde, is death,

[16] A new Angel appeared in our time, haughty and shy, in this lower world; then, as
beautiful as she had come, bright and alive she flew back to the upper spheres.
   O happy heaven, now thou showest thyself adorned with that light of which earth
has been deprived; and you, blessed souls, are glad to see forever my divine beloved
before your eyes.
   But thou, blind world, hast reason to complain; thy glory has faded, thy valor is
dead; thy supremacy has been overthrown.
   I see only one remedy to our short life, that, since man has such a deep ocean to
cross, he should gather the sails, and die in the harbor.

> But when thou from this world wilt goe,
>   The whole world vapors with thy breath.

The accent is here dramatic and passionate; there is none of that splendid fustian about the "intrinsique balm," the "preservative," and similar pseudo-scientific paraphernalia.

> Or if, when thou, the worlds soule, goest,
>   It stay, tis but thy carkasse then,
> The fairest woman, but thy ghost,
>   But corrupt wormes, the worthyest men.

I suppose when Donne wrote:

> For there's a kinde of World remaining still,
> Though shee which did inanimate and fill
> The world, be gone . . .
> .   .   .   .
> The twilight of her memory doth stay;
> Which, from the carcasse of the old world, free,
> Creates a new world . . .

he meant more or less the same thing; but the dramatic liveliness of the shorter poem makes all the difference. And the rapid change of intonation is continued in the next stanza:

> O wrangling schooles, that search what firre
>   Shall burne this world, had none the wit
> Unto this knowledge to aspire,
>   That this her feaver might be it? [17]

There is in this poem a nervous elasticity which seems worlds apart from the ponderous redundancy of the "Anatomy of the World," and was to be equalled only by another among English poets, Robert Browning. No

[17] A similar use of the theory of the end of the world through fire had been made by Tasso when he attributed to Providence the illness which was casting a shadow on the beauty of Eleonora d'Este. For, he argued, should that beauty appear in its full brightness

> incenerite ed arse
> Morrian le genti. . . .
> .   .   .   .
> E ciò che il Fato pur minaccia, allora
> In faville converso il mondo fora.

[The nations would be burnt to ashes. . . . And, what Fate still threatens, the world then would be turned into sparks (i.e., the Day of Wrath would take place).]

doubt most of Donne's poems appeal to our modern taste thanks to that dramatic quality of their style.

Donne's "Holy Sonnets" come next in interest after his songs. Though they have none of the originality of the latter, they can vie with those of Michelangelo for earnestness and intensity of religious thought: indeed, they are remarkably close to them in inspiration. In both poets the "devout fitts come and go away/Like a fantastique Ague"; faith has proved such a difficult conquest for them, that they are continually afraid of slackening in zeal. The moments of grace are so rare that Michelangelo asks God to make haste:

> Ché con più tempo il buon voler men dura.[18]

Both of them try to overcome the aridity of their hearts; they feel between their heart and God a barrier, which only God can break:

> Batter my heart, three person'd God. . . .
> . . . .
> I, like an unsurpt towne, to'another due,
> Labour to'admit you, but Oh, to no end. . . .

> Tra 'l foco e 'l cor di ghiaccio un vel s'asconde. . . .
>
> . . . .
> I' t'amo con la lingua e poi mi doglio,
> Ch'amor non giungie al cor. . . .
> . . . .
> Squarcia 'l vel tu, Signior! Rompi quel muro
> Che con la sua durezza ne ritarda
> Il sol della tua luce. . . .[19]

Also Donne could have repeated Michelangelo's appeal to God:

[18] . . . for here
With lengthening days good thought and wishes fail.
                              (Symonds' translation)
[19] Between it [my heart] and the fire a veil of ice
Deadens the fire. . . .
    . . . .
I love Thee with my tongue, then mourn my fill;
For love warms not my heart. . . .
    . . . .
Rend Thou the veil, dear Lord! Break Thou that wall
Which with its stubbornness retards the rays
Of that bright sun. . . .
                              (Symonds' translation)

Manca la speme, e pur cresce il desio
. . . .
Ammezzami la strada, ch'al ciel sale,
Signior mio caro, e, a quel mezzo solo
Salir, m'è di bisognio la tua 'ita.[20]

Except thou rise and for thine owne worke fight,
Oh I shall soone despaire . . . .

Non mirin con justizia i tuo' sant'occhi
Il mio passato, e 'l gastigato orecchio
Non tenda a quello il tuo braccio severo.
Tuo sangue sol mie colpe lavi e tocchi
E più abondi, quant'i' son più vecchio,
Di pronta aita e di perdono intero.[21]

. . . Oh! of thine onely worthy blood,
And my teares, make a heavenly Lethean flood,
And drowne in it my sinnes blacke memorie;
That thou remember them, some claime as debt,
I thinke it mercy, if thou wilt forget.

One may say that these are more or less commonplaces of religious poetry, but it is all the same remarkable that both Michelangelo and Donne strike the same notes, and only these. Idle as it perhaps would be to speculate on affinities between Donne and Michelangelo, I cannot forbear to record here another curious coincidence. Michelangelo had said in a famous sonnet:

Non ha l'ottimo artista alcun concetto
Ch'un marmo solo in sé non circoscriva

[20] Hope fades, but still desire ascends
. . . .
Shorten half-way my road to heaven from earth!
Dear Lord, I cannot even half-way rise,
Unless thou help me on this pilgrimage.
(Symonds' translation)

[21] Let not Thy holy eyes be just to see
My evil past, Thy chastened ears to hear
And stretch the arm of judgment to my crime:
Let Thy blood only lave and succour me,
Yielding more perfect pardon, better cheer,
As older still I grow with lengthening time.
(Symonds' translation)

>   Col suo soverchio, e solo a quello arriva
>   La man, che ubbidisce all'intelletto.[22]

The same image occurs in "The Cross":

>   As perchance, Carvers do not faces make,
>   But that away, which hid them there, do take.

Donne, of course, could not have known of Michelangelo's sonnets, which were posthumously published in 1623. But in his peculiar mixture of realism and Platonism, in the dramatic turn of his genius as well as in his laborious yearnings for beauty and religion, in that double character of half-baffled, half-triumphant struggle, in his power of depicting the horrors of sin and death, and the terrible effects of the wrath of God, Donne is perhaps nearer to Michelangelo than to anybody else.

[22] The best of artists hath no thought to show
Which the rough stone in its superfluous shell
Doth not include: to break the visible spell
Is all the hand that serves the brain can do.
                              (Symonds' translation)

John Donne: a Reconsideration

by J. E. V. Crofts

Donne came of age in 1593, at that uncomfortable moment when the gale of Elizabethan enthusiasm had nearly blown itself out and a chill was in the air. He was in time to take part in the last "heroick" exploit of the age, the capture of Cadiz (1596); but in the next year its glories were effaced by the miserable Islands Voyage and the outbreak of those open factions and animosities which darkened the remaining years of the reign. It was the age of Hamlet: indeed, if we suppose Hamlet to have been thirty at the date of the play, Donne was exactly his contemporary. "This goodly frame, the Earth, seemes to me a sterrill Promontory; this most excellent Canopy the Ayre, . . . why, it appeares no other thing to mee, then a foule and pestilent congregation of vapours." No more of Petrarch now; no more talk of Plato and the Divine Idea. The smart young man now plucked his hat over his eyes; wrote gritty satires in a Roman vein; and joined that School of Darkness presided over by Raleigh, where fierce young atheists read papers questioning and abolishing everything under the sun. Gloriana still reigned; and in districts remote from the capital the horns of her Elfland were still to be heard faintly blowing; but in London the pageant was paling under the light of an intellectual dawn, and her surviving knights and seneschals were revealed as a group of tired and pouchy-faced old men standing about the throne of a dreadfully painted old woman. Even the most radiant stars of her legend were losing their fire: even Astrophel, it was said, had been "no pleasant man in countenance, his face being spoilt with pimples." [1] And into this scene of disillusionment and dwindling

"John Donne: A Reconsideration." (Original title: "John Donne.") Contributed by J. E. V. Crofts to *Essays and Studies by Members of the English Association*, vol. xxii (Oxford, 1937). Reprinted by permission of the author. [Professor Crofts's quotations from Donne's poems are mainly taken from E. K. Chambers' text (The Muses' Library, 1896), but he does not follow its punctuation exactly and at times appears to be quoting from memory. *Ed.*]

[1] Jonson, "Conversations with Drummond," *Works*, ed. Herford and Simpson, vol. i (Oxford, 1925), p. 139.

reputations enter John Donne, as its expositor and coryphaeus; alert, critical, ruthless; "not dissolute but very neat, a great visitor of Ladies, a great frequenter of Playes, a great writer of conceited Verses."

Ah yes, he saw through it all. An "age of rusty iron" [2] he calls it in one of his early satires (very modern satires in the manner of Persius, full of knaves and fools and spades called spades). "Away, thou changeling motley humourist," he cries to the fashionable friend who would take him out for a walk,

> Leave me; and in this standing wooden chest,
> Consorted with these few books let me lie
> In prison, and here be coffined when I die. . . .
> Shall I leave all this constant company
> And follow headlong, wild, uncertain thee? [3]

What, after all, was there to see? The Court? Tush! he knew all about the Court. He had crowded with the rest into the Presence and had watched the typical courtier doing his stuff.

> . . . He enters, and a Lady which owes
> Him not so much as good will he arrests,
> And unto her protests, protests, protests
> So much as at Rome would serve to have thrown
> Ten Cardinals into the Inquisition,
> And whispered "by Jesu" so often that a
> Pursuivant would have ravished him away
> For saying of our Lady's psalter. But 'tis fit
> That they each other plague; they merit it. [4]

He had passed through the great Chamber ("Why is it hung with the Seven Deadly Sins?") and had seen there the royal power and majesty embodied at last—in what? Why, in the yeomen of the guard! That is what it all came down to: stupid and gigantic beefeaters.

> . . . Men that do know
> No token of worth but "Queen's man," and fine
> Living,—barrels of beef, flagons of wine. [5]

The Court! It was theme for a Savonarola. Somewhere in the background he knew that the glare and glitter culminated in a blaze of diamonds and

[2] Satire V, 35.   [3] Satire I, 2-4, 11-12.
[4] Satire IV, 210-18.   [5] *Ibid.*, 230.

that formidable old fairy, the Queen. But was she quite real? Was she in touch with things? Had she any idea, for instance, of the rapine and injustice daily perpetrated in her name?

> Alas! no more than Thames' clear head doth know
> Whose meads her arms drown, or whose corn o'erflow.[6]

No, he had seen through the Queen. Indeed, how could it be otherwise? For the Queen, after all, was a woman, and he had seen through women.

> Hope not for mind in women; at their best
> Sweetness and wit, they are but Mummy possest.[7]

His researches into this subject had been extensive, or he liked to have them thought so. His reading in the more crabbed texts of old-fashioned theology had taught him that woman was inferior to man not merely in mental equipment but in spiritual essence. Her faith was not as valid: her truth was not as true. And hence it followed that the love that she could feel must ever remain inferior to the love that she could inspire. This doleful notion is to be found in *Paradise Lost* and is sometimes regarded as an aberration typical of a Puritan poet. But it runs through the poems of Donne like spilt acid, producing the oddest effects of corrosion and distortion, yields, for instance, that quiet insult at the end of "Air and Angels":

> I saw I had love's pinnace overfraught;
>   Thy every hair for love to work upon
> Is much too much; some fitter must be sought;
>   For, nor in nothing, nor in things
> Extreme, and scattering bright, can love inhere;
>   Then as an angel face and wings
> Of air, not pure as it, yet pure doth wear,
>   So thy love may be my love's sphere;
>   Just such disparity
> As is 'twixt air's and angel's purity,
> 'Twixt women's love and men's will ever be.

Ah yes, he had seen through love. He knew all about "the marriage of true minds." "I say we will have no more marriages. Those that are married already shall live; the rest shall keep as they are"; or rather, keep as they were in that blissful imagined state of nature, before the

"tyrant Custom" had laid chains on man, and "Honor" and "Constancy"
had been elevated into moral imperatives.

> Will no other vice content you?
> Will it not serve your turn to do as did your mothers?
> Or have you all old vices spent and now would find out others?
> Or doth a fear that men are true torment you?
> O we are not, be not you so;
> Let me, and do you, twenty know;
> Rob me, but bind me not, and let me go.
> Must I, who came to travel thorough you,
> Grow your fix'd subject, because you are true?[8]

And so in a number of studiously scandalous "elegies" and "songs" he
unfolds his sage and serious doctrine of promiscuity; presents that view of
human nature which Othello greeted simply with the words "Goats
and monkeys" as the only true view; describes his adventures on these
unlit levels; boasts of his conquests, mocks at injured husbands, and, in
short, is at pains to present himself as one of the most egregious and
offensive young coxcombs that even the Elizabethan age produced.

True, he does not remain at that level. Life in terms of appetite is a
theme which soon yields him intellectual thistles instead of fleshly figs,
and these elaborately licentious verses are interspersed with others in
which the spiritual mystery of love is, after all, grudgingly admitted, and
even the outworn language of "Constancy," "Honor," and the rest is
found to have a meaning. So impossible did it prove, alas, to "turn and
live with the animals." But his coxcombry still adheres to him. Love,
when it comes, is not an experience which reilluminates his life and
wipes away the trivial, fond records of youthful apostasy. It is simply the
peripeteia in the coxcomb's drama. What we see is not the new man, the
lover transfigured, but the coxcomb defeated: the man who in spite of
all his cynical professions has gone and fallen in love after all. It is not
love that inspires him so much as exasperation at feeling love. It is all
imposture; he knew it, he knew it. Woman has nothing to offer; man has
nothing to gain.[9] The whole thing is an elaborate and diabolical
swindle by which we are made to give our substance for a shadow.[10] All
this he knew, and yet—

> For Godsake hold your tongue, and let me love.[11]

The whole body of his love-poetry is held together by this implicit drama
of the defeated coxcomb: the man who is impelled to adore what he
would fain despise, and who, when the truth of his feelings is extorted

---

[8] "The Indifferent."   [9] "Love's Alchemy."
[10] "Love's Exchange."   [11] "The Canonization."

from him, gives rein to hyperbole and grotesque exaggeration as a kind of sneering commentary on his own seriousness.

I may seem to be overemphasizing this aspect of Donne's literary character. Some critics have tried, by rearranging his poems and then using them as biographical data, to trace the evolution of the lascivious prig into the grave lover who subsequently took holy orders and became a famous Dean of St. Paul's. The turning-point in this Platonic process is supposed to have been his love for Anne More, whom he met as a ward in the house of his patron, Sir Thomas Egerton, and whom he married secretly in 1601. But this is really no more than sentimental conjecture, very difficult to square with the facts. All that we know about the dates of Donne's "Songs and Sonnets" is contained in the statement of Ben Jonson that "all his best pieces" (which must surely include some of the more grave and decorous) were written "ere he was twenty five years of age": [12] that is, if we take it literally, before the end of 1597, when he entered Egerton's household and met Anne More for the first time. As for the purifying and restraining influence of his love for her, assumed in the story, it is surely worth remark that the most deliberately outrageous of all his poems, a poem which would certainly have landed him in jail if he had allowed it to circulate before the Queen's death, was written in August 1601, after he had known Anne More for nearly four years, and only about four months before he married her. This is "Metempsychosis": a work evidently planned as his *magnum opus*. He was going to make an end. He was going to smite once and smite no more. He was going to demolish—to sweep away—all the sentimental pasteboard and puppetry of the Elizabethan era. He was going to take that wretched thing, a woman's soul, and having traced its dirty transmigrations from the primeval slime through the bodies of shark and sparrow, ape and bitch, was going to leave it—where? Why, in Queen Elizabeth. In Gloriana. In our

> Faith's pure shield, the Christian Diana.

The thing was to be an attack not only on the Queen herself, but on all the sentiment with which she had ever been regarded: on that whole system of half-chivalrous, half-Platonic idealism which had animated her servants of the pre-Armada generation, and still lingered in the hearts of the older men. It was to be a great act of liberation, and like most literary enterprises of the kind it was never finished. But it is characteristic of Donne that, although the poem peters out after some fifty stanzas, the preface is already carefully written:

> Others at the Porches and entries of their Buildings set their Armes; I my picture; if any colours can deliver a minde so plaine and flat and thorough-light as mine. . . .

[12] "Conversations with Drummond," *Works, ed. cit.,* i. 135.

The liberation may not be completed, but the statue to the liberator is up. The fragment stands among Donne's works like a huge and mutilated inscription. The object of the verb is uncertain; the verb itself is obscure; but there is no doubt that the sentence begins with the pronoun "I." And for Donne everything did so begin, and end. Throughout his life he was a man self-haunted, unable to escape from his own drama, unable to find any window that would not give him back the image of himself. Even the mistress of his most passionate love-verses, who must (one supposes) have been a real person, remains for him a mere abstraction of sex: a thing given. He cannot see her—does not apparently want to see her; for it is not of her that he writes, but of his relation to her; not of love, but of himself loving. And so in later life, though the stuff of his meditations changes, this inability to lose himself remains. It is not of God that he thinks so often or so deeply as of his relation to God; of the torturing drama of his sin and its expiation, the sowing and the reaping, the wheat and the tares. The great commonplace of his sermons, it has been said, is death; but in truth it is not death that inspires his frightful eloquence so much as the image of himself dying; and the preoccupation culminates in that ghastly charade of his last hours, described by Walton, when he lay contemplating the portrait of himself in his winding sheet like a grim and mortified Narcissus. There was no *incognito* for him in death; and even in his vision of the life beyond death the wearisome drama went on.

> As upon my expiration, my transmigration from hence, as soon as my soul enters into Heaven I shall be able to say to the Angels, "I am of the same stuff as you, spirit and spirit, and therefore let me stand with you, and look upon the face of your God, and my God,"—so at the resurrection of this body I shall be able to say to the Angel of the great Councell, the Son of God, Jesus Christ himself: "I am of the same stuff as you, body and body, flesh and flesh, and therefore let me sit down with you, at the right hand of the Father, in an everlasting security from this last enemy, who is now destroyed, Death." [13]

One may admire the eloquence and sincerity of such a passage; but are saints usually so much concerned with precedence, and does their Heaven usually look so like the House of Convocation?

I stress this peculiarity in Donne's make-up because it accounts in part for the powerful fascination which his writings exert. Just because he is so conscious of himself we are aware of him—the man speaking—in a manner and to a degree hardly to be paralleled in our reading of lyric poetry. Every word is resonant with his voice; every line seems to bear the stamp of his peculiar personality. And this impression is not something which we fancy or invent for ourselves. It is deliberately forced upon us

[13] *LXXX Sermons* (1640), p. 145.

by a technique which has no other object. The affected brusqueness of the language, the wilful fractures of the verse, the frequent use of startling or disgusting analogies—in short, the persistent violation of poetic decorum as decorum was then understood—are devices to ensure that we shall read these poems not as the expression of any man or every man, but as the expression of this one man and no other. His personality, or the idea that he contrives to give us of it, is a necessary part of his instrument as a writer. It is a sort of context, an invisible cavern-wall about his poems, reverberating and corroborating what they say. Many of them would strike us as merely curious experiments if we found them standing alone. But in their proper matrix, the "Songs and Sonnets," they acquire an expressiveness often quite out of proportion to their intrinsic qualities. Who can say how much a poem like "Negative Love," for instance, owes to the fact that we come upon it suddenly among the tirades and objurgations, sneers and ribaldries of the defeated coxcomb?

> I never stoop'd so low, as they
> Which on an eye, cheek, lip, can prey;
>   Seldom to them which soar no higher
>   Than virtue, or the mind to admire.
> For sense and understanding may
>   Know what gives fuel to their fire;
> My love, though silly, is more brave;
> For may I miss, whene'er I crave
> If I know yet what I would have.

It is the intensely personal quality of Donne's writing that distinguishes it sharply from that of the so-called Classical School. To Dryden and his followers a lyric was an object almost as impersonal as a china bowl, and the skill of its craftsman was shown not in subjecting the material to the needs of his individual expression but rather in the opposite, in subjecting his individual desires and purposes to an idea conceived of as existing already in the material. Language was stuff that had poems in it if you could find them: perfect word-statues awaiting release from the block. They did not habitually reflect that in nine cases out of ten we understand a man not by what he says but by what we can suppose him to mean, that the same form of words may acquire a fresh meaning with every new situation in which it is used, and that in the last resort language is rather the symptom of expression than the substance. They thought of it habitually as the substance: the meanable crystallized and fixed in the sayable by the usage of their enlightened age. And out of this amalgam of the thing said which all could mean, and the thing meant which all could nearly say, they were able to fashion a bold, impersonal, comely sort of poetry, molded by social pressures and brightly glazed with civil decorum. It is impossible to imagine anything more unlike the art of Donne:

> Mark but this flea, and mark in this
> How little that which thou deny'st me is;
> It suck'd me first, and now sucks thee. . . .

Every decorum of civil life is deliberately shattered in order that this ruthless individual may emerge. Pope's poetry admits us to a social group, and gives us a sense of sharing in its amenities. But Donne's harsh voice breaks up any party; the social Airs and Graces flutter away, and we are left with a solitary figure, darkly pondering:

> When my grave is broke up again
> Some second guest to entertain
> —For graves have learn'd that woman-head,
> To be to more than one a bed—
> And he that digs it, spies
> A bracelet of bright hair about the bone. . . .[14]

It is like a soliloquy in a play by Webster, and demands an empty stage.

It was inevitable that a man so constituted should rebel against literary conventions; but the nature of his rebellion, and the direction that it took, were determined by the extraordinary deficiencies of his equipment as a poet. The beauty of the visible world meant nothing to him and yielded him no imagery for serious purpose. I am not forgetting

> Her pure and eloquent blood
> Spoke in her cheeks, and so distinctly wrought
> That one might almost say, her body thought.[15]

This is always quoted. But it is quoted because it is the only passage in all his works which seems to record an intense visual experience; the one oasis in a visual desert. Nor can it be said that he is much sensitive to beauty as perceived by the ear. His poems often begin with a noble resonance, but it is seldom maintained beyond a few lines and nearly always degenerates before the end into an ugly cross-hatching of verbal noises. In some cases this is of course deliberate:

> Good we must love and must hate ill,
> For ill is ill and good good still.[16]

Plug-ugly verse of this kind is evidently intended to jolt the ear. But even in later years, when he has given up these vanities and is humbly using the sonnet-form which he had at first despised, the same cacophony often

[14] "The Relic."   [15] *The Second Anniversary*, 244-6.
[16] "Community."

howls from his pen. One may defend it by attaching some new and recondite value to ugliness, and this is often done. But it remains ugliness. The only sense-impressions which seem to have had much value for Donne were tactual, or related to tactual experience. Space and the disposition of solid objects in space; continuity, distance, height, and depth; progress from point to point, curving or rectilinear, continuous or interrupted; the motion of the spiral, the smoothness and density of the sphere, the varying angles of a hinge; all that fabric of palpable fact which we must suppose to make the world of a man born blind and deaf—it is from this, or from material closely allied to it, that Donne draws his most energetic imagery. His poems are pestered with the apparatus by which contemporary science endeavored to extend man's tactual apprehension of the universe, and reduce the immeasurable or mysterious to something which he could hold in the palm of his hand: globes, orreries, compasses, deep-sea plummets; a model of the planets consisting of beads threaded on a string; a model of the nervous system done in hair; a dissecting-table, with evidence of gory rummagings thereon; a stone cut from the bladder; a dessicated mandrake; jelly said to have been a falling star; a whole Tradescant's houseful of rarities, jumbled together and viewed under the cold, white light of a window facing north. To Peter Bell the primrose was at least yellow. To Donne it is a five-pointed object suggestive of mathematical analogies with the nature of woman: all that remains of a primrose in the dark.[17] And yet such is the intensity with which he contemplates this narrow field of sensation which nature made significant for him, such the zeal with which he explores and improves and exploits it, that he is able out of this dismal lumber to evolve an imagery far more powerfully expressive than that of many poets more happily endowed. This is indeed one of the things that make his work so fascinating and so difficult to judge fairly. It is all in some measure a *tour de force,* and our sense of its poetic quality is liable to be surcharged with the kind of admiration which we give to the complete model of a frigate made out of mutton bones by a prisoner of war.

Certainly, a sense of difficulty overcome is an important element in the effect which Donne's poetry makes upon us, and was evidently felt and intended to be so by himself. This is shown in his technique throughout. One might have expected a poet who jangles the instrument of meter so impatiently to forgo fixed patterns altogether and use some kind of free verse. But, as Professor Legouis has pointed out, only one of the verse-forms used in the "Songs and Sonnets" could be said to belong to this category, and most of them consist of highly intricate and exacting patterns which he had apparently invented for himself. What makes it more curious is that, having gone to the trouble of inventing these

[17] "The Primrose, being at Montgomery Castle."

patterns, he persistently effaces and makes us forget them by allowing the natural rhythm of his language to pour over them, like a flood over a harrow, drowning them out of sight. It is not just a matter of "the sense variously drawn out from one verse into another." His verse is often definitely out of phase in the sense that the metrical shape and the rhythmical movement have no discernible relation. He seems to have regarded the pattern of verse (when he thought about it) not as an aid or an instrument of expression, but as a kind of obstacle, like the intricate words of a lock; and the game of versification consisted in cutting the key of words so cunningly that it would move through them all without touching, as though they were not there. Viewed in this way versification becomes simply a form of wit, and it ends logically enough in those typographical pillars and altars and Easter-wings which diversify the pages of Herbert's *Temple*. Once it is admitted that the pattern is merely an obstacle, there is no reason why it should not take a visual form as well as any other. But Donne's impulse to create a difficulty for his art to surmount was in itself defensible, and thoroughly characteristic of the man.

It is seen again, I think, in that quickest hedge of "metaphysical" wit which guards the center of so many of his poems. Much has been written about this, and no one can doubt that the peculiar merits as well as the defects of his poetry proceed from it. To mention nothing else, it is by this restless cerebration that the drama of the defeated coxcomb is kept present to the mind. But as "thought" this intellectual content of his poetry seems to me a good deal less important than some critics have made it out, and the attempt to represent Donne as a philosophical poet, like Lucretius or even like Chapman, is surely going too far. For Donne's "rebellion," if the term may be used, was social and ethical rather than intellectual. Little evidence has been adduced by those competent to judge that he was ever in any sense a constructive thinker. Though he questions much, he establishes nothing new, and the fabric of his ideas, as Miss Ramsay and others have shown, is still mediaeval. In spite of the scientific lumber that figures in his poems the new scientific movement really meant nothing to him. When he refers to it it is with dismay, as an added complication of an already too complicated world.[18] Like so many of his contemporaries he felt himself to be living in the latter twilight of Time.

> The skye lookes dusky: the Sunne puts forth a drowsie head; as if hee were no longer as David once described him, like a *Bride-groome comming out of his chamber, or a strong man rejoycing to runne his race.* The Moone looks pale, as if she were sicke with age: and the starres doe but twinckle; as if they were dimme, and look'd upon the earth with spectacles.

[18] *The First Anniversary*, 205.

The Colours of the Rainbow are not so radiant, and the whole earth shewes
but like a garment often dy'd, destitute of the native hew.[19]

Everything had been tried; every avenue had been explored, and nothing yet was certain. It was high time for man to turn away from this
fading wreck of a world and fix his eyes on Heaven. This is Donne's intellectual position as expounded in the first and almost only poem which
he allowed to be published. "The Anatomy of the World."

> Have not all souls thought
> For many ages that our body's wrought
> Of air, and fire, and other elements?
> And now they think of new ingredients:
> And one soul thinks one, and another way
> Another thinks, and 'tis an even lay.
> Know'st thou but how the stone doth enter in
> The bladder's cave, and never break the skin?
> Know'st thou how blood, which to the heart doth flow,
> Doth from one ventricle to th' other go?
> And for the putrid stuff which thou dost spit,
> Know'st thou how thy lungs have attracted it?
> There are no passages, so that there is
> —For aught thou know'st—piercing of substances. . . .
> What hope have we to know ourselves, when we
> Know not the least things which for our use be?
> We see in authors, too stiff to recant,
> A thousand controversies of an ant. . . .
> When wilt thou shake off this pedantry
> Of being taught by sense and fantasy?
> Thou look'st through spectacles; small things seem great
> Below; but up into the watch-tower get,
> And see all things despoil'd of fallacies;
> Thou shalt not peep through lattices of eyes,
> Nor hear through labyrinths of ears, nor learn
> By circuit or collections to discern.
> In heaven thou straight know'st all concerning it.[20]

This skepticism regarding the very instrument of knowledge colors
Donne's poetry throughout. His thinking never seems to be quite valid,
even to himself. He is sometimes careful of the steps in his logic, but he
is nearly always careless of its direction, and will use it to defend a manifest sophistry as readily as to serve what may be truth. He seems to value

[19] Adams, *Sermons* (1630).
[20] *The Second Anniversary*, 263 *et seq*.

it, as others value fancy, more for the strange things it may suggest than for any sober certainties it can yield. Logic is the Mephistophiles by whose aid he can conjure up Helen or swindle a horse-courser: a means of peopling the unknown with the phantoms of what might be. Even in his most somber poems the thought is seldom more than half serious:

> Whoever comes to shroud me, do not harm
>> Nor question much,
> That subtle wreath of hair which crowns my arm;
> The mystery, the sign you must not touch;
>> For 'tis my outward soul,
> Viceroy to that, which unto heaven being gone,
>> Will leave this to control
> And keep these limbs, her provinces, from dissolution.
>
> For if the sinewy thread my brain lets fall
>> Through every part
> Can tie those parts, and make me one of all,
> Those hairs which upward grew, and strength and art
>> Have from a better brain,
> Can better do't; except she meant that I
>> By this should know my pain,
> As prisoners then are manacled, when they're condemn'd to die.
>
> Whate'er she meant by it, bury it with me,
>> For since I am
> Love's martyr, it might breed idolatry,
> If into other hands these relics came.
>> As 'twas humility
> To afford to it all that a soul can do,
>> So 'tis some bravery,
> That since you would have none of me, I bury some of you.[21]

The argument that *because* the thread-like nerves from his own brain hold his body together, *therefore* the nerve-like threads from her much better brain will do it much better is a typical piece of trifling. And yet the final effect of the poem is grave enough: all the graver, perhaps, for the suggestion of brain-sickness which these futile ingenuities convey. The twaddling logic has been used to suspend and thus somehow to intensify the expression of powerful feeling. And this seems to me to be what happens in all Donne's successful poetry. He was never really interested enough in his own thought to take it as seriously as his critics. Mr. Eliot has said that "A thought for Donne was an experience; it modified his sensibility." But in so far as this is more than a truism—for I suppose

---

[21] "The Funeral."

that any man's thought modifies his sensibility to some extent—it seems to me to suggest the exact opposite of the truth. It was Donne's sensibility that modified his thought, mammocked it, made a guy of it in poem after poem. Yet this "thought," this convolvulus-growth of intellectual whim-whams, is an organic part of his poetry, and cannot be dismissed in Johnson's short way as a kind of foreign body entangled in his art by accident. Its value might perhaps best be compared with that of the Fool in *King Lear*, as providing an undercurrent of half-relevant commentary which, while it never really touches the core of the situation, serves to heighten our sense of it by creating a kind of suspense. In the poem quoted above, the futile analogy between the hair-like threads descending from one head and the thread-like hairs ascending from the other helps by its dawdling irrelevance and teasing of the mind to accentuate the sense of passionate release in the words.

> Whate'er she meant by it, bury it with me

So again in the poem called "A Valediction: of Weeping": his round tears are coins because they bear her image reflected in them; they bear his whole world reflected in them, therefore they are worlds; they are globes made by a map-maker, and his tears are the sea drawn up by her (the moon); and if she weeps too there will be too much sea and his world will be drowned—thus the brain-sick fancies are piled up, twaddle upon twaddle, until the whole thing explodes with a passionate outcry and a familiar image:

> O more than moon,
> Draw not up seas to drown me in thy sphere;
> Weep me not dead in thine arms, but forbear
> To teach the sea what it may do too soon.

In such passages one seems to detect the same principle of opposition that governs the technique of his verse. Just as his intricate verse-patterns are like the wards of a lock menacing the free movement of his language, so these figments of his intellect are used as obstacles endangering and making more arduous his heart's right of way. When the technique is successful his poems are enriched with the intensity of feeling which springs from the idea of difficulty surmounted. But it is surely not the technique of a philosophical poet. It suggests rather a man who felt that in the last resort the structures of the intellect were useless, and that contact with ultimate reality could be found only in passion: the passion of love, or the passion of faith.

Donne and Love Poetry
in the Seventeenth Century

by C. S. Lewis

The great central movement of love poetry, and of fiction about love, in Donne's time is that represented by Shakespeare and Spenser. This movement consisted in the final transmutation of the mediaeval courtly love or romance of adultery into an equally romantic love that looked to marriage as its natural conclusion. The process, of course, had begun far earlier—as early, indeed, as the *Kingis Quhair*—but its triumph belongs to the sixteenth century. It is most powerfully expressed by Spenser, but more clearly and philosophically by Chapman in that underestimated poem, his *Hero and Leander*. These poets were engaged, as Professor Vinaver would say, in reconciling Carbonek and Camelot, virtue and courtesy, divine and human love; and incidentally in laying down the lines which love-poetry was to follow till the nineteenth century. We who live at the end of the dispensation which they inaugurated and in reaction against it are not well placed for evaluating their work. Precisely what is revolutionary and creative in it seems to us platitudinous, orthodox, and stale. If there were a poet, and a strong poet, alive in their time who was failing to move with them, he would inevitably appear to us more "modern" than they.

But was Donne such a poet? A great critic has assigned him an almost opposite role, and it behoves us to proceed with caution. It may be admitted at once that Donne's work is not, in this respect, all of a piece; no poet fits perfectly into such a scheme as I have outlined—it can be true only by round and by large. There are poems in which Donne attempts to sing a love perfectly in harmony with the moral law, but they are not very numerous and I do not think they are usually his best pieces. Donne never for long gets rid of a mediaeval sense of the sinfulness of sexuality; indeed, just because the old conventional division be-

"Donne and Love Poetry in the Seventeenth Century." The latter part of an essay contributed by C. S. Lewis to *Seventeenth-Century Studies Presented to Sir Herbert Grierson* (Oxford, 1938), pp. 73-84. Reprinted by permission of the author and The Clarendon Press. [For a modification of the views expressed here, see C. S. Lewis, *English Literature in the Sixteenth Century* (Oxford, 1954), pp. 546-551. *Ed.*]

tween Carbonek and Camelot is breaking up, he feels this more continuously and restively than any poet of the Middle Ages.

Donne was bred a Roman Catholic. The significance of this in relation to his learned and scholastic imagery can be exaggerated; scraps of Calvin, or, for that matter, of Euclid or Bacon, might have much the same poetical effect as his scraps of Aquinas. But it is all-important for his treatment of love. This is not easily understood by the modern reader, for later-day conceptions of the Puritan and the Roman Catholic stand in the way. We have come to use the word "Puritan" to mean what should rather be called "rigorist" or "ascetic," and we tend to assume that the sixteenth century Puritans were "puritanical" in this sense. Calvin's rigorist theocracy at Geneva lends color to the error. But there is no understanding the period of the Reformation in England until we have grasped the fact that the quarrel between the Puritans and the Papists was not primarily a quarrel between rigorism and indulgence, and that, in so far as it was, the rigorism was on the Roman side. On many questions, and specially in their view of the marriage bed, the Puritans were the indulgent party; if we may without disrespect so use the name of a great Roman Catholic, a great writer, and a great man, they were much more Chestertonian than their adversaries. The idea that a Puritan was a repressed and repressive person would have astonished Sir Thomas More and Luther about equally. On the contrary, More thought of a Puritan as one who "loved no lenten fast nor lightly no fast else, saving breakfast and eat fast and drink fast and luske fast in their lechery"— a person only too likely to end up in the "abominable heresies" of the Anabaptists about communism of goods and wives. And Puritan theology, so far from being grim and gloomy, seemed to More to err in the direction of fantastic optimism. "I could for my part," he writes, "be very well content that sin and pain and all were as shortly gone as Tindall telleth us: but I were loth that he deceved us if it be not so." More would not have understood the idea, sometimes found in the modern writers, that he and his friends were defending a "merry" Catholic England against sour precisions; they were rather defending necessary severity and sternly realistic theology against wanton labefaction—penance and "works" and vows of celibacy and mortification and Purgatory against the easy doctrine, the mere wish-fulfilment dream, of salvation by faith. Hence when we turn from the religious work of More to Luther's *Table-talk* we are at once struck by the geniality of the latter. If Luther is right, we have waked from nightmare into sunshine: if he is wrong, we have entered a fools' paradise. The burden of his charge against the Catholics is that they have needlessly tormented us with scruples; and, in particular, that "Antichrist will regard neither God nor the love of women." "On what pretence have they forbidden us marriage? 'Tis as though we were forbidden to eat, to drink, to sleep." "Where women are not honoured, temporal and domestic government are despised." He praises women repeatedly: More, it will be remembered, though apparently an excellent husband and father, hardly ever mentions a woman save to ridicule her. It is easy to see why Luther's marriage (as he called it) or Luther's "abominable bichery" (if you prefer) became almost a symbol. More can never keep off the subject for more than a few pages.

This antithesis, if once understood, explains many things in the history of sentiment, and many differences, noticeable to the present day, between the Protestant and the Catholic parts of Europe. It explains why the conversion of courtly love into romantic monogamous love was so largely the work of English, and even of Puritan, poets; and it goes far to explain why Donne contributes so little to that movement.

I trace in his poetry three levels of sentiment. On the lowest level (lowest, that is, in order of complexity), we have the celebration of simple appetite, as in Elegy XIX. If I call this a pornographic poem, I must be understood to use that ugly word as a descriptive, not a dyslogistic, term. I mean by it that this poem, in my opinion, is intended to arouse the appetite it describes, to affect not only the imagination but the nervous system of the reader.[1] And I may as well say at once—but who would willingly claim to be a judge in such matters?—that it seems to me to be very nearly perfect in its kind. Nor would I call it an immoral poem. Under what conditions the reading of it could be an innocent act is a real moral question; but the poem itself contains nothing intrinsically evil.

On the highest, or what Donne supposed to be the highest, level we have the poems of ostentatiously virtuous love, "The Undertaking," "A Valediction: forbidding Mourning," and "The Ecstasy." It is here that the contrast between Donne and his happier contemporaries is most marked. He is trying to follow them into the new age, to be at once passionate and innocent; and if any reader will make the experiment of imagining Beatrice or Juliet or Perdita, or again, Amoret or Britomart, or even Philoclea or Pamela, as the auditress throughout these poems, he will quickly feel that something is wrong. You may deny, as perhaps some do, that the romantic conception of "pure" passion has any meaning; but certainly, if there is such a thing, it is not like this. It does not prove itself pure by talking about purity. It does not keep on drawing distinctions between spirit and flesh to the detriment of the latter and then explaining why the flesh is, after all, to be used. This is what Donne does, and the result is singularly unpleasant. The more he labors the deeper "Dun is in the mire," and it is quite arguable that "The Ecstasy" is a much nastier poem than the nineteenth Elegy. What any sensible woman

---

[1] The restatement of this in terms acceptable to the Richardsian School (for whom all poetry equally is addressed to the nervous system) should present no difficulty. For them it will be a distinction between parts, or functions, of the system.

would make of such a wooing it is difficult to imagine—or would be difficult if we forget the amazing protective faculty which each sex possesses of not listening to the other.

Between these two extremes falls the great body of Donne's love poetry. In certain obvious, but superficial, respects it continues the mediaeval tradition. Love is still a god and lovers his "clergie"; oaths may be made in "reverentiall feare" of his "wrath"; and the man who resists him is "rebell and atheist." Donne can even doubt, like Soredamors, whether those who admit Love after a struggle have not forfeited his grace by their resistance, like

> Small townes which stand stiffe, til great shot
> Enforce them.

He can personify the attributes of his mistress, the "enormous gyant" her Disdain and the "enchantress *Honor,*" quite in the manner of *The Romance of the Rose.* He writes *Albas* for both sexes, and in the "Holy Sonnets" repents of his love poetry, writing his palinode, in true mediaeval fashion. A reader may wonder, at first, why the total effect is so foreign to the Middle Ages: but Donne himself has explained this when he says, speaking of the god of Love,

> If he wroung from mee a teare, I brin'd it so
> With scorne or shame, that him it nourish'd not.

This admirable couplet not only tells us, in brief, what Donne has effected but shows us that he knew what he was doing. It does not, of course, cover every single poem. A few pieces admittedly express delighted love and they are among Donne's most popular works; such are "The Goodmorrow" and "The Anniversary"—poems that again remind us of the difference between his best and his typical. But the majority of the poems ring the changes on five themes, all of them grim ones—on the sorrow of parting (including death), the miseries of secrecy, the falseness of the mistress, the fickleness of Donne, and finally on contempt for love itself. The poems of parting stand next to the poems of happy love in general popularity and are often extremely affecting. We may hear little of the delights of Donne's loves, and dislike what we hear of their "purity"; the pains ring true. The song "Sweetest love, I do not goe" is remarkable for its broken, but haunting, melody, and nowhere else has Donne fused argument, conceit, and classical imitation into a more perfect unity. "The Fever" is equally remarkable, and that for a merit very rare in Donne—its inevitability. It is a single jet of music and feeling, a straight flight without appearance of effort. The remaining four of our

five themes are all various articulations of the "scorne or shame" with
which Donne "brines" his reluctantly extorted tributes to the god of
Love; monuments, unparalleled outside Catullus, to the close kinship
between certain kinds of love and certain kinds of hate. The faithlessness
of women is sometimes treated, in a sense, playfully; but there is always
something—the clever surprise in "Woman's Constancy" or the grotesque
in "Goe and catche a fallinge starre"—which stops these poems short of a
true anacreontic gaiety. The theme of faithlessness rouses Donne to a more
characteristic, and also a better, poetry in such a hymn of hate as "The
Apparition," or in the sad mingling of fear, contempt, and self-
contempt in "A Lecture upon the Shadow." The pains of secrecy give
opportunity for equally fierce and turbulent writing. I may be deceived
when I find in the sixteenth Elegy, along with many other nauseas and
indignations, a sickened male contempt for the whole female world of
nurses and "midnight startings" and hysterics; but "The Curse" is
unambiguous. The ending here is particularly delicious just because the
main theme—an attack on *Jalosie* or the "lozengiers"—is so mediaeval
and so associated with the "honor of love." Of the poet's own fickleness
one might expect, at last, a merry treatment; and perhaps in "The Indifferent" we get it. But I am not sure. Even this seems to have a sting in
it. And of "Love's Usury" what shall I say? The struggle between lust
and reason, the struggle between love and reason, these we know; but
Donne is perhaps the first poet who has ever painted lust holding love at
arm's length, in the hope "that there's no need to trouble himself with
any such thoughts yet"—and all this only as an introduction to the
crowning paradox that in old age even a reciprocated love must be en-
dured. The poem is, in its way, a masterpiece, and a powerful indirect
expression of Donne's habitual "shame and scorne." For, in the long
run, it must be admitted that "the love of hatred and the hate of love" is
the main, though not the only, theme of the "Songs and Sonnets." A man
is a fool for loving and a double fool for saying so in "whining poetry";
the only excuse is that the sheer difficulty of drawing one's pains through
rhyme's vexation "allays" them. A woman's love at best will be only
the "spheare" of a man's—inferior to it as the heavenly spheres are to
their intelligences or air to angels. Love is a spider that can transub-
stantiate all sweets into bitter: a devil who differs from his fellow devils at
court by taking the soul and giving nothing in exchange. The mystery
which the Petrarchans or their mediaeval predecessors made of it is "imposture all," like the claims of alchemists. It is a very simple matter (*foeda
et brevis voluptas*), and all it comes to in the end is

> that my man
> Can be as happy as I can.

Unsuccessful love is a plague and tyranny; but there is a plague even
worse—Love might try

> A deeper plague, to make her love mee too!

Love enjoyed is like gingerbread with the gilt off. What pleased the
whole man now pleases one sense only—

> And that so lamely, as it leaves behinde
> A kinde of sorrowing dulnesse to the minde.

The doctors say it shortens life.

It may be urged that this is an unfair selection of quotations, or even
that I have arrived at my picture of Donne by leaving out all his best
poems, for one reason or another, as "exceptions," and then describing
what remains. There is one sense in which I admit this. Any account of
Donne which concentrates on his love-poetry must be unfair to the poet,
for it leaves out much of his best work. By hypothesis, it must neglect the
dazzling sublimity of his best religious poems, the grotesque charm of
The Progress of the Soul [*Metempsychosis*], and those scattered, but exquisite, patches of poetry that appear from time to time amidst the
insanity of *The First and Second Anniversaries*. Even in the Epistles there
are good passages. But as far as concerns his love poetry, I believe I am
just. I have no wish to rule out the exceptions, provided that they are
admitted to be exceptions. I am attempting to describe the prevailing
tone of his work, and in my description no judgment is yet implied.

To judgment let us now proceed. Here is a collection of verse describing with unusual and disturbing energy the torments of a mind which
has been baffled in its relation to sexual love by certain temporary and
highly special conditions. What is its value? To admit the "unusual and
disturbing energy" is, of course, to admit that Donne is a poet; he has,
in the modern phrase, "put his stuff across." Those who believe that
criticism can separate inquiry into the success of communication from
that into the value of the thing communicated will demand that we
should now proceed to evaluate the "stuff"; and if we do so, it would
not be hard to point out how transitory and limited and, as it were,
accidental the appeal of such "stuff" must be. But something of the real
problem escapes under this treatment. It would not be impossible to
imagine a poet dealing with this same stuff, marginal and precarious as
it is, in a way that would permanently engage our attention. Donne's
real limitation is not that he writes *about*, but that he writes *in*, a chaos
of violent and transitory passions. He is perpetually excited and therefore perpetually cut off from the deeper and more permanent springs of

his own excitement. But how is this to be separated from his technique—
the nagging, nudging, quibbling stridency of his manner? If a man writes
thus, what can he communicate but excitement? Or again, if he finds
nothing but excitement to communicate, how else should he write? It
is impossible here to distinguish cause from effect. Our concern, in the
long run, must be with the actual poetry (the "stuff" *thus* communicated,
this communication of such "stuff") and with the question how far that
total phenomenon is calculated to interest human imagination. And to
this question I can see only one answer: that its interest, save for a mind
specially predisposed in its favor, must be short-lived and superficial,
though intense. Paradoxical as it may seem, Donne's poetry is too simple
to satisfy. Its complexity is all on the surface—an intellectual and
fully conscious complexity that we soon come to the end of. Beneath
this we find nothing but a limited series of "passions"—explicit,
mutually exclusive passions which can be instantly and adequately
labelled as such—things which can be readily talked about, and
indeed, must be talked about because, in silence, they begin to lose
their hard outlines and overlap, to betray themselves as partly fic-
titious. That is why Donne is always arguing. There are puzzles in his
work, but we can solve them all if we are clever enough; there is none of
the depth and ambiguity of real experience in him, such as underlies the
apparent simplicity of "How sleep the brave" or *Songs of Innocence,* or
even A'ιᾶι Λειψύδριον.[2] The same is true, for the most part, of the
specifically "metaphysical" comparisons. One idea has been put into
each and nothing more can come out of it. Hence they tend to die on our
hands, where some seemingly banal comparison of a woman to a flower or
God's anger to flame can touch us at innumerable levels and renew its
virginity at every reading. Of all literary virtues "originality," in the
vulgar sense, has, for this reason, the shortest life. When we have once
mastered a poem by Donne there is nothing more to do with it. To use
his own simile, he deals in earthquakes, not in that "trepidation of the
spheres" which is so much less violent but "greater far."

Some, of course, will contend that his love poems should interest me
permanently because of their "truth." They will say that he has shown
me passion with the mask off, and catch at my word "uncomfortable"
to prove that I am running away from him because he tells me more truth
than I can bear. But this is the mere frenzy of anti-romanticism. Of
course, Donne is true in the sense that passions such as he presents do
occur in human experience. So do a great many other things. He makes
his own selection, like Dickens, or Gower, or Herrick, and his world is
neither more nor less "real" than theirs; while it is obviously less real
than the world of Homer, or Virgil, or Tolstoy. In one way, indeed,

---

[2] The superficial simplicity here is obvious; the deeper ambiguity becomes evident
if we ask whether Lipsydrion is an object of detestation or of nostalgic affection.

Donne's love-poetry is less true than that of the Petrarchans, in so far as it largely omits the very thing that all the pother is about. Donne shows us a variety of sorrows, scorns, angers, disgusts, and the like which arise out of love. But if any one asked "What is all this *about*? What is the attraction which makes these partings so sorrowful? What is the peculiarity about this physical pleasure which he speaks of so contemptuously, and how has it got tangled up with such a storm of emotions?" I do not know how we could reply except by pointing to some ordinary love-poetry. The feeblest sonnet, almost, of the other school would give us an answer with coral lips and Cupid's golden wings and the opening rose, with perfumes and instruments of music, with some attempt, however trite, to paint that iridescence which explains why people write poems about love at all. In this sense Donne's love-poetry is parasitic. I do not use this word as a term of reproach; there are so many good poets, by now, in the world that one particular poet is entitled to take for granted the depth of a passion and deal with its froth. But as a purely descriptive term, "parasitic" seems to me true. Donne's love poems could not exist unless love poems of a more genial character existed first. He shows us amazing shadows cast by love upon the intellect, the passions, and the appetite; to learn of the substance which cast them we must go to other poets, more balanced, more magnanimous, and more humane. There are, I well remember, poems (some two or three) in which Donne himself presents the substance; and the fact that he does so without much luxury of language and symbol endears them to our temporarily austere taste. But in the main, his love-poetry is *Hamlet* without the prince.

Donne's influence on the poets of the seventeenth century is a commonplace of criticism. Of that influence at its best, as it is seen in the great devotional poetry of the period, I have not now to speak. In love-poetry he was not, perhaps, so dominant. His *nequitiae* probably encouraged the cynical and licentious songs of his successors, but, if so, the imitation is very different from the model. Suckling's impudence, at its best, is light-hearted and very unlike the ferocity of Donne; and Suckling's chief fault in this vein—a stolid fleshliness which sometimes leads him to speak of his mistress's body more like a butcher than a lecher—is entirely his own. The more strictly metaphysical elements in Donne are, of course, lavishly reproduced; but I doubt if the reproduction succeeds best when it is most faithful. Thus Carew's stanzas "When thou, poor Excommunicate" or Lovelace's "To Lucasta, going beyond the Seas" are built up on Donne's favorite plan, but both, as it seems to me, fail in that startling and energetic quality which this kind of thing demands. They have no edge. When these poets succeed it is by adding something else to what they have learned from Donne—in fact by reuniting Donne's manner with something much more like ordinary poetry. Beauty (like cheerfulness) is always breaking in. Thus the conceit of asking where various

evanescent, beautiful phenomena go when they vanish and replying
that they are all to be found in one's mistress is the sort of conceit that
Donne might have used; and, starting from that end, we could easily
work it up into something tolerably like bad Donne. As thus:

> Oh fooles that aske whether of odours burn'd
> The seminall forme live, and from that death
> Conjure the same with chymique arte—'tis turn'd
> To that quintessence call'd her Breath!

But if we use the same idea as Carew uses it we get a wholly different
effect:

> Ask me no more where Jove bestows
> When June is past, the fading rose:
> For in your beauty's orient deep
> These flowers, as in their causes, sleep.

The idea is the same. But the choice of the obvious and obviously beautiful rose, instead of the recondite seminal form of vegetables, the great
regal name of Jove, the alliteration, the stately voluptuousness of a
quatrain where all the accented syllables are also long in quantity (a
secret little known)—all this smothers the sharpness of thought in sweetness. Compared with Donne, it is almost soporific; compared with it,
Donne is shrill. But the conceit is there; and "as in their causes, sleep"
which looks at first like a blunder, is in fact a paradox that Donne might
have envied. So again, the conceit that the lady's hair outshines the sun,
though not much more than an Elizabethan conceit, might well have
appeared in the "Songs and Sonnets"; but Donne would neither have
wished, nor been able, to attain the radiance of Lovelace's

> But shake your head and scatter day!

This process of enchanting, or, in Shakespeare's sense, "translating"
Donne was carried to its furthest point by Marvell. Almost every element
of Donne—except his metrical roughness—appears in the "Coy Mistress."
Nothing could be more like Donne, both in the grimness of its content
and in its impudently argumentative function, than the conceit that

> worms shall try
> That long preserved virginity.

All the more admirable is the art by which this and everything else
in that poem, however abstruse, dismaying, or sophistical, is subordinated

to a sort of golden tranquillity. What was death to Donne is mere play to Marvell. "Out of the strong," we are tempted to say, "has come sweetness," but in reality the strength is all on Marvell's side. He is an Olympian, ruling at ease for his own good purposes, all that intellectual and passionate mobility of which Donne was the slave, and leading Donne himself, bound, behind his chariot.

From all this we may conclude that Donne was a "good influence"—a better influence than many greater poets. It would hardly be too much to say that the final cause of Donne's poetry is the poetry of Herbert, Crashaw, and Marvell; for the very qualities which make Donne's kind of poetry unsatisfying poetic food make it a valuable ingredient.

The Language of Paradox:
"The Canonization"

by Cleanth Brooks

Even the apparently simple and straightforward poet is forced into paradoxes by the nature of his instrument. Seeing this, we should not be surprised to find poets who consciously employ it to gain a compression and precision otherwise unobtainable. Such a method, like any other, carries with it its own perils. But the dangers are not overpowering; the poem is not predetermined to a shallow and glittering sophistry. The method is an extension of the normal language of poetry, not a perversion of it.

I should like to refer the reader to a concrete case. Donne's "Canonization" ought to provide a sufficiently extreme instance.

> For Godsake hold your tongue, and let me love
>   Or chide my palsie, or my gout,
> My five gray haires, or ruin'd fortune flout,
>   With wealth your state, your minde with Arts improve,
>   Take you a course, get you a place,
>   Observe his honour, or his grace,
> Or the Kings reall, or his stamped face
>   Contemplate, what you will, approve,
>   So you will let me love.
>
> Alas, alas, who's injur'd by my love?
>   What merchants ships have my sighs drown'd?
> Who saies my teares have overflow'd his ground?
>   When did my colds a forward spring remove?
>   When did the heats which my veines fill
>   Adde one more to the plaguie Bill?
> Soldiers finde warres, and Lawyers finde out still

Litigious men, which quarrels move,
Though she and I do love.

Call us what you will, wee are made such by love;
Call her one, mee another flye,
We'are Tapers too, and at our owne cost die,
And wee in us finde the Eagle and the Dove.
The Phœnix ridle hath more wit
By us, we two being one, are it.
So to one neutrall thing both sexes fit,
Wee dye and rise the same, and prove
Mysterious by this love.

Wee can dye by it, if not live by love,
And if unfit for tombes and hearse
Our legend bee, it will be fit for verse;
And if no peece of Chronicle wee prove,
We'll build in sonnets pretty roomes;
As well a well wrought urne becomes
The greatest ashes, as halfe-acre tombes,
And by these hymnes, all shall approve
Us Canoniz'd for Love:

And thus invoke us; You whom reverend love
Made one anothers hermitage;
You, to whom love was peace, that now is rage;
Who did the whole worlds soule contract, and drove
Into the glasses of your eyes
(So made such mirrors, and such spies,
That they did all to you epitomize,)
Countries, Townes, Courts: Beg from above
A patterne of your love!

The basic metaphor which underlies the poem (and which is reflected in the title) involves a sort of paradox. For the poet daringly treats profane love as if it were divine love. The canonization is not that of a pair of holy anchorites who have renounced the world and the flesh. The hermitage of each is the other's body; but they do renounce the world, and so their title to sainthood is cunningly argued. The poem then is a parody of Christian sainthood; but it is an intensely serious parody of a sort that modern man, habituated as he is to an easy yes or no, can hardly understand. He refuses to accept the paradox as a serious rhetorical device; and since he is able to accept it only as a cheap trick, he is forced into this dilemma. Either: Donne does not take love seriously; here he is merely sharpening his wit as a sort of mechanical exercise. Or:

Donne does not take sainthood seriously; here he is merely indulging in a cynical and bawdy parody.

Neither account is true; a reading of the poem will show that Donne takes both love and religion seriously; it will show, further, that the paradox is here his inevitable instrument. But to see this plainly will require a closer reading than most of us give to poetry.

The poem opens dramatically on a note of exasperation. The "you" whom the speaker addresses is not identified. We can imagine that it is a person, perhaps a friend, who is objecting to the speaker's love affair. At any rate, the person represents the practical world which regards love as a silly affectation. To use the metaphor on which the poem is built, the friend represents the secular world which the lovers have renounced.

Donne begins to suggest this metaphor in the first stanza by the contemptuous alternatives which he suggests to the friend:

> . . . chide my palsie, or my gout,
> My five gray haires, or ruin'd fortune flout. . . .

The implications are: (1) All right, consider my love as an infirmity, as a disease, if you will, but confine yourself to my other infirmities, my palsy, my approaching old age, my ruined fortune. You stand a better chance of curing those; in chiding me for this one, you are simply wasting your time as well as mine. (2) Why don't you pay attention to your own welfare—go on and get wealth and honor for yourself. What should you care if I do give these up in pursuing my love.

The two main categories of secular success are neatly, and contemptuously epitomized in the line

> Or the Kings reall, or his stamped face . . .

Cultivate the court and gaze at the king's face there, or, if you prefer, get into business and look at his face stamped on coins. But let me alone.

This conflict between the "real" world and the lover absorbed in the world of love runs through the poem; it dominates the second stanza in which the torments of love, so vivid to the lover, affect the real world not at all—

> What merchants ships have my sighs drown'd?

It is touched on in the fourth stanza in the contrast between the word "Chronicle" which suggests secular history with its pomp and magnificence, the history of kings and princes, and the word "sonnets" with its suggestions of trivial and precious intricacy. The conflict appears again in the last stanza, only to be resolved when the unworldly lovers, love's saints who have given up the world, paradoxically achieve a more intense world. But here the paradox is still contained in, and supported by, the dominant metaphor: so does the holy anchorite win a better world by giving up this one.

But before going on to discuss this development of the theme, it is important to see what else the second stanza does. For it is in this second stanza and the third, that the poet shifts the tone of the poem, modulating from the note of irritation with which the poem opens into the quite different tone with which it closes.

Donne accomplishes the modulation of tone by what may be called an analysis of love-metaphor. Here, as in many of his poems, he shows that he is thoroughly self-conscious about what he is doing. This second stanza, he fills with the conventionalized figures of the Petrarchan tradition: the wind of lovers' sighs, the floods of lovers' tears, etc.—extravagant figures with which the contemptuous secular friend might be expected to tease the lover. The implication is that the poet himself recognizes the absurdity of the Petrarchan love metaphors. But what of it? The very absurdity of the jargon which lovers are expected to talk makes for his argument: their love, however absurd it may appear to the world, does no harm to the world. The practical friend need have no fears: there will still be wars to fight and lawsuits to argue.

The opening of the third stanza suggests that this vein of irony is to be maintained. The poet points out to his friend the infinite fund of such absurdities which can be applied to lovers:

> Call her one, mee another flye,
> We'are Tapers too, and at our owne cost die. . . .

For that matter, the lovers can conjure up for themselves plenty of such fantastic comparisons: *they* know what the world thinks of them. But these figures of the third stanza are no longer the threadbare Petrarchan conventionalities; they have sharpness and bite. The last one, the likening of the lovers to the phoenix, is fully serious, and with it, the tone has shifted from ironic banter into a defiant but controlled tenderness.

The effect of the poet's implied awareness of the lovers' apparent madness is to cleanse and revivify metaphor; to indicate the sense in which the poet accepts it, and thus to prepare us for accepting seriously the fine and seriously intended metaphors which dominate the last two stanzas of the poem.

The opening line of the fourth stanza,

> Wee can dye by it, if not live by love,

achieves an effect of tenderness and deliberate resolution. The lovers are ready to die to the world; they are committed; they are not callow but confident. (The basic metaphor of the saint, one notices, is being carried on; the lovers in their renunciation of the world, have something of the confident resolution of the saint. By the bye, the word "legend"—

> . . . if unfit for tombes and hearse
> Our legend bee—

in Donne's time meant "the life of a saint.") The lovers are willing to forego the ponderous and stately chronicle and to accept the trifling and insubstantial "sonnet" instead; but then if the urn be well wrought, it provides a finer memorial for one's ashes than does the pompous and grotesque monument. With the finely contemptuous, yet quiet phrase, "halfe-acre tombes," the world which the lovers reject expands into something gross and vulgar. But the figure works further; the pretty sonnets will not merely hold their ashes as a decent earthly memorial. Their legend, their story, will gain them canonization; and approved as love's saints, other lovers will invoke them.

In this last stanza, the theme receives a final complication. The lovers in rejecting life actually win to the most intense life. This paradox has been hinted at earlier in the phoenix metaphor. Here it receives a powerful dramatization. The lovers in becoming hermits, find that they have not lost the world, but have gained the world in each other, now a more intense, more meaningful world. Donne is not content to treat the lovers' discovery as something which comes to them passively, but rather as something which they actively achieve. They are like the saint, God's athlete:

> Who did the whole worlds soule contract, and drove
> Into the glasses of your eyes. . . .

The image is that of a violent squeezing as of a powerful hand. And what do the lovers "drive" into each other's eyes? The "Countries, Townes," and "Courtes," which they renounced in the first stanza of the poem. The unworldly lovers thus become the most "worldly" of all.

The tone with which the poem closes is one of triumphant achievement, but the tone is a development contributed to by various earlier elements. One of the more important elements which works toward our acceptance of the final paradox is the figure of the phoenix, which will bear a little further analysis.

The comparison of the lovers to the phoenix is very skillfully related to the two earlier comparisons, that in which the lovers are like burning tapers, and that in which they are like the eagle and the dove. The phoenix comparison gathers up both: the phoenix is a bird, and like the tapers, it burns. We have a selected series of items: the phoenix figure seems to come in a natural stream of association. "Call us what you will," the lover says, and rattles off in his desperation the first comparisons that occur to him. The comparison to the phoenix seems thus merely another outlandish one, the most outrageous of all. But it is this most fantastic one, stumbled over apparently in his haste, that the poet goes on to develop. It really describes the lovers best and justifies their renunciation. For the phoenix is not two but one, "we two being one, are it"; and it burns, not like the taper at its own cost, but to live again. Its death is life: "Wee dye and rise the same . . ." The poet literally justifies the fantastic assertion. In the sixteenth and seventeenth centuries to "die" means to experience the consummation of the act of love. The lovers after the act are the same. Their love is not exhausted in mere lust. This is their title to canonization. Their love is like the phoenix.

I hope that I do not seem to juggle the meaning of *die*. The meaning that I have cited can be abundantly justified in the literature of the period; Shakespeare uses "die" in this sense; so does Dryden. Moreover, I do not think that I give it undue emphasis. The word is in a crucial position. On it is pivoted the transition to the next stanza.

> Wee can dye by it, if not live by love,
> And if unfit for tombes . . .

Most important of all, the sexual submeaning of "die" does not contradict the other meanings: the poet is saying: "Our death is really a more intense life"; "We can afford to trade life (the world) for death (love), for that death is the consummation of life"; "After all, one does not expect to live *by* love, one expects, and wants, to die *by* it." But in the total passage he is also saying: "Because our love is not mundane, we can give up the world"; "Because our love is not merely lust, we can give up the other lusts, the lust for wealth and power"; "because," and this is said with an inflection of irony as by one who knows the world too well, "because our love can outlast its consummation, we are a minor miracle, we are love's saints." This passage with its ironical tenderness and its realism feeds and supports the brilliant paradox with which the poem closes.

There is one more factor in developing and sustaining the final effect. The poem is an instance of the doctrine which it asserts; it is both the assertion and the realization of the assertion. The poet has actually before our eyes built within the song the "pretty room" with which he says the lovers can be content. The poem itself is the well-wrought urn which can hold the lovers' ashes and which will not suffer in comparison with the prince's "halfe-acre tomb."

And how necessary are the paradoxes? Donne might have said directly, "Love in a cottage is enough." "The Canonization" contains this admirable thesis, but it contains a great deal more. He might have been as forthright as a later lyricist who wrote, "We'll build a sweet little nest, / Somewhere out in the West, / And let the rest of the world go by."

He might even have imitated that more metaphysical lyric, which maintains, "You're the cream in my coffee." "The Canonization" touches on all these observations, but it goes beyond them, not merely in dignity, but in precision.

I submit that the only way by which the poet could say what "The Canonization" says is by paradox. More direct methods may be tempting, but all of them enfeeble and distort what is to be said. This statement may seem the less surprising when we reflect on how many of the important things which the poet has to say have to be said by means of paradox: most of the language of lovers is such—"The Canonization" is a good example; so is most of the language of religion—"He who would save his life, must lose it"; "The last shall be first." Indeed, almost any insight important enough to warrant a great poem apparently has to be stated in such terms. Deprived of the character of paradox with its twin concomitants of irony and wonder, the matter of Donne's poem unravels into "facts," biological, sociological, and economic. What happens to Donne's lovers if we consider them "scientifically," without benefit of the supernaturalism which the poet confers upon them? Well, what happens to Shakespeare's lovers, for Shakespeare uses the basic metaphor of "The Canonization" in his *Romeo and Juliet?* In their first conversation, the lovers play with the analogy between the lover and the pilgrim to the Holy Land. Juliet says:

> For saints have hands that pilgrims' hands do touch
> And palm to palm is holy palmers' kiss.

Considered scientifically, the lovers become Mr. Aldous Huxley's animals, "quietly sweating, palm to palm."

For us today, Donne's imagination seems obsessed with the problem of unity; the sense in which the lovers become one—the sense in which the soul is united with God. Frequently, as we have seen, one type of union becomes a metaphor for the other. It may not be too far-fetched to see both as instances of, and metaphors for, the union which the creative imagination itself effects. For that fusion is not logical; it apparently violates science and common sense; it welds together the discordant and the contradictory. Coleridge has of course given us the classic description of its nature and power. It "reveals itself in the balance or reconcilement of opposite or discordant qualities: of sameness, with difference; of the general, with the concrete; the idea, with the image; the individual, with the representative; the sense of novelty and freshness, with old and familiar objects; a more than usual state of emotion, with more than usual order. . . ." It is a great and illuminating statement, but is a series of paradoxes. Apparently Coleridge could describe the effect of the imagination in no other way.

Shakespeare, in one of his poems, has given a description that oddly parallels that of Coleridge.

> Reason in it selfe confounded,
> Saw Division grow together,
> To themselves yet either neither,
> Simple were so well compounded.

I do not know what his "The Phoenix and the Turtle" celebrates. Perhaps it *was* written to honor the marriage of Sir John Salisbury and Ursula Stanley; or perhaps the Phoenix is Lucy, Countess of Bedford; or perhaps the poem is merely an essay on Platonic love. But the scholars themselves are so uncertain, that I think we will do little violence to established habits of thinking, if we boldly pre-empt the poem for our own purposes. Certainly the poem is an instance of that magic power which Coleridge sought to describe. I propose that we take it for a moment as a poem about that power;

> So they loved as love in twaine,
> Had the essence but in one,
> Two distincts, Division none,
> Number there in love was slaine.
>
> Hearts remote, yet not asunder;
> Distance and no space was seene,
> Twixt this Turtle and his Queene;
> But in them it were a wonder. . . .
>
> Propertie was thus appalled,
> That the selfe was not the same;
> Single Natures double name,
> Neither two nor one was called.

Precisely! The nature is single, one, unified. But the name is double, and today with our multiplication of sciences, it is multiple. If the poet is to be true to his poetry, he must call it neither two nor one: the paradox is his only solution. The difficulty has intensified since Shakespeare's day: the timid poet, when confronted with the problem of "Single Natures double name," has too often funked it. A history of poetry from Dryden's time to our own might bear as its subtitle "The Half-Hearted Phoenix."

In Shakespeare's poem, Reason is "in it selfe confounded" at the union of the Phoenix and the Turtle; but it recovers to admit its own bankruptcy:

> Love hath Reason, Reason none,
> If what parts, can so remaine. . . .

and it is Reason which goes on to utter the beautiful threnos with which
the poem concludes:

> Beautie, Truth, and Raritie,
> Grace in all simplicitie,
> Here enclosde, in cinders lie.
>
> Death is now the Phoenix nest,
> And the Turtles loyall brest,
> To eternitie doth rest. . . .
>
> Truth may seeme, but cannot be,
> Beautie bragge, but tis not she,
> Truth and Beautie buried be.
>
> To this urne let those repaire,
> That are either true or faire,
> For these dead Birds, sigh a prayer.

Having pre-empted the poem for our own purposes, it may not be too
outrageous to go on to make one further observation. The urn to which
we are summoned, the urn which holds the ashes of the phoenix, is like
the well-wrought urn of Donne's "Canonization" which holds the phoenix-
lovers' ashes: it is the poem itself. One is reminded of still another urn,
Keats's Grecian urn, which contained for Keats, Truth and Beauty, as
Shakespeare's urn encloses "Beautie, Truth, and Raritie." But there is
a sense in which all such well-wrought urns contain the ashes of a
phoenix. The urns are not meant for memorial purposes only, though
that often seems to be their chief significance to the professors of literature. The phoenix rises from its ashes; or ought to rise; but it will not
arise for all our mere sifting and measuring the ashes, or testing them
for their chemical content. We must be prepared to accept the paradox
of the imagination itself; else "Beautie, Truth, and Raritie" remain
enclosed in their cinders and we shall end with essential cinders, for all
our pains.

Donne and Seventeenth Century Poetry

by J. B. Leishman

In the historical consideration of literature there are three dangers against which we should be continually on our guard: the danger that we may lose sight of the larger differences and distinctions through concentrating too much attention upon the subsidiary ones; the danger that we may pervert these subsidiary distinctions into antitheses; the danger that within these subsidiary distinctions we may insist too much upon identity and too little upon difference. In the present field of study we have,·on the one hand, heard perhaps too much of a School of Jonson and a School of Donne, of the classical and the so-called metaphysical strains in seventeenth century poetry, and not enough of those larger differences between the characteristic nondramatic poetry of the Age of Elizabeth and that of the Jacobean and Caroline periods, differences in which both Jonson and Donne equally share; while on the other hand, we have had, perhaps, too many generalizations about the so-called metaphysical poets and not enough insistence on the very important differences between them. It is, indeed, easier to perceive certain obvious differences between the poetry of Donne and Jonson than to perceive certain important resemblances, just as it is easier to perceive certain superficial resemblances between, say, Donne and Crashaw than to become aware of their fundamental differences. The ultimate purpose of such generalizations, classifications, and distinctions is to increase awareness, to enable us, by analysis and comparison, to achieve a clearer recognition, a more intense appreciation, of the peculiar virtue, the essential *thisness,* of whatever literature we may be studying; this, though, is a strenuous task, and most of us, I fear, tend unconsciously to manipulate these generalizations, classifications, and distinctions, disregarding here, overemphasizing there, until we have spread over every-

"Donne and Seventeenth Century Poetry." Chapter I of *The Monarch of Wit,* by J. B. Leishman, 5th edition, revised (London, 1962). Copyright 1951 by Hutchinson's University Library. Reprinted by permission of the author, the Hutchinson Publishing Group, and Hillary House Publishers, Ltd. [With the author's approval the footnotes have been reduced. *Ed.*]

thing a veil of custom and a film of familiarity which shall save us as much as possible from the insupportable fatigue of thought. Donne has been too often considered as a so-called metaphysical poet and too little as a seventeenth century poet (many characteristic seventeenth century poets began to write during the reign of Elizabeth); let us begin, then, by trying to reach some not too inadequate conception of the characteristics of seventeenth century poetry in general and of the principal differences and varieties within that fundamental identity.

That such a conception is both real and necessary is proved by the fact that the poetry of those two very individual and very different poets, Ben Jonson and John Donne, who are commonly regarded as the founders of two different schools, has many important characteristics in common. They were—to begin with an important fact which has received too little attention—they were both, in a sense, coterie-poets, poets who made their initial impact not upon the common reader but upon comparatively small circles of intellectuals and literary amateurs. Apart from his contributions to the facetious commendations of Thomas Coryat in the latter *Crudities* (1611) and to the elegies on Prince Henry in *Lachrymae Lachrymarum* (1613), the only poems Donne printed during his lifetime were the two *Anniversaries* upon the religious death of Mistris Elizabeth Drury, in 1611 and 1612. The first collected edition of his poems was not published until 1633, two years after his death, and his great reputation as a poet during his lifetime was gained entirely through the circulation of his poems in manuscript. Jonson, it is true, was a much more public poet than Donne: he wrote plays, which were not only acted, but published, under very careful supervision, by himself. Nevertheless, the great body of his nondramatic verse was not published until after his death, and he too, though less exclusively and remotely than Donne, was the master, the *arbiter elegantiarum,* of a circle, of a coterie, of various young Templars and Courtiers who gathered round him in taverns, hung upon his words, begged copies of his verses, and were proud to be known as his sons.

When we speak, as we often do, of Jonson and Donne as the two great influences on the nondramatic poetry of the first half of the seventeenth century, and when we think, as we often do, of that poetry chiefly in its relation to either or both of them, we should not forget that we are speaking and thinking only of that portion of seventeenth century poetry which we now chiefly read and remember, and that much even of this poetry, easy, familiar, *harmlos* (to borrow a German word) as it now seems to us, may well have seemed quite exceptionally choice and sophisticated to its writers and first readers. There are many seventeenth century poems which may seem to us only very superficially like Donne's, but, which at the time may well have seemed astonishingly *dernier cri* and quite beyond the reach of simple-minded admirers of Forests of

Arden and Bowers of Bliss. Both Jonson and Donne were superior persons, and both seem to have been well aware of their superiority, but Donne, though far more urbane, was a much more superior person than Jonson, and, except superficially, much less imitable. Contemporary allusions to his poetry are few and far between, and even quite advanced men seem to have remained ignorant of it for an incredibly long time.[1] In the various miscellanies published between 1640 and 1660, whose contents seem to have been derived partly from printed texts and partly from manuscript commonplace-books, and which may be regarded as reflecting fairly accurately the taste of the average cultivated gentleman of the time of Charles I, both the number of Donne's poems included and any obvious traces of his influence are remarkably small. The influence of Jonson, the epigrammatic rather than the moral Jonson, the Jonson of "Still to be neat, still to be drest," "Come my Celia, let us prove," and "If I freely may discover," is far more striking. It is in the wittily, often impudently, argumentative love-poem, and in the indecently, sometimes obscenely, witty elegy, epigram, or paradox, that Donne's influence upon the secular poetry of the seventeenth century is chiefly apparent.[2] Such poems, though, are more frequent in the published works of particular poets (Carew, Suckling, Lovelace, Cowley), and in certain manuscript collections, than in the miscellanies, where the persistence both of the hearty Elizabethan song and of the Elizabethan pastoral tradition is far more noticeable. In the main, Donne's dialectic is simplified and his wit coarsened by his imitators. One wonders what Donne thought of them. (It must sometimes have been an embarrassment to him that, at the time when he was preaching in St. Paul's, various obscene epigrams were being handed about and attributed to "Dr. Donne.") Jonson, so often prickly and dogmatic, was probably a more indulgent parent: when he declared that "my son Cartwright writes all like a man," the modern reader finds it hard to know just what he meant, and will perhaps reflect that, after all, it's a wise father who knows his own children.

William Drummond of Hawthornden, a disciple of Spenser and of the Italians, has recorded that when Ben Jonson visited him in 1619 he told him that his poems "were all good . . . save that they smelled too much of the Schooles, and were not after the fancie of the tyme." Jonson, no doubt, was speaking for himself and for those who agreed with him, but it is really impossible to know just how many did agree with him, or to

---

[1] All hitherto known contemporary allusions to Donne's poetry have been collected (together with many discoveries of his own) by Mr. W. Milgate in a series of articles in *Notes and Queries* (27th May, 10th June, 8th July, 2nd September, 1950).

[2] His influence in a narrower and more specialized field, that of eulogy and funeral elegy (or, as he himself would have called it, "epicede"), was perhaps still more immediate and decisive. Poems of this kind, though, are more frequently in the manuscript commonplace books than in the miscellanies, except in such essentially academic miscellanies as *Parnassus Biceps*.

form even a rough estimate of the proportion of then readers of English poetry who shared this "fancie of the tyme." [3] In saying that the poetry of Jonson and of Donne was in a sense coterie poetry, I want to insist upon the fact that it is almost impossible to know just how far the coterie extended, whom it included, who, so to speak, were in the inner circle and who were merely on the fringe. Where fashion and mode are active the detection and disintrication of "influences" become formidably difficult. Milton admired Homer and Virgil and Ovid, Tasso and della Casa, not because anyone had told him to do so, but because he believed that was how great poetry should be written: one often feels, though, that many of his contemporaries admired Donne because to admire Donne was the done thing. Similarly, although today one constantly hears it said that contemporary English poets have been greatly influenced by Hopkins, by Mr. Eliot, and even by Rilke, it may well be that future generations will find the business of detecting these "influences" a most baffling task. Generalizations even about those seventeenth century poets whose work is available in modern editions can at best be tentative. Not even the well-known poets will fit neatly into categories: even in them we encounter all manner of paradoxes and tergiversations. Cowley has related that it was the discovery of a volume of Spenser in his mother's parlor that made him irrecoverably a poet; when, however, he went out into the world he discovered that not Spenser but Donne was the man, and set himself to imitate Donne—"to a fault," as Dryden said, who himself

---

[3] In an undated letter to the physician and celebrated Latin poet, Dr. Arthur Johnston, published in the folio edition of his *Works* (1711, p. 143), Drummond has expressed his own opinion of a certain "fancie of the tyme." Although he admired Donne as an "epigrammatist" and praised his second Elegy, "The Anagram," it is almost impossible not to suppose that Drummond is here alluding to Donne and to some of Donne's imitators. The letter begins abruptly with a Sidneian encomium on the antiquity and dignity of poetry, and then proceeds as follows:

In vain have some Men of late (Transformers of every Thing) consulted upon her Reformation, and endeavoured to abstract her to *Metaphysical* Ideas, and *Scholastical* Quiddities, denuding her of her own Habits, and those Ornaments with which she hath amused the World some Thousand Years. *Poesy* is not a Thing that is yet in the finding and search, or which may be otherwise found out, being already condescended upon by all Nations, and as it were established *jure Gentium*, amongst *Greeks, Romans, Italians, French, Spaniards.* Neither do I think that a good Piece of *Poesy*, which *Homer, Virgil, Ovid, Petrarch, Bartas, Ronsard, Boscan, Garcilasso* (if they were alive, and had that Language) could not understand, and reach the Sense of the Writer. Suppose these Men could find out some other new *Idea* like *Poesy*, it should be held as if Nature should bring forth some new *Animal*, neither Man, Horse, Lyon, Dog, but which had some Members of all, if they had been proportionably and by right Symmetry set together. What is not like the Ancients and conform to those Rules which hath been agreed unto by all Times, may (indeed) be something like unto *Poesy*, but it is no more *Poesy* than a Monster is a Man. Monsters breed Admiration at the First, but have ever some strange Loathsomness in them at last.

Milton would probably have subscribed to every word of this.

confessed that Cowley had been the darling of his youth. When, though, one turns from the poets whose works are available in modern editions to the miscellanies and manuscript commonplace books of the age, the task of generalizing about seventeenth century poetry, seventeenth century taste, and seventeenth century sensibility seems almost impossible. If I am now attempting to generalize myself, it is with an almost overwhelming conviction of the vanity of dogmatizing.

Each of these two very characteristic seventeenth century poets, Jonson and Donne, was born during the reign of Elizabeth, and each had begun to establish his reputation during the last decade of the sixteenth century. Nevertheless, great as are the differences between them, the poetry of each has more in common with that of the other than it has with the poetry of Spenser, or of the Sonneteers, or with the lyrics in the song-books, or with such poems as *Venus and Adonis* and *The Rape of Lucrece.* On the one hand, neither Jonson nor Donne seems ever to have shared the ambition of Spenser and of several of Spenser's disciples to write a large-scale heroic or narrative poem. On the other hand, they both took the short poem more seriously than the typical Elizabethan poets did. Even if one leaves out of account the great mass of utterly undistinguished Elizabethan lyric, where the same rhymes, phrases, and properties appear over and over again with wearisome iteration, where nymphs and swains on the plains trip at leisure in a measure, view with pleasure Flora's treasure in meadows fresh and gay where fleecy lambs do play, weave in bowers crowns of flowers, or where fountains spring from mountains sigh and languish in their anguish—even if one forgets what the great majority of the poems (including Spenser's and Sidney's), in, say, *England's Helicon* are really like—even if one confines oneself to the long-sifted contents of modern anthologies, one often feels that even the best Elizabethan poets just tossed off their delightful lyrics: partly, perhaps, because they were generally intended to be sung and therefore ought not to be too weighty or condensed. And one's general impression of the Elizabethan sonneteers is that they wrote too many sonnets and wrote them too easily. Jonson's foolish Matheo in *Every Man in His Humour* would, when melancholy, "write you your halfe score or your dozen of sonnets at a sitting." Both Jonson and Donne seem to have set a new fashion of writing short but very concentrated poems—Donne's always and Jonson's often intended to be handed round in manuscript and admired by connoisseurs. For it cannot be too strongly insisted that most of what we now chiefly remember of the nondramatic poetry of the first half of the seventeenth century was poetry that for years had been circulating in manuscript before it finally found its way into print, while most of the nondramatic poets who were publishing were either belated Elizabethans or pertinacious disciples of Spenser, and were regarded by the young intellectuals of the Court, the Inns of Court, and the Universities as old-fashioned and out of date. (One can go a good way toward

"placing" the younger Milton among his contemporaries by saying that
for him neither the *Faerie Queene* nor Ovid's *Metamorphoses* was out of
date.) It is significant and almost symbolic that that grand old Elizabethan,
Michael Drayton, who was born a year earlier than Shakespeare and who
lived and wrote and published until 1631, should have twice rather
bitterly and contemptuously protested against this new fashion for short
poems circulated in manuscript. In 1612, in the Preface to the first part
of his immense *Poly-olbion,* that "chorographical description of all the
tracts, rivers, mountains, forests, and other parts of this renowned isle
of Great Britain," he declared that

> in publishing this Essay of my Poeme, there is this great disadvantage
> against me; that it commeth out at this time, when Verses are wholly
> deduc't to Chambers, and nothing esteem'd in this lunatique Age, but
> what is kept in Cabinets, and must only passe by Transcription;

and in his "Epistle to Henry Reynolds, Esquire, of Poets and Poesie,"
published in 1627, after reaching the end of his description of English
poets from Chaucer to the two Beaumonts and William Browne, he
added that he was not concerned with those poets who were too proud to
publish and who chose to be known only through the circulation of their
poems in manuscript.

Jonson, as I have admitted, was a less exclusive, a more public, poet
than Donne, but he too wrote what he most valued for an audience fit
though few. Spenser, one might almost say, wrote for all who cared for
poetry at all; both Jonson and Donne wrote very emphatically for those
who knew what was what. There is some analogy, though only a slight
one, between the literary situation then and that which exists today; there
was something, though only something, of the same gulf between "serious"
and "popular" poetry. The position of Spenser had been in some ways
similar to that of Tennyson; the position of Jonson and Donne was in
some ways similar to that of Mr. Eliot. The Jacobean intellectuals, or
some of them, reacted against the Elizabethans somewhat as the inter-war
intellectuals did against the Victorians. This analogy, though, must not
be pressed too far:[4] it is sufficient to insist that much of the most memo-

[4] The chief danger of such analogies is that they tend to make us forget what I may
call the Elizabethan time-scale and the fact that scarcely anything of what now seems
to us most memorable in Elizabethan poetry and drama had been published or acted
before the last decade of the sixteenth century. One may perhaps describe the situation
with some approximation to truth by saying that the poetry of Spenser, of Jonson
and of Donne and of their several disciples and imitators was all simultaneously com-
peting for public favor, but that during the first half of the seventeenth century,
among the more intellectual and sophisticated, the examples of Jonson and of Donne
on the whole prevailed. When we speak of nineteenth or twentieth century literary
"movements" or "reactions," we are generally thinking in terms of generations; if we
transfer these phrases to the Elizabethan literary scene we must learn to think in
terms of a few years, or even, sometimes, of a few months.

rable nondramatic poetry of the first half of the seventeenth century,
a poetry very greatly influenced by the example of either Jonson or Donne
or both, is a more exclusive and critical and intellectual kind of poetry
than that which is typically Elizabethan. The phrase "strong-lined" is
often used by seventeenth century writers to describe the new qualities
which they admired in the poetry both of Jonson and of Donne: something close-packed and strenuous, requiring some effort and connoisseur-
ship to appreciate it, as distinguished from the easily appreciated, "the
soft, melting, and diffuse style of the Spenserians." [5] The facts, not merely
that no one has ever thought of calling Jonson a metaphysical poet, but
that his poetry shares many typical seventeenth century characteristics
with Donne's, should suggest to us that it is worthwhile to try to consider
Donne more as a typical seventeenth century or "strong-lined" poet, and
less as a so-called metaphysical one.

Jonson addressed two very encomiastic epigrams to Donne (xxiii and
xcvi), as well as one (xciv) commanding a manuscript of his Satires to the
Countess of Bedford, and Donne, who never condescended to praise any
other contemporary poet, contributed some very flattering Latin verses
to the quarto edition of Jonson's *Volpone*. They had, indeed, much in
common. Both, one might almost say, wrote as though Spenser had never
lived: Spenser's national and patriotic strain, his Platonic idealism, his
elaborate description, his amplification and ornamentation—all these
find no place in their verse. They rejected too what one may call the
Petrarchan tradition, the too often merely extravagant and conventional
adoration of the sonneteers, and they rejected the elaborate and mainly
frigid decoration of such poems as *Venus and Adonis* and *The Rape of
Lucrece*. Both insisted on what Jonson called "language such as men do
use," and would have disagreed with Gray and agreed with Wordsworth
(in theory, though not always in practice) that there should be no essential
difference between the diction of poetry and that of conversation. Both
wrote much poetry that was satirical and realistic. Both—a very notable
characteristic of the typical seventeenth century as distinguished from
the typical Elizabethan lyrist—stamped an image of themselves upon
nearly all they wrote; for, while one of the chief characteristics of the
Elizabethan lyric is a certain anonymousness, the song rather than the
singer, seventeenth century lyrists, as Professor Moorman has observed,
lyrists otherwise so different as Crashaw, Vaughan, Suckling, or Herrick,
"whether their poetry be intense or not, stand revealed to us in what
they write." Finally—to conclude this brief review of affinities—both
Jonson and Donne wrote poems more sequacious, organic, and untransposable than their predecessors, although with Donne this new sense of
structure seems to have been stimulated by scholastic logic, with Jonson
by the example of the classical lyric.

Seventeenth century poetry, then, or much of seventeenth century

[5] See an article by G. Williamson, "Strong Lines," in *English Studies*, 1936, pp. 152ff.

poetry, is colloquial in diction, undecorative and untraditional in imagery, dispensing with what Carew, in his elegy on Donne, called

> the goodly exil'd traine
> Of gods and goddesses, which in thy just raigne
> Were banish'd nobler Poems,

personal in tone and logical in structure. In these respects both Jonson and Donne are characteristic seventeenth century poets. "But," some readers may be inclined to ask at this point, "what about Donne's metaphysics, what about his famous metaphysical wit?" In the pages that follow I shall hope to demonstrate, among other things, first, that Donne is certainly not a metaphysical poet in the wider sense of being a philosophic one; secondly, that although, in the narrower sense which Dryden had in mind when he declared that Donne "affected the metaphysics," he does indeed occasionally draw illustrations and analogies from the realms of philosophy, theology, and popular science, what, probably, most readers have in mind when they call him a metaphysical poet is an often syllogistic argumentation and argumentativeness which might, however, be more appropriately called scholastic or dialectical than metaphysical; thirdly, that in almost all Donne's best poetry there is a dramatic element, an element of personal drama, which is no less characteristic than the argumentative, scholastic, or dialectical strain; and fourthly, closely connected with this element of drama, that there is in many of his poems a very strong element of sheer wit and paradox. Now if one regards Donne's poetry chiefly in this way, as what I have called the dialectical expression of personal drama, one will, I think, perceive more clearly what are the really important resemblances and differences, on the one hand, between his poetry and that of other so-called metaphysical poets, and, on the other hand, between his poetry and that of Jonson and of poets who are commonly regarded as belonging to the School of Jonson. What, looked at in one way, seem differences in kind appear, when looked at in another way, to be rather differences in degree. The important thing, perhaps, is to decide what is the right way of looking, which is the viewpoint that will enable us to distinguish rightly between differences in degree and differences in kind, and to decide precisely at what point differences which at first seem merely differences in degree pass into differences in kind.

Consider, for example, the stylistic relationship between Herbert and Donne: the best poetry of both might equally well be described as the dialectical expression of personal drama. Herbert, like Donne, can make the purest poetry out of almost bare argument, and Herbert's expression of his relationship to God is no less dramatic than Donne's expression of various imaginary relationships with women and of his actual relationship with his wife: true though it be that Donne's dialectic is more ingenious than Herbert's and his analogies more various and, as it often seems to us, more far-fetched, and although in much of Donne's poetry there is an element of sheer invention, sheer wit and sheer paradox which we do not find in Herbert's. How much of the poetry of other so-called metaphysical poets may be appropriately described as the dialectical expression of personal drama? Certainly Marvell's "To his Coy Mistress" and "The Definition of Love," although in most of Marvell's poetry the dialectical element is more apparent than the dramatic, and although the "Horatian Ode" is nearer to Jonson's kind of poetry than to Donne's. Crashaw's poetry is personal and often dramatic, but is it dialectical? Vaughan's poetry is personal, but less intimately so than Herbert's; dialectical, but less tightly and consistently so than Herbert's; occasionally, but not pervasively, dramatic, and with a strong element of vision and visual imagery that is found neither in Herbert's poetry nor in Donne's.

Now, on the other hand, between Donne's kind of poetry and Jonson's, which are the differences in degree and which are the differences in kind? Although the differences between Donne's kind of poetry and Jonson's are greater than those between Donne's kind of poetry and Herbert's, although very little, if any, of Jonson's poetry could be described as the dialectical expression of personal drama, and although the element of sheer wit is as absent from Jonson's poetry (though Jonson could admire it in Donne's) as it is from Herbert's, there still remain many differences which may perhaps be profitably regarded as differences within a fundamental identity, that, namely, of seventeenth century poetry in general, differences in degree rather than in kind. Both Donne's language and Jonson's language is colloquial, "language such as men do use," but Donne's is more defiantly and resolutely colloquial. Jonson's poetry, in comparison with the typical Elizabethan lyric or with Spenser or with the sonneteers, is free from decoration, but Jonson does not exile the gods and goddesses so rigorously or reject the whole apparatus of classical mythology and allusion so utterly and consistently as Donne. Jonson's lyrics, in comparison with typical Elizabethan lyrics, are organic and untransposable, but they are seldom so rigorously logical, so capable of prose-analysis, as Donne's, Donne's dialectical method here introducing what almost amounts to a difference in kind. And although, in comparison with the anonymity of the typical Elizabethan lyric, Jonson's lyrics are personal and individual, they are so rather in the way in which Horace's Odes are so than in the way in which Donne's poems are. The style and tone are individual, but, as with Horace, never, or very seldom, eccentrically and unclassically individual, and the matter, as with Horace, is essentially public, "what oft was thought, but ne'er so well expressed."

Indeed, the idea or-ideal of the kind of poetry that Jonson most wanted to write and was continually trying to write, a poetry memorably expressing that "high and noble matter" of which he spoke in his Epistle "To

Elizabeth Countess of Rutland," has been, I cannot but think, most perfectly realized in some of Horace's Odes. Were I limited to the choice of one ode which should represent as completely as possible both the manner and the matter of the graver Horace, I think I should choose the sixteenth of his Second Book, of which I here offer a translation "according to the Latin measure, as near as the language will permit":

> Peace is what one, caught on the open sea, will
> beg of heav'n above when the somber storm clouds
> hide the moon, and stars are no longer certain
> guides for the sailor.

> Peace the savage fighters of Thracia pray for,
> peace, the Mede resplendent with broidered quiver,
> peace, unbought, dear Grosphus, with proffered gold or
> purple or jewels.

> Ah, for neither treasure nor lictors bearing
> rods before a Consul can check the spirit's
> wretched civil strife or the cares that circle
> costliest ceilings.

> Well can fare no little, his humble table's
> brightest piece of plate the ancestral salt-dish,
> one of whose light sleep not a fear or sordid
> wish has deprived him.

> Why, with such short span, do we so contend for
> large possessions? Why do we seek for countries
> warmed with other suns? Has an exile ever
> quitted himself then?

> Sickly Care can clamber aboard the brass-bound
> galleys, keep abreast of the knightly riders,
> swifter far than stags or the cloud-compelling
> easterly breezes.

> Let the soul, content with the present, scorn to
> reck what lies beyond, and with stubborn smiling
> sweeten what seems bitter. From ev'ry aspect
> nothing is perfect.

> Early death removed the renowned Achilles,
> age prolonged left little to cheer Tithonus;
> me perhaps some blessing denied to you some
> hour will have granted.

> Flocks in hundreds bleat and Sicilian cattle
> low around your folds, in the stables whinny

chariot-racing horses, and doubly-dyed in
African purple

glows the wool you're clad with; to me, with small do-
main, the subtle spirit of Grecian Muses
came as Fate's mixed gift, and a soul aloof from
envious throngers.

It was, I say, towards poetry of this kind, individual indeed, but both in manner and in matter essentially public and classical, a poetry of statement and of weighty generalization, that Jonson was continually striving. I need not multiply examples: consider the concluding lines of "To the World: A farewell for a Gentle-woman, vertuous and noble":

> My tender, first, and simple yeeres
>   Thou did'st abuse, and then betray;
> Since stird'st up jealousies and feares,
>   When all the causes were away.
> Then, in a soile hast planted me,
>   Where breathe the basest of thy fooles;
> Where envious arts professed be,
>   And pride, and ignorance the schooles,
> Where nothing is examin'd, weigh'd,
>   But, as 'tis rumor'd, so beleev'd:
> Where every freedome is betray'd,
>   And every goodnesse tax'd, or griev'd.
> But, what we'are borne for, we must beare:
>   Our fraile condition it is such,
> That, what to all may happen here,
>   If't chance to me, I must not grutch.
> Else, I my state should much mistake,
>   To harbour, a divided thought
> From all my kinde: that, for my sake,
>   There should a miracle be wrought.
> No, I doe know, that I was borne
>   To age, misfortune, sicknesse, griefe:
> But I will beare these, with that scorne,
>   As shall not need thy false reliefe.
> Nor for my peace will I goe farre,
>   As wandrers doe, that still doe rome,
> But make my strength, such as they are,
>   Here in my bosome, and at home.

Or consider one of the most Horatian, I might almost say, one of the most Roman, things Jonson ever wrote, the verses "To Sir Robert Wroth," penetrated with that characteristically Roman reverence for the traditional pursuits and festivals of the countryman which recurs so often, and with equal spontaneity, in the poems of Jonson's disciple Herrick. After describing, in magnificently animated and colorful verse, the varied activities of the estate and the hospitality of its owner, Jonson concludes with a passage which, in part at any rate, is no less Virgilian than Horatian, and which was probably inspired by some famous lines at the end of Virgil's second Georgic:

> Let others watch in guiltie armes, and stand
>   The furie of a rash command,
> Goe enter breaches, meet the cannons rage,
>   That they may sleepe with scarres in age.
> And shew their feathers shot, and cullors torne,
>   And brag, that they were therefore borne.
> Let this man sweat, and wrangle at the barre,
>   For every price, in every jarre,
> And change possessions, oftner with his breath,
>   Then either money, warre, or death:
> Let him, then hardest sires, more disinherit,
>   And each where boast it as his merit,
> To blow up orphanes, widdowes, and their states;
>   And thinke his power doth equall *Fates*.
> Let that goe heape a masse of wretched wealth,
>   Purchas'd by rapine, worse than stealth,
> And brooding o'er it sit, with broadest eyes,
>   Not doing good, scarce when he dyes.
> Let thousands more goe flatter vice, and winne,
>   By being organes to great sinne,
> Get place, and honor, and be glad to keepe
>   The secrets, that shall breake their sleepe:
> And, so they ride in purple, eate in plate,
>   Though poyson, thinke it a great fate.
> But thou, My WROTH, if I can truth apply,
>   Shalt neither that, nor this envy:
> Thy peace is made: and, when man's state is well,
>   'Tis better, if he there can dwell.
> God wisheth, none should wracke on a strange shelfe:
>   To him, man's dearer than t'himselfe.
> And, howsoever we may thinke things sweet,
>   He always gives what he knowes meet;
> Which who can use is happy: Such be thou.
>   Thy morning's and thy evening's vow
> Be thankes to him, and earnest prayer, to finde
>   A body sound, with sounder minde;

> To doe thy countrey service, thy selfe right;
> That neither want doe thee affright,
> Nor death; but when thy latest sand is spent,
> Thou maist thinke life, a thing but lent.

It is in what may be called, in a wide sense, his moral poetry, that portion of his nondramatic verse which is still far less widely known than it deserves to be, that Jonson is most fundamentally akin to Horace and, at the same time, most representative of one of the most characteristic strains in seventeenth century and Augustan verse. From Wotton's

> How happy is he born and taught
> That serveth not another's will

to the youthful Pope's

> Happy the man whose wish and care
> A few paternal acres bound,
> Content to breathe his native air
> In his own ground

how much of the morality, one might almost say, how much of the religion, of English poets seems almost indistinguishable from that blend of Stoicism and Epicureanism which has been so perfectly expressed by Horace! How often we find it, the disintrication of the mean from its extremes, the exposure and rebuke of immoderate ambitions and desires and of every kind of too-muchness, the praise of moderate hospitality, of good talk and good wine, of the healthfulness of country life as distinguished from that of the city and the court, the celebration of antique virtue and simplicity—these, together with exhortations not to be too cast down by grief or ill-fortune, but to recognize and accept the conditions of human life.[6]

Although they both share in varying degrees those common characteristics of seventeenth century poetry in general which I have tried to indicate, there is a very great difference, a difference not merely in degree but in kind, between Donne's exercises in sheer wit, Donne's dialectical expression of personal drama, and that essentially classical and public poetry towards which Jonson was always striving. Jonson's most memorable lines (often adapted from classical authors) are weighty and general:

---

[6] There is, of course, another way of looking at the matter, which may be suggested by the following entry in the Diary of John Manningham, of the Middle Temple, under 12th February, 1602: "Ben Jonson the poet nowe lives upon one Townesend and scornes the world. (*Tho: Overbury.*)" (ed. Bruce, Camden Society, London, 1868, p. 130).

Men have beene great, but never good by chance.[7]

Man may securely sinne, but safely never.[8]

A good *Poet's* made, as well as borne.[9]

'Tis wisdom, and that high
For men to use their fortune reverently,
Even in youth.[10]

Donne's most memorable lines are personal and dramatic:

I wonder by my troth, what thou, and I
Did, till we lov'd? [11]

For Godsake hold your tongue, and let me love.[12]

If yet I have not all thy love,
Deare, I shall never have it all.[13]

Donne's style and manner are not only individual, but, in comparison
with Horace's or Jonson's, eccentrically and unclassically individual. And
as for the matter of his poetry, where he is being mainly witty and
paradoxical, it is public only in the sense that we can imagine its being
publicly recited and enjoyed in companies whose conceptions of wit,
whose tastes, in comparison with Horace's or Pope's or Dr. Johnson's
(for Ben Jonson, although his own practice was very different, could
admire Donne's wit), were eccentric and unclassical. Where, on the other
hand, Donne is being serious, or mainly serious, the matter of his poetry,
in comparison with that of Ben Jonson or Horace, is essentially private,
not "What oft was thought, but ne'er so well expressed," but something
"seldom thought and seldom so expressed." A. N. Whitehead once defined
religion as "What the individual does with his own solitariness":[14] nearly
all Donne's serious poetry, his love-poetry no less than his religious poetry,
and nearly all Herbert's poetry and Vaughan's, is in this sense essentially,
not merely nominally, religious, is a record of what the poet has been
doing with his solitariness. This solitariness, this privateness, this self-
containedness, this, together with the often dialectical and dramatic
expression of it, is, it seems to me, the most important difference between
the serious poetry of Donne and the so-called Metaphysical School and
that of Jonson and the Classical or Horatian School.

[7] "An Epistle to Sir Edward Sackville," l. 124.
[8] "Epode": "Not to know vice at all."
[9] "To the Memory of my beloved, the Author Mr. William Shakespeare."
[10] "An Ode": "High-spirited friend."   [11] "The Good-morrow."
[12] "The Canonization."   [13] "Lovers infinitenesse."
[14] *Religion in the Making* (London, 1927), p. 6.

The Religious Poetry of John Donne

by Helen Gardner

*   *   *

With the probable exception of "The Cross," for which no precise date can be suggested, and which is more a verse-letter than a divine poem, the earliest of Donne's Divine Poems appears to be *"La Corona."* *"La Corona"* is a single poem, made up of seven linked sonnets, each of which celebrates not so much an event in the life of Christ as a mystery of faith. Those brought up in a different tradition might well wonder why Donne should devote one sonnet of his seven to the Finding in the Temple, and omit all reference to the events of the Ministry, except for a brief reference to miracles. The emphasis on the beginning and close of the life of Christ is characteristic of mediaeval art, whether we think of a series of windows like those at Fairford, or of the mediaeval dramatic cycles. It was dictated by the desire to present with simplicity the Christian scheme of man's redemption. The popular devotional equivalent of this emphasis upon the plan of salvation was the meditation on the Fifteen Mysteries of the Rosary, and reference to them explains at once why Donne would find it natural to pass directly from the Finding in the Temple to the events of Holy Week.[1] Habits of prayer, like other early habits, can survive modifications of a man's intellectual position. It is doubtful whether Donne felt there was anything particularly Catholic in concentrating on the Mysteries of the Faith, or in addressing his second and third sonnets to the Blessed Virgin, or in apostrophizing St. Joseph in his fourth; but it is also doubtful whether anyone who had been brought up as a Protestant would have done so.

"La Corona" has been undervalued as a poem by comparison with the

"The Religious Poetry of John Donne." From Part I of the General Introduction to *The Divine Poems of John Donne*, edited by Helen Gardner (Oxford, 1952), pp. xxi-xxxvii. Reprinted by permission of The Clarendon Press. [Some footnotes have been omitted. *Ed.*]

[1] The Joyful Mysteries are the Annunciation, Visitation, Nativity, Presentation, Finding in the Temple; the Sorrowful Mysteries are the Agony, Scourging, Crowning with Thorns, Bearing of the Cross, Crucifixion; the Glorious Mysteries are the Resurrection, Ascension, Coming of the Holy Ghost, Assumption, Coronation. Donne's "rectified devotion" naturally omits the last two, which have no basis in Scripture.

"Holy Sonnets," because the difference of intention behind the two sets of sonnets has not been recognized. The *"La Corona"* sonnets are inspired by liturgical prayer and praise—oral prayer; not by private meditation and the tradition of mental prayer. They echo the language of collects and office hymns, which expound the doctrines of the Catholic Faith, recalling the events from which those doctrines are derived, but not attempting to picture them in detail. Instead of the scene of the maiden alone in her room at Nazareth, there is a theological paradox: "Thy Makers maker, and thy Fathers mother." The scandal of the Cross is presented not by a vivid picture of its actual ignomiy and agony, but by the thought that here the Lord of Fate suffered a fate at the hand of his creatures. The petitions with which the last three poems end, though couched in the singular, are petitions which any man might pray. Each is the appropriate response to the mystery propounded. It is not surprising to find that the first sonnet of the set is a weaving together of phrases from the Advent Offices in the Breviary, and that the second draws on the Hours of the Blessed Virgin. As always happens with Donne, direct dependence on sources weakens as he proceeds.[2] But the impulse with which he began *"La Corona"* is clearly visible in the first two sonnets. His "crowne of prayer and praise" was to be woven from the prayers and praises of the Church. It is possible that he chose to use the sonnet, a form he had used before this only for epistles, because he wished to write formally and impersonally: to create an offering of beauty and dignity. *"La Corona"* is perhaps no more than a religious exercise, but it is an accomplished one. The sonnets are packed with meaning, with striking and memorable expressions of the commonplaces of Christian belief. The last line of each, repeated as the first line of the next, is both a fine climax and a fine opening. Unlike the majority of Elizabethan sonneteers, Donne has chosen the more difficult form of the sonnet. He follows Sidney in limiting the rhymes of the octave to two, and employs Sidney's most favored arrangement of those rhymes in two closed quatrains. He alternates between two arrangements of the rhymes of the sestet.[3] His seventh sonnet pre-

---

[2] This process can be seen in the "Holy Sonnets," and, to take a very different kind of poetry, the Elegies. Donne appears to have begun his career as a love poet by a close imitation of the Ovidian elegy, but he transforms it by a passion outside Ovid's range, a dramatic intensity Ovid did not attempt, and a kind of wit beyond the scope of the "sweet witty soul of Ovid," so that the finest of the Elegies do not suggest Ovid at all.

[3] The first, third, and fifth sonnets have a closed quatrain and a couplet; the second, fourth, sixth, and seventh, an open quatrain and a couplet. This second arrangement is Sidney's favorite; the first is also found in *Astrophel and Stella* but only in three sonnets. Apart from the obvious attraction of the drama and wit of *Astrophel and Stella,* a work whose relation to the "Songs and Sonnets" has not been sufficiently discussed, Donne would naturally be drawn to Sidney's, rather than to the looser "Elizabethan" form of the sonnet. Sidney combined the final couplet, which suits his and Donne's natural rhetorical gift so well, with a stricter organization of the whole poem. Donne could find in the Sidneian form, as he did in his own complex stanzas, the artistic pleasure of overcoming "Rimes vexation."

sented a problem; if it contrasted with his sixth, it would be the same as his first. He chose the lesser evil, and repeated the form of the sixth sonnet in the seventh, in order to make the last lead round again to the first and form a circle.

"A Litany," which is probably the next important divine poem, is less successful than *"La Corona,"* but more interesting. Donne has cast his "meditation in verse" into the formal mould of a litany. On the other hand, he has employed a stanza of his own invention. The contrast between the simple traditional outline of the poem and the intricacies of the separate stanzas is the formal expression of the poem's ambiguity. It appears impersonal, but is, in fact, highly personal. It tells us much, though indirectly, of its author's mind at the time when it was written, not least because it is in some ways uncharacteristic of him. It has the special interest of poems which are the product of a period of transition, when in the process of reshaping a personality some elements are stressed to the exclusion of others. "A Litany" is remarkable for a quality that is rare in Donne's poetry, though it is often found in his letters and sermons: sobriety. Although it is the wittiest of the Divine Poems, startling in paradox, precise in antithesis, and packed with allusions, its intellectual ingenuity and verbal audacity are employed to define an ideal of moderation in all things. Sir Herbert Grierson called it "wire-drawn and tormented." "Wire-drawn" it may be called with justice; it analyzes temptations with scrupulosity, and shows a wary sense of the distinctions that divide the tainted from the innocent act or motive. But "tormented" seems less just, even if we confine the word to the style. The ideal which is aspired to is simplicity of motive, "evennesse" of piety, and a keeping of "meane waies." Something of this ideal is already realized in the deliberate care with which the aspiration is expressed. At first sight the poem may appear overingenious. On further acquaintance it comes to seem not so much ingenious as exact; less witty, and more wise.

We know from Donne's letter to Goodyer, in which he refers to its composition,[4] that "A Litany" was written during an illness and in a mood of dejection. The "low devout melancholie" of *"La Corona"* has deepened into a sin from which Donne prays to be delivered in the first verse. It is very closely connected with Donne's two long exercises in casuistry: *Biathanatos,* in which he argued the most searching problem in personal ethics, whether a man may ever rightly take his own life; and *Pseudo-Martyr,* in which he debated under its pressing topical form the perennial problem of which things are Caesar's. It is a casuist's poem and shows traces both of the current debate on the Oath of Allegiance[5] and of Donne's personal searchings of conscience in his years of failure, when he was still hoping for worldly success and, if Walton is right, had already been offered and had rejected advancement in the Church. Donne, who

---

[4] *Letters* (1651), pp. 31-37.
[5] See the reference to "equivocation" in Stanza XIX.

was "subtle to plague himself," must have been conscious of the contrast between his relatives, who for conscience' sake had chosen exile, imprisonment or death, and himself. He had conformed to the Established Church and was using his powers in its defence, and had even been offered a means of maintenance in its ministry. The rather exaggerated stress in "A Litany" on the compatibility of the service of God with "this worlds sweet" may reflect his need, at this time, to assure himself that the way that appears easier is not, for that reason, necessarily wrong. Intransigence may even, he hints, be a form of self-indulgence, an easy way out of the strain of conflicting duties:

> for Oh, to some
> Not to be Martyrs, is a martyrdome.[6]

But if this seems an oversubtle explanation, there is another reason why Donne should at this period pray more strongly to be delivered from contempt of the world than from overvaluing it. The temptation to despise what one has not obtained and to cry, because one has been unsuccessful, "the world's not worth my care" is strong to ambitious natures. It must have been strong to Donne who had by nature both the melancholy and the scorn of the satirist. If we remember the circumstances of his life at Mitcham—his anxiety for his wife whom he had brought to poverty and for the future of his growing family, his inability to find secure employment and his broken health—the petitions of "A Litany" gain in meaning. We see the passionate and hyperbolical Donne, the proud and irritable young man of the Satires and Elegies, attempting to school himself to patience, not rejecting with scorn a world that has disappointed him, but praying that he may accept what life brings in a religious spirit. His declarations that happiness may exist in courts, and that the earth is not our prison, show an affinity with the contemporary movement in France, which Bremond described under the name of "l'humanisme dévot." [7] They also contrast most interestingly with the pessimism of some Jacobean writers, particularly Webster, with whom Donne is often compared. The dying Antonio's cry, "And let my Sonne, flie the Courts of Princess," and Vittoria's last words, "O happy they that never saw the Court," only sum up the constant Senecan despising of the world in Webster's two greatest plays. "A Litany" has none of this

---

[6] Trollope analyzed this state of mind well in describing young Mr. Arabin's hesitations after Newman's secession: "Everything was against him: all his worldly interests required him to remain a Protestant; and he looked on his worldly interests as a legion of foes, to get the better of whom was a point of extremest honor. In his then state of ecstatic agony such a conquest would have cost him little; he could easily have thrown away all his livelihood; but it cost him much to get over the idea that by choosing the Church of England he should be open in his own mind to the charge that he had been led to such a choice by unworthy motives." (*Barchester Towers*, ch. XX.)

[7] See the first volume of his *Histoire littéraire du sentiment religieux en France.*

cynicism. It is, whatever else we may say of it, a singularly unbitter poem, although it was written at a bitter time.

In many ways it is the most Anglican of the Divine Poems and continually anticipates Donne's leading ideas as a preacher. Although we may see in his restoration of the saints, whom Cranmer had banished from the Litany, a further sign of his loyalty to "the ancient ways," his own praise of his poem in his letter to Goodyer makes the typical Anglican claim of avoiding both excess and defect:

> That by which it will deserve best acceptation, is, That neither the Roman Church need call it defective, because it abhors not the particular mention of the blessed Triumphers in heaven; nor the Reformed can discreetly accuse it, of attributing more then a rectified devotion ought to doe.

We may also see in the whole poem a habit of mind which has been shaped by the practice of systematic self-examination, and thinks more in terms of particular sins and failings than in terms of general and total unworthiness; but the particular sins which Donne prays to be delivered from are not the traditional sins. There is no trace of the old classifications under which the conscience can be examined: sins against God and sins against my neighbor, or the seven deadly sins and their branches. Instead the sins in "A Litany" can all be referred back to two general philosophic conceptions: the conception of virtue as the mean between two extremes, and the related conception of virtue as the proper use of all the faculties. Donne anticipates here that ideal of "reasonable piety" which is so familiar later in the century in the manuals of the Caroline divines. The resolute rejection of otherworldliness, the antiascetic and antimystical bias of the poem, the concentration on "a daily beauty" and the sanctification of ordinary life, with the consequent ignoring of any conception of sanctity as something extraordinary and heroic, the exaltation of the undramatic virtues of patience, discretion, and a sober cheerfulness— all these things are characteristic of Anglican piety in the seventeenth century and after.[8] In comparison with the Roman Catholic books of

[8] Cf. Taylor's *Holy Living, The Whole Duty of Man*, and Law's *A Serious Call to a Devout and Holy Life*, and such classic expressions of the Anglican spirit as Bishop Ken's Morning and Evening Hymns and Keble's Hymn "New every morning is the love":

> We need not bid, for cloistered cell,
> Our neighbor and our work farewell,
> Nor strive to wind ourselves too high
> For sinful man beneath the sky:
>
> The trivial round, the common task,
> Would furnish all we ought to ask—
> Room to deny ourselves, a road
> To bring us daily nearer God.

See H. R. McAdoo, *The Structure of Caroline Moral Theology* (London, 1949), for an extended discussion of the Caroline manuals.

devotion, which they frequently drew upon and adapted, the Anglican manuals seem to some tastes rather dry, with their stress on edification and "practical piety" and the "duties of daily life." "A Litany" has something of this dryness. It has neither the warmth of mediaeval religious devotion, nor the exalted note of the Counter-Reformation. It reflects the intellectuality which Anglicanism derived from its break with mediaeval tradition and its return to the patristic ages.

But in spite of its many felicities in thought and expression, its beauty of temper, its interest in what it tells us of Donne's mind, and its historical interest as an early expression by a writer of genius of a piety characteristic of the Church of England, "A Litany" cannot be regarded as a wholly successful poem. It is an elaborate private prayer, rather incongruously cast into a liturgical form. Donne's letter to Goodyer shows he was aware of the discrepancy between such a "divine and publique" name and his "own little thoughts." He attempted to defend himself by the examples of two Latin litanies which he had found "amongst ancient annals." [9] The defense is not a very cogent one. The litanies he refers to, although written by individuals, are genuine litanies, suitable for general use. Donne's poem could hardly be prayed by anyone but himself. Although he preserves the structure of a litany (Invocations, Deprecations, Obsecrations, and Intercessions), he does not preserve the most important formal element in a litany, the unvarying responses in each section. His opening invocations to the Persons of the Trinity have each a particular petition in place of the repeated "Miserere nobis." He is, of course, debarred by his membership of a Reformed Church from using the response "Ora pro nobis"; instead he exercises his ingenuity in finding suitable petitions for each group of saints to make, or for us to make as we remember them. There is some awkwardness in this "rectified devotion," which, accepting that the saints pray for men, avoids direct requests for their suffrages while suggesting fitting subjects for their intercessions; and the absence of any response makes these stanzas formally unsatisfactory. With the Deprecations, Obsecrations, and Intercessions, he makes use of the responses "Libera nos" and "Audi nos"; but he treats them as refrains to be modified according to each stanza, as he had loved to adapt and twist refrains in his love-poetry. In one place he goes so far as to invert his response, and beg the Lord not to hear. One may sympathize with Donne's desire to find a form for his meditation; but the incompatibility between the material of the poem and the chosen form is too great. The form has had to be too much twisted to fit the material, and the material has been moulded to the form rather than expressed by it.

Most critics have agreed in regarding *"La Corona"* and "A Litany" as inferior to the "Holy Sonnets," which give an immediate impression

---

[9] The two poems Donne refers to can be found in Migne, P[atrologia] L[atina] lxxxvii. 39 and 42. They are of no interest; Donne only cites them because they afford a precedent for a private litany.

of spontaneity. Their superiority has been ascribed to their having been written ten years later, and their vehemence and anguished intensity have been connected with a deepening of Donne's religious experience after the death of his wife. There can be no question of their poetic greatness, nor of their difference from *"La Corona"* and "A Litany"; but I do not believe that greatness or that difference to be due to the reasons which are usually given. The accepted date rests on an assumption which the textual history of the sonnets does not support: the assumption that the three "Holy Sonnets" which the Westmoreland manuscript alone preserves were written at the same time as the other sixteen. These three sonnets are, as Sir Herbert Grierson called all the "Holy Sonnets," "separate ejaculations"; but the other sixteen fall into clearly recognizable sets of sonnets on familiar themes for meditation.[10] They are as traditional in their way as *"La Corona"* and "A Litany" are, and as the three Hymns are not. The Hymns are truly occasional; each arises out of a particular situation and a personal mood. But in theme and treatment the "Holy Sonnets," if we ignore the three Westmoreland sonnets, depend on a long-established form of religious exercise: not oral prayer, but the simplest method of mental prayer, meditation. To say this is not to impugn their originality or their power. Donne has used the tradition of meditation in his own way; and it suits his genius as a poet far better than do the more formal ways of prayer he drew upon in *"La Corona"* and "A Litany." Yet although, with the possible exception of the Hymns, the "Holy Sonnets" are his greatest divine poems, I do not myself feel that they spring from a deeper religious experience than that which lies behind "A Litany." The evidence which points to a date in 1609 does not seem to me to conflict with their character as religious poems; on the contrary it accords rather better with it than does the hitherto accepted date.

Many readers have felt a discrepancy between the "Holy Sonnets" and the picture which Walton gives of Donne's later years, and between the "Holy Sonnets" and the sermons and Hymns. There is a note of exaggeration in them. This is apparent, not only in the violence of such a colloquy as "Batter my heart," but also in the strained note of such lines as these:

> But who am I, that dare dispute with thee?
> O God, Oh! of thine onely worthy blood,
> And my teares, make a heavenly Lethean flood,
> And drowne in it my sinnes blacke memorie.
> That thou remember them, some claime as debt,
> I thinke it mercy, if thou wilt forget.

---

[10] For the arguments for an earlier date for the main body of the "Holy Sonnets," and the demonstration of their dependence on the tradition of formal meditation see my edition of the *Divine Poems* (1952), pp. xxxvii-lv.

At first sight the closing couplet seems the expression of a deep humility; but it cannot be compared for depth of religious feeling with the "Hymn to God the Father," where, however great the sin is, the mercy of God is implied to be the greater, or with such passages as the following, on the phrase *virga irae*:

> But truely, beloved, there is a blessed comfort ministred unto us, even in that word; for that word *Gnabar,* which we translate *Anger, wrath,* hath another ordinary signification in Scripture, which, though that may seem to be an easier, would prove a heavier sense for us to beare, than this of *wrath* and *anger;* this is, *preteritio, conniventia,* God's forbearing to take knowledge of our transgressions; when God shall say of us, as he does of *Israel, Why should ye be smitten any more?* when God leaves us to our selves, and studies our recovery no farther, by any more corrections; for, in this case, there is the lesse comfort, because there is the lesse *anger* show'd. And therefore *S. Bernard,* who was heartily afraid of this sense of our word, heartily afraid of this preterition, that God should forget him, leave him out, affectionately, passionately embraces this sense of the word in our Text, *Anger;* and he sayes, *Irascaris mihi Domine, Domine mihi irascaris, Be angry with me O Lord, O Lord be angry with me, lest I perish!* [11]

This is the tone of the last lines of "Good Friday":

> O thinke mee worth thine anger, punish mee,
> Burne off my rusts, and my deformity,
> Restore thine Image, so much, by thy grace,
> That thou may'st know mee, and I'll turne my face.

Both make the close of the sonnet seem facile.

The almost histrionic note of the "Holy Sonnets" may be attributed partly to the meditation's deliberate stimulation of emotion; it is the special danger of this exercise that, in stimulating feeling, it may falsify it, and overdramatize the spiritual life. But Donne's choice of subjects and his whole-hearted use of the method are symptoms of a condition of mind very different from the mood of *"La Corona"* or even from the conflicts which can be felt behind "A Litany." The meditation on sin and on judgment is strong medicine; the mere fact that his mind turned to it suggests some sickness in the soul. The "low devout melancholie" of *"La Corona,"* the "dejection" of "A Litany" are replaced by something darker. In both his preparatory prayers Donne uses a more terrible word, despair. The note of anguish is unmistakable. The image of a soul in meditation which the "Holy Sonnets" present is an image of a soul working out of its salvation in fear and trembling. The two poles between which it oscillates are faith in the mercy of God in Christ, and a sense of personal unworthi-

[11] *Fifty Semons* (1649), xlviii. 455.

ness that is very near to despair. The flaws in their spiritual temper are a part of their peculiar power. No other religious poems make us feel so acutely the predicament of the natural man called to be the spiritual man. None present more vividly man's recognition of the gulf that divides him from God and the effort of faith to lay hold on the miracle by which Christianity declares that the gulf has been bridged.

Donne's art in writing them was to seem "to use no art at all." His language has the ring of a living voice, admonishing his own soul, expostulating with his Maker, defying Death, or pouring itself out in supplication. He creates, as much as in some of the "Songs and Sonnets," the illusion of a present experience, throwing his stress on such words as "now" and "here" and "this." And, as often there, he gives an extreme emphasis to the personal pronouns:

> Take mee to you, imprison mee, for I
> Except you'enthrall mee, never shall be free,
> Nor ever chast, except you ravish mee.

The plain unadorned speech, with its idiomatic turns, its rapid questions, its exclamatory Oh's and Ah's, wrests the movement of the sonnet to its own movement. The line is weighted with heavy monosyllables, or lengthened by heavy secondary stresses, which demand the same emphasis as the main stress takes. It may be stretched out to

> All whom warre, dearth, age, agues, tyrannies,

after it has been contracted to

> From death, you numberlesse infinities.

Many lines can be reduced to ten syllables only by a more drastic use of elision than Donne allowed himself elsewhere, except in the Satires; and others, if we are to trust the best manuscripts, are a syllable short and fill out the line by a pause. This dramatic language has a magic that is unanalyzable: words, movement, and feeling have a unity in which no element outweighs the other.

The effect of completely natural speech is achieved by exploiting to the full the potentialities of the sonnet.[12] The formal distinction of octave and sestet becomes a dramatic contrast. The openings of Donne's sestets are as dramatic as the openings of the sonnets themselves: impatient as in

> Why doth the devill then usurpe in mee?

---

[12] As in *"La Corona,"* Donne keeps to two rhymes in the octave, and varies his sestet, using either *cddcee* or *cdcdee*. No general plan governs his choice here of which type of sestet he uses.

or gentle as in

> Yet grace, if thou repent, thou canst not lacke;

or imploring as in

> But let them sleepe, Lord, and mee mourne a space.

Though the *turn* in each of these is different, in all three there is that sudden difference in tension that makes a change dramatic. Donne avoids also the main danger of the couplet ending: that it may seem an afterthought, or an addition, or a mere summary. His final couplets, whether separate or running on from the preceding line, are true rhetorical climaxes, with the weight of the poem behind them. Except for Hopkins, no poet has crammed more into the sonnet than Donne. In spite of all the liberties he takes with his line, he succeeds in the one essential of the sonnet: he appears to need exactly fourteen lines to say exactly what he has to say. Donne possibly chose the sonnet form as appropriate for a set of formal meditations, but both in meditation and in the writing of his sonnets he converts traditional material to his own use. He was not, I believe, aiming at originality, and therefore the originality of the "Holy Sonnets" is the more profound.

With the exception of "The Lamentations of Jeremy," in which Donne, like so many of his contemporaries, but with more success than most, attempted the unrewarding task of paraphrasing the Scriptures, the remainder of the Divine Poems are occasional. The poem "Upon the Annunciation and Passion" is very near in mood and style to *"La Corona."* As there, Donne writes with strict objectivity. He contemplates two mysteries which are facets of one supreme mystery, and tries to express what any Christian might feel.[13] On the other hand, "Good Friday, Riding Westward" is a highly personal poem: a free, discursive meditation arising out of a particular situation. The elaborate preliminary conceit of the contrary motions of the heavenly bodies extends itself into astronomical images, until the recollection of the Passion sweeps away all thoughts but penitence. As in some of the finest of the "Songs and Sonnets," Donne draws out an initial conceit to its limit in order, as it seems, to throw it away when "to brave clearnesse all things are reduc'd." What he first sees as an incongruity—his turning his back on his crucified Savior—he comes

---

[13] Dr. F. E. Hutchinson told me that he once had the experience of being invited to preach a Lady Day Sermon in a year when Good Friday fell on the same day, and when, having written his sermon, he looked up Donne's poem, he found that he had done little but expand Donne's couplet:

> Or 'twas in him the same humility,
> That he would be a man, and leave to be.

to see as perhaps the better posture, and finally as congruous for a sinner. The poem hinges on the sudden apostrophe:

> and thou look'st towards mee,
> O Saviour, as thou hang'st upon the tree.

After this, discursive meditation contracts itself to penitent prayer. The mounting tension of the poem—from leisurely speculation, through the imagination kindled by "that spectacle of too much weight for mee," to passionate humility—makes it a dramatic monologue. So also does the sense it gives us of a second person present—the silent figure whose eyes the poet feels watching him as he rides away to the west.

"Good Friday" is the last divine poem Donne wrote before his ordination and it points forward to the Hymns. They also arise from particular situations, are free, not formal meditations, and have the same unforced feeling. They are the only lyrics among the Divine Poems, and it is not only in their use of the pun and conceit that they remind us of the "Songs and Sonnets." They have the spontaneity which *"La Corona"* and "A Litany" lack, without the overemphasis of the "Holy Sonnets." In them Donne's imagination has room for play. Each sprang from a moment of crisis. The "Hymn to Christ" was written on the eve of his journey overseas with Doncaster, a journey from which, as his Valediction Sermon shows, he felt he might not return. It is a finer treatment of the subject of the sonnet written after his wife's death in the Westmoreland manuscript. While the sonnet is general and reflective, in the Hymn his imagination is fired by his immediate circumstances and he translates his thoughts into striking and moving symbols. The "Hymn to God the Father" was written, according to Walton, during Donne's grave illness of 1623, and the "Hymn to God my God, in my sickness," whether it should be dated during the same illness or in 1631, was written when he thought himself at the point of death. In both the conclusion is the same: "So, in his purple wrapp'd receive mee Lord," and "Sweare by thy selfe." Donne's earliest poem on religion, the third Satire, ended with the words "God himselfe to trust," and it is fitting that what is possibly his last divine poem, and certainly one of his best known, should end with the memory of the promise to Abraham, the type of the faithful.[14] For the Divine Poems are poems of faith, not of vision. Donne goes by a road

---

[14] Cf. Gen. xxii. 16: "By myself have I sworn, saith the Lord"; and Heb. vi. 13-18: For when God made promise to Abraham, because he could swear by no greater, he sware by himself. . . . For men verily swear by the greater: and an oath for confirmation is to them an end of all strife. Wherein God, willing more abundantly to shew unto the heirs of promise the immutability of his counsel, confirmed it by an oath: that by two immutable things, in which it was impossible for God to lie, we might have a strong consolation, who have fled for refuge to lay hold upon the hope set before us.

which is not lit by any flashes of ecstasy, and, in the words he had carved on his tomb, "aspicit Eum cujus nomen est Oriens." The absence of ecstasy makes his divine poems so different from his love poems. There is an ecstasy of joy and an ecstasy of grief in his love-poetry; in his divine poetry we are conscious almost always of an effort of will. In the "Holy Sonnets" there is passion and longing, and in the Hymns some of the "modest assurance" which Walton attributed to Donne's last hours, but there is no rapture.

If Donne's spiritual and moral achievement are to be assessed, we must go to the sermons rather than to the Divine Poems. Their moral wisdom, their power to admonish or console, their faith in God's mercy, and their constant thankfulness for his bounty are the testimony of "a clear knowing soul, and of a Conscience at peace with it self." [15] What raises Donne as a preacher above the level of his contemporaries in his Evangelical fervor, the Pauline note which is everywhere in his sermons.[16] He speaks to sinners, as a sinner who has found mercy. The generous and affectionate side of his nature found its outlet here. As he said in a sermon:

> Till we come to that joy, which the heart cannot conceive, it is, I thinke, the greatest joy that the soule of man is capable of in this life, (especially where a man hath been any occasion of sinne to others) to assist the salvation of others.[17]

We should not expect to find in the religious poetry of a man who speaks like this a foretaste of bliss, or even the expectation of it.

Donne was a man of strong passions, in whom an appetite for life was crossed by a deep distaste for it. He is satirist and elegist at the same period, and even in the same poem. The scorn of the satirist invades the world of amorous elegy; his gayest poems have a note of bitterness, his most passionate lyrics are rarely free from a note of contempt, even if it is only a sardonic aside or illustration. In his love-poetry he set the ecstasy of lovers over against the dull, foolish, or sordid business of the world, or exalted one member of her sex by depreciating all the rest, or, in revulsion from the "queasie pain of being belov'd and loving," turned on his partner with savagery or mockery. But he was also a man of strong and loyal affections: a good son, a devoted husband, a loving father, and a warm and constant friend. From the beginning there is this other side to Donne. In moral and psychological terms, Donne's problem was to come to terms with a world which alternately enthralled and disgusted him, to be the master and not the slave of his temperament. Like Wordsworth in his middle years, he came to long for "a repose that ever is the same." He did

---

[15] Walton, *Lives* (Worlds' Classics), p. 83.

[16] "The cross of Christ is dimly seen in Taylor's works. Compare him in this respect with Donne, and you will feel the difference in a moment" (Coleridge, *Table Talk*, London, 1835, i. 168). Coleridge might well have mentioned Andrewes with Taylor.

[17] *LXXX Sermons*, liii. 532.

not look to religion for an ecstasy of the spirit which would efface the memory of the ecstasy of the flesh; but for an "evennesse" of piety which would preserve him from despair. In the boldest of the "Holy Sonnets" it is in order that he may "rise and stand" that he prays to be overthrown, and in order that he may be ever chaste that he prays God to ravish him. The struggles and conflicts to which the Divine Poems witness did not lead to the secret heights and depths of the contemplative life, but to the public life of duty and charity which Walton describes. That Donne had to wrestle to the end is clear. Like Dr. Johnson, with whom, in his natural melancholy and as a practical moralist, he has much in common, he remained burdened by the consciousness of his sins and aware of his need for mercy at the judgment.

Donne's divine poems are the product of conflict between his will and his temperament. They lack, therefore, the greatness of his love-poetry, whose power lies in its "unchartered freedom": in the energy of will with which he explores and expresses the range of his temperament. In his love-poetry he is not concerned with what he ought or ought not to feel, but with the expression of feeling itself. Passion is there its own justification, and so is disgust, or hatred or grief. In his divine poetry feeling and thought are judged by the standard of what a Christian should feel or think. As a love poet he seems to owe nothing to what any other man in love had ever felt or said before him; his language is all his own. As a divine poet he cannot escape using the language of the Bible, and of hymns and prayers, or remembering the words of Christian writers. Christianity is a revealed religion, contained in the Scriptures and the experience of Christian souls; the Christian poet cannot voyage alone. The truths of Donne's love-poetry are truths of the imagination, which freely transmutes personal experience. They are his own discoveries. The truths of revelation are the accepted basis of his religious poetry, and imagination has here another task. It is, to some extent, fettered. Donne anticipated Johnson's criticism of "poetical devotion," and was perhaps his own best critic, when he wrote to Sir Robert Carr, apologizing for his poem on Hamilton:

> You know my uttermost when it was best, and even then I did best when I had least truth for my subjects. In this present case there is so much truth as it defeats all Poetry. . . . If you had commanded mee to have waited on his body to Scotland and preached there, I would have embraced the obligation with more alacrity.[18]

But although the Divine Poems are not the record of discoveries, but of struggles to appropriate a truth which has been revealed, that truth does not "defeat all Poetry," but gives us a poetry whose intensity is a moral intensity. Some religious poetry, Herbert's perhaps, can be regarded as a

[18] *Poems*, ed. Grierson (Oxford, 1912), i. 288.

species of love-poetry; but Donne's is not of that kind. The image of Christ as Lover appears in only two of his poems—both written soon after the death of his wife. The image which dominates his divine poetry is the image of Christ as Savior, the victor over sin and death. The strength with which his imagination presents this figure is the measure of his need, and that need is the subject of the finest of his religious poems.

The Literary Value of Donne's Sermons

by Evelyn M. Simpson

John Donne was essentially a poet. It is as a poet, primarily, that he holds and will continue to hold his place in English literature. But in the later years of his life his creative power had to express itself for the most part in "that other harmony of prose." To his contemporaries it would have seemed hardly fitting that a Dean of St. Paul's should spend his time in idle versemaking. Occasionally the poetic impulse was too strong for him, and he composed one of his great sonnets or hymns, but for most of his time he labored in his vocation of preaching, and in this way he produced his finest prose.

Prose was a medium of literary expression which he had already used in the *Paradoxes and Problems, Biathanatos, Ignatius his Conclave,* and *Essays in Divinity.* He became an artist in prose as well as in verse. He had the poet's feeling for the color and sound of words, and the instinct for the right word in the right place. He was able to please, or surprise, or shock, in prose as he had done in verse. His prose lacks something of the concentrated intensity of his verse, it is true. Prose by its very nature tends to be more diffuse than poetry, and less individual. Yet Donne's prose conveys to us the unmistakable flavor of the man's personality, and the study of it is an exciting experience.

In prose Donne belongs to the school of Hooker and Jeremy Taylor, of Milton and Sir Thomas Browne. Like them he had been trained to write Latin prose, and he carried into his writing of his native language that mastery of the long period, that control of subordinate clauses, which is one of the marks of a Latin stylist. His greatest effects, such as that at the close of the terrible and majestic passage on damnation, are obtained by the marshaling of clause on clause, till the climax comes like a peal of thunder.

Donne did not attain at once to this mastery of the long period. One of his early attempts in prose, the "Character of a Dunce," consists of one enormous sentence which in a modern edition occupies three pages of print. This sentence has, however, no organic unity; it is really a string of sentences separated from one another at intervals by commas, and colons, and its structure would be much improved if all the colons and some of the commas were replaced by full stops. But in the interval between the writing of the "Character of a Dunce" and the sermons, Donne gave himself the severe intellectual exercise of composing a whole book, *Conclave Ignati,* in Latin. Also he trained himself in the writing of English in *Biathanatos, Pseudo-Martyr,* and *Essays in Divinity.* None of these works can approach the great sermons in style, but in all of them are passages in which Donne begins to try his powers and to give hints of greatness. . . .*

*   *   *

> He brought light out of darknesse, not out of a lesser light; he can bring thy Summer out of Winter, though thou have no Spring; though in the wayes of fortune, or understanding, or conscience, thou have been benighted till now, wintred and frozen, clouded and eclypsed, damped and benummed, smothered and stupified till now, now God comes to thee, not as in the dawning of the day, not as in the bud of the spring, but as the Sun at noon to illustrate all shadowes, as the sheaves in harvest, to fill all penuries, all occasions invite his mercies, and all times are his seasons.[1]

As we reread this passage, so exquisite in its cadences that the attempt to analyze its technique seems almost profane, we become conscious not only of Donne's subtle use of alliteration and antithesis, but also of music deriving from a kind of parallelism characteristic of another form of poetry, the Hebrew poetry of the Psalms and Prophets. This form of poetry has been at home in English ever since Tindale's great translation of 1534, though indeed we may trace its influence right back to the Old English period and the days of Caedmon and Cynewulf. Donne was a Hebrew scholar, and he studied the Old Testament in three different languages—in the original Hebrew, which he quotes at times to show the force of some particular word; in the Latin of the Vulgate, with which he had been familiar from childhood; and finally, in the English of the Geneva Bible and the Authorized Version. His Sermons are saturated with the language of Hebrew poetry, and also with its parallelism and antithesis.

Two or three examples must suffice to show the skill with which Donne chooses passages from the English Bible, dwells on them, and incorporates them into his own prose. Here is one from a Whitsunday sermon in which Donne had taken as his text, "And the Spirit of God moved upon the

---

* [A discussion of Donne's use of alliteration, antithesis, and repetition is omitted here. *Ed.*]

[1] *LXXX Sermons,* No. 2, p. 13.

face of the waters." He has, in mystical fashion, interpreted the waters in divers ways. Finally he remembers a verse in one of the great stories of the Old Testament, the tragedy of David and Absalom. He turns from the waters of baptism, and the waters of affliction, to the last and deepest waters of all, the waters of death:

> To end all with the end of all, Death comes to us in the name, and notion of waters too, in the Scriptures. The Widow of Tekoah said to *David* in the behalfe of *Absalon*, by the Counsaile of *Joab*, The water of death over-flowes all; *we must needs dye, saies she, and are as water spilt upon the ground, which cannot be gathered up againe:* yet God devises meanes, that his banished, be not expelled from him. So the Spirit of God moves upon the face of these waters, the Spirit of life upon the danger of death.[2]

The incorporation of these words into Donne's own prose is carried a stage further in one of his meditations upon death. "Looke upon the *water,* and we are as that, and as that spilt upon the ground." [3]

An Easter sermon contains a passage leading up, with fine effect, to two verses of Scripture which might seem to contradict each other. Donne does not quote the second verse from the Authorized Version; he para-phrases the last few words in order to emphasize the contrast at which he is aiming.

> Little know we, how little a way a soule hath to goe to heaven, when it departs from the body; Whether it must passe locally, through Moone, and Sun, and Firmament, (and if all that must be done, all that may be done, in lesse time then I have proposed the doubt in) or whether that soule finde new light in the same roome, and be not carried into any other, but that the glory of heaven be diffused over all, I know not, I dispute not, I inquire not. Without disputing, or inquiring, I know, that when Christ sayes, *That God is not the God of the dead,* he saies that to assure me, that those whom I call dead, are alive. And when the Apostle tels me, *That God is not ashamed to be called the God of the dead,* he tels me that to assure me, That Gods servants lose nothing by dying.[4]

Elsewhere Donne brings together two familiar verses from the Epistle to the Hebrews and a much less familiar one from the Prophet Jeremiah, and weaves them into the structure of his own prose:

> *Here we have no continuing City;* first, no City, no such large being, and then no continuing at all, it is but a sojourning. . . . Here we are but *Viatores,* Passengers, wayfaring men; This life is but the high-way, and thou canst not build thy hopes here. . . . What the Prophet sayes to thy Saviour (*O the hope of Israel, the Saviour thereof in time of trouble, why shouldest*

[2] *Ibid.,* No. 31, p. 311.   [3] *Fifty Sermons,* No. 30, p. 270.
[4] *LXXX Sermons,* No. 22, pp. 219-220.

thou be a stranger in the land, and as a wayfaring man, that turnes aside to
tarry for a night?) say thou to thy soule, Since thou art a stranger in the
land, a wayfaring man, turned aside to tarry for a night, since the night is
past, *Arise and depart, for here is not thy rest. . . .*[5]

These are not purple passages, but paragraphs which occur in the
ordinary course of Donne's argument. The poetry of the Hebrew prophets
mingles naturally with his own stately English prose. We are accustomed
to think of the Authorized Version as a monument of the English language, using chiefly words of native origin, plain, direct, and vigorous.
Donne's vocabulary, which incorporates so much of the phraseology of the
Bible, is distinguished by the same qualities. At times Donne uses Latin-
isms and turns of phrase derived from Latin syntax, but in the sermons
the English Bible is the most potent of all the influences which have
helped to mold his style.

The vocabulary used by Donne in the sermons is much larger than that
employed in his poems. It includes such words as *agnomination, binom-*
inous, colluctation, commonefaction, conculcation, consubstantiality, in-
choation, inintelligibleness, innotescence, longanimity, lycanthropy,
maciiency, significative, supergression, superplusage, and the like, as well
as theological terms like the *hypostatical union of two natures* in Christ,
the *impassibility* of the Divine Nature, or the *impenitablenesse* of those
who sin against the Holy Ghost. However useful such words may be in theological controversy, they do little to increase the effectiveness of Donne's
style. As soon as he is moved by a strong emotion, they drop out of his
speech, which returns to the native idiom that he could use so well. On
death, a subject which always moved him deeply, he says:

> It comes equally to us all, and makes us all equall when it comes. The
> ashes of an Oak in the Chimney, are no Epitaph of that Oak, to tell me how
> high or how large that was; It tels me not what flocks it sheltered while
> it stood, nor what men it hurt when it fell. The dust of great persons graves
> is speechlesse too, it sayes nothing, it distinguishes nothing: As soon as the dust
> of a wretch whom thou wouldest not, as of a Prince whom thou couldest
> not look upon, will trouble thine eyes, if the winde blow it thither; and
> when a whirle-wind hath blowne the dust of the Church-yard into the
> Church, and the man sweeps out the dust of the Church into the Churchyard,
> who will undertake to sift those dusts again, and to pronounce, This is the
> Patrician, this is the noble flowre, and this the yeomanly, this the Plebeian
> bran? [6]

> Death is not a banishing of you out of this world; but it is a visitation of
> your kindred that lie in the earth; neither are any nearer of kin to you, then
> the earth it selfe, and the wormes of the earth. You heap earth upon your
> soules, and encumber them with more and more flesh, by a superfluous and

[5] *Ibid.*, No. 39, pp. 390-391.   [6] *Ibid.*, No. 15, p. 148.

luxuriant diet; You adde earth to earth in new purchases, and measure not by Acres, but by Manors, nor by Manors, but by Shires; And there is a little Quillet, a little Close, worth all these, A quiet Grave.[7]

Donne's sentences, when he chooses, can be as terse, pithy, and colloquial as Bunyan's, or as eloquent and rhetorical as Milton's. To illustrate this, we may set side by side two passages in which his theme is the same —his consciousness that his repentance for his early sins has been accepted. by God.

> I doubt not of mine own salvation, and in whom can I have so much occasion of doubt, as in myself? When I come to heaven, shall I be able to say to any there, Lord, how got you hither? Was any man less likely to come thither than I?[8]

The colloquial vigor of these sentences is in strong contrast with the sustained eloquence of the second passage, taken from a Lenten sermon on Job's cry, "O earth, cover not thou my blood."

> And truly, so may I, so may every soule say, that is rectified, refreshed, restored, re-established by the seales of Gods pardon, and his mercy, so the world would take knowledge of the consequences of my sins, as well as of the sins themselves, and read my leafes on both sides, and heare the second part of my story, as well as the first; so the world would look upon my temporall calamities, the bodily sicknesses, and the penuriousnesse of my fortune contracted by my sins, and upon my spirituall calamities, dejections of spirit, sadnesse of heart, declinations towards a diffidence and distrust in the mercy of God, and then, when the world sees me in this agony and bloody sweat would also see the Angels of heaven ministring comforts unto me; so they would consider me in my *Peccavi*, and God in his *Transtulit*, Me in my earnest Confessions, God in his powerfull Absolutions, Me drawne out of one Sea of blood, the blood of mine owne soule, and cast into another Sea, the bottomlesse Sea of the blood of Christ Jesus; so they would know as well what God hath done for my soule, as what my soule and body have done against my God; so they would reade me throughout, and look upon me altogether, I would joyne with *Job*, in his confident adjuration, *O Earth cover not thou my blood;* Let all the world know all the sins of my youth, and of mine age too, and I would not doubt, but God should receive more glory, and the world more benefit, then if I had never sinned.[9]

Though the theme is essentially the same, the difference in treatment corresponds to a significant change in the thought. In the first passage Donne is thinking primarily of his hearers. He wishes to console some dejected soul by the mention of his own assurance that God has shown

[7] *Ibid.*, No. 46, p. 463.   [8] *Ibid.*, No. 24, p. 241.
[9] *Ibid.*, No. 13, p. 132.

mercy to himself a sinner. He is using prose of the plainest and most direct kind for its ordinary purpose, the communication of a fact by the speaker to his hearers. But in the second passage his imagination is fired by a metaphysical idea—the possibility that evil may be transmuted into good. From the thought of his own repentance accepted by God's mercy, he rises to the contemplation of an active divine energy which can make evil itself an instrument of a greater good. This was an idea peculiarly dear to Donne. He had given crude expression to it in his early *Paradoxes*, and he elaborated it in several of his sermons. Here he almost forgets his hearers in order on the one hand to meditate aloud on his own agonies and calamities, and on the other to consider that "bottomlesse Sea of the blood of Christ Jesus" in which his sins have been drowned. The words kindle and glow, "the wheels take fire from the mere rapidity of their motion," as Coleridge finely said of Donne's poetry,[10] and so the sentences take to themselves something of the music and rhythm of poetry.

This paradoxical idea, that evil may be transformed into an instrument for good, leads us to a consideration of Donne's use of paradox in general. In the poems, both secular and divine, he had constantly employed paradox, and it is characteristic of him that his earliest attempts at literary prose were short pieces modeled on the Italian *paradossi*. In the sermons he delights to expound the great paradoxes of the Christian religion—God made man in order that man may be made one with God; Christ who is Very God of Very God bearing every humiliation even to the death of the cross; or the believer who dies to live contrasted with the natural man who lives to die. Of the Crucifixion, Donne writes:

> . . . I see those hands stretched out, that stretched out the heavens, and those feet racked, to which they that racked them are foot-stooles; I heare him, from whom his nearest friends fled, pray for his enemies, and him, whom his Father forsooke, not forsake his brethren; I see him that cloathes this body with his creatures, or else it would wither, and cloathes this soule with his Righteousness, or else it would perish, hang naked upon the Crosse; And him that hath, him that is, *the Fountain of the Water of Life*, cry out, *He thirsts. . . .*[11]

[10] *Biographia Literaria* (Oxford, 1907), ii. 56.
[11] *LXXX Sermons*, No. 40, p. 401. The whole of this passage should be compared with Donne's poem "Good Friday," lines 21-27 (ed. Grierson, i. 336-337):

> Could I behold those hands which span the Poles,
> And turn all spheares at once, peirc'd with those holes?
> Could I behold that endlesse height which is
> Zenith to us, and our Antipodes,
> Humbled below us? or that blood which is
> The seat of all our Soules, if not of his,
> Made durt of dust, or that fleshe which was worne
> By God, for his apparell, rag'd, and torne?

Of the faithful who died in the great plague epidemic of 1625 he says to their friends and relatives:

> But are all these dead? *They were,* says the Text; they were in your eyes, and therefore we forbid not that office of the eye, that holy tenderness, to weep for them that are so dead. But there was a part in every one of them, that could not die; which the God of life, who breathed it into them, from his own mouth, hath suck'd into his own bosome. . . . When time shall be no more, when death shall be no more, they shall renew, or rather continue their being.[12]

Paradox can be used in a very different fashion for the purpose of sarcastic rebuke. Donne has sharp words for the insincerity and irreverence of some of his hearers:

> *God's House is the house of Prayers;* It is his Court of Requests; There he receives petitions, there he gives Order upon them. And you come to God in his House, as though you came to keepe him company, to sit downe, and talke with him halfe an houre; or you come as Ambassadors, covered in his presence, as though ye came from as great a Prince as he. You meet below, and there make your bargaines, for biting, for devouring Usury, and then you come up hither to prayers, and so make God your Broker. You rob, and spoile, and eat his people as bread, by Extortion, and bribery, and deceitful waights and measures, and deluding oathes in buying and selling, and then come hither, and so make God your Receiver, and his house a den of Thieves. His house is *Sanctum Sanctorum.* The holiest of holies, and you make it onely *Sanctuarium;* It should be a place sanctified by your devotions, and you make it onely a Sanctuary to privilege Malefactors, A place that may redeeme you from the ill opinion of men, who must in charity be bound to thinke well of you, because they see you here.[13]

Paradox and irony are closely linked, for there is often an ironical intention behind the paradox. Donne has a keen eye for life's little ironies, while at the same time he never forgets the final and tremendous irony of death. Thus to the heavy paterfamilias, inclined to become a domestic tyrant, he gives a word of advice.

> Call not light faults by heavie Names; Call not all sociablenesse, and Conversation, Disloyaltie in thy Wife; Nor all levitie, or pleasurablenesse, Incorrigiblenesse in thy Sonne; nor all negligence or forgetfulnesse, perfidiousnesse in thy Servants; Nor let every light disorder within doores, shut thee out of doores, or make thee a stranger in thine owne House. In a smoakie roome, it may bee enough to open a Windowe without leaving the place; . . .[14]

---

[12] *XXVI Sermons,* No. 21, pp. 296-297.
[13] *LXXX Sermons,* No. 68, p. 692.
[14] *The First Sermon Preached to King Charles,* 1625, p. 53.

This irony, sometimes humorous, sometimes bitter, pervades the sermons, giving them a characteristic flavor. Donne applies it even to himself in a remorseless analysis of his own failures in prayer:

> I throw my selfe down in my Chamber, and I call in, and invite God, and his Angels thither, and when they are there, I neglect God and his Angels, for the noise of a Flie, for the ratling of a Coach, for the whining of a doore; I talke on, in the same posture of praying; Eyes lifted up; knees bowed downe; as though I prayed to God; and, if God, or his Angels should aske me, when I thought last of God in that prayer, I cannot tell: Sometimes I finde that I had forgot what I was about, but when I began to forget it, I cannot tell. A memory of yesterdays pleasures, a feare of to morrows dangers, a straw under my knee, a noise in mine eare, a light in mine eye, an anything, a nothing, a fancy, a Chimera in my braine, troubles me in my prayer. So certainely is there nothing, nothing in spirituall things, perfect in this world.[15]

Nothing is more characteristic of Donne's poetry than his startlingly original imagery. In the sermons he is less deliberately bent on surprising his hearers, so that flowers and birds are not excluded from his metaphorical garden. Of the everlasting day of eternity he remarks: "And all the powerful Kings, and all the beautifull Queenes of this world, were but as a bed of flowers, some gathered at six, some at seaven, some at eight, All in one Morning, in respect of this Day." [16]

Even more beautiful is the picture of the soul rising in dazzling whiteness "like a Lily in Paradise, out of red earth" from the enfolding blade of Christ's protecting merit.[17] Yet even in these comparisons there is usually some trace of that "fundamental brain-work" which distinguished Donne's imagery from that of lesser men. In the last-mentioned passage the "red earth" is not merely a vivid contrast to the whiteness of the lily; it is also a reminder that in Donne's theology man was created from red soil. "In the great field of clay, of red earth, that man was made of, and mankind, I am a clod." [18]

There are some images in the sermons which surprise us by their homeliness. The preacher who indulges in empty rhetoric is described as a man who "having made a Pye of Plums, without meat, offers it to sale in every Market." [19] The worldly man is likened to a foolish mother who "in the midst of many sweet children" wastes her time in making dolls for her own amusement, or to a man who pushes into a village fair to look upon "sixpenny pictures, and three-farthing prints," while at home he has "Chamber and Galleries . . . full of curious masterpeeces." [20] Or Donne goes to the poultry yard for a metaphor: "All egges are not hatched that

[15] *LXXX Sermons*, No. 80, p. 820.
[17] *Ibid.*, No. 27, p. 274.
[19] *Ibid.*, No. 12, p. 114.
[16] *Ibid.*, No. 73, p. 748.
[18] *Ibid.*, No. 34, p. 338.
[20] *Fifty Sermons*, No. 29, p. 256.

the hen sits upon; neither could Christ himselfe get all the chickens that were hatched, to come, and to stay under his wings." [21]

Some of Donne's images are grotesque or macabre. The monstrously large, such as elephants[22] and whales, or the absurdly small, such as flies and fleas, appear in his prose works as well as in his poems. He has an elaborate comparison in which the preacher rebuking sin is likened to a fisherman harpooning a whale:

> The rebuke of sin, is like the fishing of *Whales;* the Marke is great enough; one can scarce misse hitting; but if there be not *sea room* and line enough, and a dexterity in letting out that line, he that hath fixed his harping Iron, in the Whale, endangers himselfe, and his boate; God hath made us *fishers of Men;* and when we have struck a *Whale,* touch'd the conscience of any person, which thought himselfe above rebuke, and increpation, it struggles, and strives, and as much as it can, endevours to draw fishers, and boate, the Man and his fortune into contempt, and danger. But if God tye *a sicknesse,* or any other calamity, to the end of the line, that will winde up this Whale againe, to the boate, bring back this rebellious sinner better advised, to the mouth of the Minister, for more counsaile, and to a better souplenesse, and inclinablenesse to conforme himselfe, to that which he shall after receive from him; onely calamity makes way for a rebuke to enter.[23]

Any anthology of Donne's prose will supply so many examples of the macabre that it is unnecessary here to do more than to quote one only, in which he adds a fresh touch to the well-worn image of life as a journey to a distant city by reminding his hearers of the gallows which were placed at a conspicuous spot outside any town of importance. "As he that travails weary, and late towards a great City, is glad when he comes to a place of execution, because he knows that is neer the town; so when thou comest to the gate of death, [be] glad of that, for it is but one step from that to thy *Jerusalem.*" [24]

The sermons contain a large number of images of that ingenious and far-fetched kind which distinguishes his poetry. As Dr. Johnson asked "Who but Donne would have thought that a good man is a telescope?" so we may ask in turn who else would have compared a good man's life to an engraving.

> Bee pleased to remember that those Pictures which are deliver'd in a minute, from a print upon a paper, had many dayes, weeks, Moneths time for the graving of those Pictures in the Copper; So this Picture of that

---

[21] *LXXX Sermons,* No. 7, p. 70.   [22] For elephants see *Fifty Sermons,* No. 40, p. 372.
[22] *Fifty Sermons,* No. 10, pp. 74-75.
[24] *XXVI Sermons,* No. 20, pp. 294-295, first numbering.

dying Man, that dies in Christ, that dies the death of the Righteous, that embraces Death as a Sleepe, was graving all his life; All his publique actions were the lights, and all his private the shadowes of this Picture.[25]

In all these examples, the image, whether used for metaphor or simile, has been portrayed in set terms. But Donne can also suggest an image by the use of the appropriate verbs. "Implicite beleevers, ignorant beleevers, the adversary may swallow; but the understanding beleever, he must chaw, and pick bones, before he come to assimilate him, and make him like himself." [26] Here the verbs "swallow," "chaw," "pick bones," at once conjure up before the reader's eye a grim figure like that of Bunyan's Giant Slay-good who "was rifling Feeble-mind, with a purpose after that to pick his bones; for he was of the nature of flesh-eaters."

There are a certain number of images in Donne's sermons which give us a shock of surprise of a different kind. There is an incongruity about metaphors taken from the theater or the gaminghouse, used as they are by Donne to illustrate some profound truth of religion; it is the converse of his use in the poems of some image drawn from theology or metaphysics in the service of profane love. We feel a shock of surprise at the sight of these unequally yoked pairs. The discovery of occult resemblances between things apparently unlike was singled out by Dr. Johnson as one of the distinctive marks of the wit of Donne and his followers. When the things coupled are sacred and secular, a suggestion of profanity arises. In the love poems Donne is sometimes deliberately profane, and it may be that in the divine poems and the sermons he occasionally uses incongruous secular metaphors with the contrary intention of reclaiming that which had been polluted for the service of the sanctuary. Thus in one of the "Holy Sonnets" he cries to the picture of Christ:

> No, no; but as in my idolatrie
> I said to all my profane mistresses,
> Beauty, of pitty, foulnesse onely is
> A signe of rigour: so I say to thee,
> To wicked spirits are horrid shapes assigned,
> This beauteous forme assures a piteous minde.[27]

So in the sermons we find: "God stoops even to the words of our foule and unchaste love, that thereby he might raise us to the heavenly love of himselfe, and his Son." [28]

It may be, however, that in these passages Donne was writing, as he usually did, with no watertight compartments in his mind. Life is one,

[25] *Ibid.*, No. 15, p. 218.   [26] *LXXX Sermons*, No. 18, p. 178.
[27] *Poems*, i. 328.   [28] *LXXX Sermons*, No. 41, p. 406.

in all its manifestations, ugly or beautiful; the reality behind is one, and is manifested in the secular as well as in the sacred. "All things that are, are equally removed from being nothing; and whatsoever hath any beeing, is by that very beeing, a glasse in which we see God, who is the roote, and the fountaine of all beeing." [29]

Thus Donne obtains for himself a range of imagery incomparably wider than that of other preachers. He can draw his metaphors from the royal court and the stage, from the tavern and the gaminghouse. Here is a striking reminder that Donne had been in his youth a great frequenter of plays. He says that God is not to be truly found by the soul in "those transitory and interlocutory prayers, which out of custome and fashion we make, and still proceed in our sin; when we pretend to speake to God, but like Comedians upon a stage, turne over our shoulder, and whisper to the Devill." [30]

The image of the gods as gamesters who sport with mankind in a game of chance is one that has found favor with atheistic philosophers, but was hardly to be expected from the pulpit of St. Paul's. Donne, however, uses it without any irreverence to condemn the deeper irreligion of those Puritan preachers who proclaimed man's predestination to damnation before his birth. The whole passage is a noble protest of a truly religious spirit against that grim doctrine:

Never propose to thyself such a God as thou wert not bound to imitate: Thou mistakest God, if thou make him to be any such thing, or make him to do any such thing, as thou in thy proportion shouldst not be, or shouldst not do. And shouldst thou curse any man that had never offended, never transgrest, never trespast thee? Can God have done so? Imagine God, as the Poet saith, *Ludere in humanis,* to play but a *game at Chesse* with this world; to sport himself with making little things great, and great things nothing: Imagine God to be but at play with us, but a gamester; yet will a gamester *curse,* before he be in danger of losing any thing? Will God curse man, before man have sinned? [31]

There is an image drawn from the game of bowls, a favorite Elizabethan pastime, in *XXVI Sermons*: "For though it may seem a degree of flattery, to preach against little sins in such a City as this, where greater sins do abound; yet because these be the materials and elements of greater sins, (and it is impossible to say where a Bowl will lie, that is let fall down a hill, though it be let never so gently out of the hand). . . ." [32]

Beauty finds strange resting places. The perplexed and tortured soul of Donne sought her not in the light of setting suns, but in the obscure processes of the mind of man. He thought of the Supreme Beauty as a

[29] *Ibid.,* No. 23, p. 227.
[31] *Fifty Sermons,* No. 26, p. 224.
[30] *Ibid.,* No. 59, p. 596.
[32] *XXVI Sermons,* No. 24, p. 335.

mathematical symbol—God the Circle. The beauty of nature was seen by him, not in sea or sky, but in "the peacefull succession, and connexion of causes, and effects." [33] "The correspondence and relation of all parts of Nature to one Author, the concinnity and dependence of every piece and joint of this frame of the world, the admirable order, the immutable succession, the lively and certain generation, and birth of effects from their Parents, the causes: in all these, though there be no sound, no voice, yet we may even see that it is an excellent song, an admirable piece of musick and harmony. . . ." [34]

We cannot read Donne's sermons aright without realizing that this preacher was essentially a poet, who when he was debarred from the ordinary forms of verse threw his energy into weaving new rhythms and harmonies in prose. There was nothing unreal or factitious in such an exercise, nothing which detracted from his profound sincerity. He could not express the truth of himself save in poetry, or in a rhythmical prose which had all the essentials of poetry. Poetry to such a man as Donne is the resolution of an inner conflict, a means of harmonizing discordant forces. There are some of his sermons, admittedly only a few, which are in effect poems. Donne planned them under the influence of some strong emotion, and their structure is fundamentally that of a poem. A good example is to be found in the sermon preached in St. Paul's on Easter Day, 1629. Donne based it on a highly poetical passage of the Book of Job, that describing the vision of Eliphaz the Temanite. At first sight no text could seem less suitable for an Easter meditation than this Hebrew vision, in which Eliphaz, a wild man out of the desert, is shaken to the very marrow of his bones by an unseen presence which declares the unapproachable holiness of God.

> Fear came upon me, and trembling,
>   which made all my bones to shake.
> Then a spirit passed before my face;
>   the hair of my flesh stood up:
> It stood still, but I could not discern the form thereof:
>   an image was before mine eyes;
> There was silence, and I heard a voice, saying,
> Shall mortal man be more just than God?
>   shall a man be more pure than his Maker?
> Behold, he put no trust in his servants;
>   and his angels he charged with folly:
> How much less in them that dwell in houses of clay,
>   whose foundation is in the dust,
>   which are crushed before the moth?

[33] *LXXX Sermons*, No. 15, p. 146. For God as a circle, *Ibid.*, No. 2, p. 14: "God is a circle himselfe, and he will make thee one."

[34] *XXVI Sermons*, No. 13, p. 181, second numbering.

> They are destroyed from morning to evening:
>
> they perish for ever, without any regarding it.[35]

Donne evidently intended to shake his hearers out of the complacency with which they anticipated an eloquent sermon on somewhat conventional lines. For several years in succession he had given them his finest discourses on the resurrection of the dead. He believed profoundly in the Christian hope of immortality, but he himself had lately passed through deep waters of sorrow and sickness. In 1627 he had lost his daughter Lucy, and two beloved friends, Magdalen Danvers and Lucy, Countess of Bedford. In the late summer of 1628 he had been attacked by a high fever and a quinsy, which confined him to his bed. For some weeks he was unable to preach, and a rumor got about that he was dead. He was now an old man by the standard of those days, and he knew that he had not much longer to live. Before the prospect of meeting the Eyes of God, he asked himself the question of the vision—"Shall mortal man be more just than God?"— and became conscious of his complete unworthiness. In the sermon, he presented to his hearers the dilemma of Eliphaz, and he arranged it in a series of paragraphs, at the end of which the text, which in the Hebrew is itself a line of poetry, is repeated as a refrain varying slightly from stanza to stanza. This was a device which he had used in several of his poems, such as "The Will," "An Epithalamion on the Lady Elizabeth and Count Palatine being married," and "Epithalamion made at Lincoln's Inn." In the sermon, the text, "Behold, he put no trust in his servants, and his Angels he charged with folly," is repeated at the end of nine paragraphs, first in the original form, and then with such modifications as "God put no trust in those servants, but . . . ," or, "In those servants he put no trust, and those Angels he charged with folly."

In the last three paragraphs the refrain is discarded, and Donne turns from the clouded vision of Eliphaz to the clearer revelation of God in Christ. He remembers that with the Lord there is mercy, and with Him is plenteous redemption. He offers to all his hearers the salvation which he himself has received. He rejoices in the multitude of those that shall be saved, and takes up into his own prose the great phrases of the *Te Deum,* which on Easter Day the Church sings with renewed gladness after the silence and austerity of Lent. "There is not only one Angel, a *Gabriel;* But *to thee all Angels cry aloud;* and Cherubim, and Seraphim, are plurall terminations; many Cherubs, many Seraphs in heaven. There is not only one Monarchall Apostle, a *Peter,* but *The glorious company of the Apostles praise thee.* There is not onely a Proto-Martyr, a *Stephen,* but *The noble army of Martyrs praise thee.*" [36]

Finally he returns to one of his favorite books, the Revelation of St.

---

[35] *Job* 4. 14-20. The text given is that of the Authorized Version, except that the parallel clauses are printed on separate lines.

[36] *LXXX Sermons,* No. 24, p. 241.

John, and recalls another version which had been in his mind for years—
that in which St. John on the Isle of Patmos saw the four angels standing
"at the round world's imagin'd corners," and then the great multitude
that no man could number of the redeemed from every nation and
kindred.

> *The key of David opens, and no man shuts.* The Son of *David,* is the key
> of *David,* Christ Jesus; He hath opened heaven for us all; let no man shut
> out himself, by diffidence in Gods mercy, nor shut out any other man, by
> overvaluing his own purity, in respect of others. . . . That so, . . . *that*
> *multitude which no man can number, of all Nations, and Kindreds, and*
> *People, and Tongues,* may enter with that acclamation, *Salvation to our*
> *God, which sitteth upon the Throne, and to the Lamb for ever.* And *unto*
> *this City of the living God, the heavenly Jerusalem, and to the innumerable*
> *company of Angels, to the general assembly, and Church of the first born,*
> *which are written in heaven, and to God the Judge of all, and to the spirits*
> *of just men made perfect, and to Jesus the Mediator of the new covenant,*
> *and to the blood of sprinkling, that speaks better things then that of Abel,*
> Blessed God bring us all, for thy Sons sake, and by the operation of thy
> Spirit. *Amen.*

Thus, though the sermon is written in prose, its underlying structure
is poetical. We are reminded of the words of a living poet who is also
well known for his prose, Sir Osbert Sitwell, who has declared: "I can
claim never to have written a book, or a short story, or an essay that I did
not conceive as if it were a poem, and in that resides the value, such as
it is, of my work." [37] We may doubt whether Donne would have made
such a claim for the large number of his sermons which are occupied
chiefly with doctrinal or controversial matters, but we can make it for
the beautiful sermon which he preached on the death of the righteous on
the first Friday in Lent 1627/1628. This is conceived as a poem on the
text, "When he had said this, he fell asleep." Sleep here is the sleep of
death, not to Donne the "sleep that knows no waking," but the sleep from
which the righteous awake to find themselves in the immediate presence
of God.

Donne opens his sermon thus: "We that will dy with Christ upon
Good-Friday, must hear his own bell toll all Lent; he that will be partaker
of his passion at last, must conform himself to his discipline of prayer
and fasting before. . . . We begin to hear Christs bell toll now, and is
not our bell in the chime?" [38]

He considers the life and death of St. Stephen as a model for the Christian, and uses prose of the ordinary kind for most of the sermon. Then,
as he nears the close, he turns from edification to ecstasy. Poetry is the
only possible vehicle, as Dante knew, for conveying even a remote

[37] *Great Morning* (London, 1948), p. 135.
[38] *XXVI Sermons,* No. 15, p. 205.

apprehension of the meaning of the Beatific Vision. Once again Donne turns to an Old Testament story for his starting point—that of Jacob in the wilderness, fleeing from his brother's vengeance, and sleeping at last in exhaustion with his head pillowed on a great stone. In his sleep he sees a ladder set up from earth to heaven, on which the angels of God ascend and descend continually, while above it stands the God against whom he has sinned, and who yet promises him mercy and guidance. "And Jacob awaked out of his sleep, and said, Surely the Lord is in this place, and I knew it not. And he was afraid, and said, How dreadful is this place! This is none other but the house of God, and this is the gate of heaven." With exquisite artistry Donne omits Jacob's fear, and chooses only those phrases which suit the awakening of the righteous. He continues:

> They shall awake as *Jacob* did,
>   and say as *Jacob* said,
> *Surely the Lord is in this place,*
>   *and this is no other but the house of God,*
>   *and the gate of heaven,*
> And into that gate they shall enter,
>   and in that house they shall dwell,
> where there shall be no Cloud nor Sun,
>   no darkenesse nor dazling,
>   but one equall light,
> no noyse nor silence,
>   but one equall musick,
> no fears nor hopes,
>   but one equall possession,
> no foes nor friends,
>   but one equall communion and Identity,
> no ends nor beginnings,
>   but one equall eternity.

Keepe us Lord so awake in the duties of our Callings, that we may thus sleepe in thy Peace, and wake in thy glory, . . .[39]

[39] *XXVI Sermons*, No. 15, p. 219. I have printed the parallel clauses on separate lines to make the construction clear.

John Donne in Meditation

by Louis L. Martz

The *Anniversaries* are not usually treated as whole poems. For one thing, the biographical facts underlying these poems lead readers to approach them with suspicion, since they were written in memory of the daughter of Donne's generous patron, Sir Robert Drury—a girl who died in her fifteenth year, and whom Donne admits he never saw.[1] As a result, the elaborate eulogies of Elizabeth Drury are frequently dismissed as venal and insincere, while interest in the poems centers on those passages which reflect Donne's awareness of the "new philosophy," on explicitly religious portions, or on any portions which provide illustrative quotations for special studies of Donne and his period.

Such fragmentary appreciation of the poems has, I think, hampered an understanding of their full significance. For each poem is carefully designed as a whole, and the full meaning of each grows out of a deliberately articulated structure. Furthermore, a close reading of each poem shows that the two *Anniversaries* are significantly different in structure and in the handling of Petrarchan imagery, and are consequently different in value. The *First Anniversary*, despite its careful structure, is, it must be admitted, successful only in brilliant patches; but I think it can be shown that the *Second Anniversary*, despite some flaws, is as a whole one of the great religious poems of the seventeenth century.

Let us look at the structure of the *First Anniversary: An Anatomie of the World. Wherein, By occasion of the untimely death of Mistris Elizabeth Drury, the frailty and the decay of this whole World is represented.* The poem is divided into an Introduction, a Conclusion, and five distinct sections which form the body of the work. Each of these five sections is subdivided into three sections: first, a meditation on some aspect of "the frailty and the decay of this whole world"; second, a eulogy of Elizabeth

"John Donne in Meditation." Part of chapter 6 of *The Poetry of Meditation,* by Louis L. Martz (New Haven, 1954), pp. 220-3, 228-48. Copyright 1954 by the Yale University Press. Reprinted by permission of the author and the Yale University Press. [In order to allow this section of Professor Martz's study to stand alone, I have made some slight alterations in the text and expanded some references. *Ed.*]

[1] Donne, *Letters* (1651), p. 219.

Drury as the "Idea" of human perfection and the source of hope, now lost, for the world; third, a refrain introducing a moral:

> Shee, shee is dead; shee's dead: when thou knowest this,
> Thou knowest how poore a trifling thing man is.
> And learn'st thus much by our Anatomie. . . .

In each section the second line of this refrain is modified so as to summarize the theme of the whole section; in the following outline of the poem I use part of the second line of each refrain as the heading for each section:

Introduction, 1-90. The world is sick, "yea, dead, yea putrified," since she, its "intrinsique balme" and "preservative," its prime example of Virtue, is dead.

Section I, 91-190: "how poore a trifling thing man is."
  1. Meditation, 91-170. Because of Original Sin man has decayed in length of life, in physical size, in mental capacity.
  2. Eulogy, 171-82. The girl was perfect virtue; she purified herself and had a purifying power over all.
  3. Refrain and Moral, 183-90. Our only hope is in religion.

Section II, 191-246: "how lame a cripple this world is."
  1. Meditation, 191-218. The "universall frame" has received injury from the sin of the Angels, and now in universe, in state, in family, " 'Tis all in peeces, all cohaerence gone."
  2. Eulogy, 219-36. Only this girl possessed the power which might have unified the world.
  3. Refrain and Moral, 237-46. Contemn and avoid this sick world.

Section III, 247-338: "how ugly a monster this world is."
  1. Meditation, 247-304. Proportion, the prime ingredient of beauty, no longer exists in the universe.
  2. Eulogy, 305-24. The girl was the "measure of all Symmetrie" and harmony.
  3. Refrain and Moral, 325-38. Human acts must be "done fitly and in proportion."

Section IV, 339-76: "how wan a Ghost this our world is."
  1. Meditation, 339-58. "Beauties other second Element, Colour, and lustre now, is as neere spent."
  2. Eulogy, 359-68. The girl had the perfection of color and gave color to the world.
  3. Refrain and Moral, 369-76. There is no pleasure in an ugly world; it is wicked to use false colors.

Section V, 377-434: "how drie a Cinder this world is."

1. Meditation, 377-98. Physical "influence" of the heavens upon the earth has been weakened.
2. Eulogy, 399-426. The girl's virtue has little effect on us now because of this weakened "correspondence" between heavens and earth; in fact the world's corruption weakened her effect while she lived.
3. Refrain and Moral, 427-34. Nothing "Is worth our travaile, griefe, or perishing," except the joys of religious virtue.

Conclusion, 435-74.

It seems clear that the religious motifs in Petrarchan lament, found at their best in Petrarch's poems "To Laura in Death," have here combined with strictly religious meditation to produce a poem which derives its form, fundamentally, from the tradition of spiritual exercises. The Jesuit exercises, we recall, normally involve a series of five exercises daily for a period of about a month, each meditation being precisely divided into points, usually into three points. . . .[*]

* * *

Various and flexible relationships exist between Donne's *Anatomy* and the tradition of methodical meditation. In particular, his fivefold sequence and his alternation of contempt and praise within each section mark the poem as a spiritual exercise. But the ultimate question remains and has no doubt already been suggested by the above parallels: is it valid to write in such a tradition when the pattern of virtue is, literally taken, only a girl? Certainly the chief problem in evaluating the poem has been very shrewdly put in the blunt objection of Ben Jonson: "That Donne's Anniversary was profane and full of blasphemies; that he told Mr. Donne, if it had been written of the Virgin Mary it had been something; to which he answered that he described the Idea of a Woman and not as she was." [2]

When does laudation of an Ideal Woman become thus objectionable in poetry with a strong religious note? It has not been generally considered so in Dante and Petrarch. Is it objectionable in Donne? An answer, so far as this poem is concerned, may be suggested by noting Petrarch's general treatment of Laura in Death. Petrarch has successfully combined eulogy with religious themes by keeping his sequence always focused on his central symbol of perfection: the *contemptus mundi*, the hyperbole of the

---

[*] [Examples of methods of religious meditation are omitted here. They are discussed at length in chapter 2 of *The Poetry of Meditation*, which gives details of books referred to in the passage here omitted. *Ed.*]

[2] "Conversations with Drummond," Ben Jonson, *Works*, ed. Herford and Simpson, i. 133 (modernized).

world's destruction, the praise of Laura in Heaven, are all justified by maintaining Laura as the origin and end of the poems' emotions, and thus making her the first Cause of the sequence.

> The chosen angels, and the spirits blest,
> Celestial tenants, on that glorious day
> My Lady join'd them, throng'd in bright array
> Around her, with amaze and awe imprest.
> "What splendor, what new beauty stands confest
> Unto our sight?"—among themselves they say;
> "No soul, in this vile age, from sinful clay
> To our high realms has risen so fair a guest."
> Delighted to have changed her mortal state,
> She ranks amid the purest of her kind;
> And ever and anon she looks behind,
> To mark my progress and my coming wait;
> Now my whole thought, my wish to heaven I cast;
> 'Tis Laura's voice I hear, and hence she bids me haste.[3]

Donne's *Anatomy* has no such focus: it has instead a central inconsistency which defeats all Donne's efforts to bring its diverse materials under control. For it is not correct to say, as Empson says, that "the complete decay of the universe" is presented as having been caused by the death of Elizabeth Drury. If this were so, the poem might achieve unity through supporting a dominant symbol of virtue's power, and one might be able to agree with Empson that the "only way to make the poem sensible is to accept Elizabeth Drury as the Logos." [4] But after the Introduction has elaborately presented this hyperbole, one discovers in the first Meditation that Elizabeth Drury has, basically, nothing to do with the sense of decay in the poem. The whole first Meditation is strictly in the religious tradition; it meditates the decline of man through sin from God's original creation:

> There is no health; Physitians say that wee,
> At best, enjoy but a neutralitie.
> And can there bee worse wicknesse, then to know
> That we are never well, nor can be so?

[3] *Rime* 346 in the translation by John Nott: *The Sonnets, Triumphs and other poems of Petrarch*, trans. "various hands," London, G. Bell and Sons, 1907 (there printed as Sonnet 75 of the sequence "To Laura in Death"). For Petrarch's use of the hyperbole of the world's destruction see *Rime* 268, 326, 338, 352; by Donne's time this had evidently become a convention of compliment, as in Donne's love-poem, "A Fever," and in a sonnet by Sannazaro pointed out by Mario Praz: see *A Garland for John Donne*, ed. Theodore Spencer (Cambridge: Harvard University Press, 1931), pp. 66-9.

[4] William Empson, *English Pastoral Poetry* (New York: W. W. Norton, 1938), p. 84.

> Wee are borne ruinous. . . .
> For that first marriage was our funerall:
> One women at one blow, then kill'd us all. . . .   (91-106)

The meditation opens with an echo of the general confession in the *Book
of Common Prayer*—"there is no health in us"—a theme developed by St.
Bernard and countless others:

> Engendered in sin, we engender sinners; born debtors, we give birth to
> debtors; corrupted, to the corrupt. . . . We are crippled souls from the
> moment when we enter into this world, and as long as we live there, and we
> shall still be so when we leave it; from the sole of our foot to the crown
> of our head there is no health in us.[5]

Continuing with a descant on traditional conceptions of the decay of man
from his first grandeur,[6] the meditation comes to a full climactic close as
(in St. Bernard's terminology) the indestructible Image of God within man
makes its traditional judgment of the ruined Likeness:

> Thus man, this worlds Vice-Emperour, in whom
> All faculties, all graces are at home . . .
> This man, so great, that all that is, is his,
> Oh what a trifle, and poore thing he is!   (161-70)

The first Meditation thus forms a unit in itself; it strikes one as having
no fundamental relation to the preceding account of the destruction of the
world by the girl's death.

    Then, clumsily and evasively, the poem comes back to the girl and to
the Petrarchan hyperbole of the world's death:

> If man were any thing, he's nothing now:
> Helpe, or at least some time to wast, allow
> T'his other wants, yet when he did depart
> With her whom we lament, hee lost his heart.   (171-4)

The Eulogy is being tacked on; and soon the difficulty of including this
hyperbole in the poem becomes embarrassingly obvious:

> shee that could drive
> The poysonous tincture, and the staine of *Eve,*

[5] St. Bernard, *Sermones de Diversis*, 42. 2; *Patrologiae cursus completus . . . Series
[latina]*, ed. Jacques Paul Migne (221 vols., Paris, 1844-65), clxxxiii. 662. I quote the
translation by Downes in Gilson's study of St. Bernard, p. 46 (see below n. 14).

[6] See St. Cyprian, *Liber ad Demetrianum,* secs. 3, 4; *Patrologiae cursus completus,*
iv. 564-7. One finds here the germ of many of Donne's comments on the world's decay
throughout the *Anatomy*.

> Out of her thoughts, and deeds; and purifie
> All, by a true religious Alchymie;
> Shee, shee is dead; shee's dead: when thou knowest this,
> Thou knowest how poore a trifling thing man is.   (179-84)

But we have known it before, and not for these reasons; thus the section comes to a flat and forced conclusion. We pause, and begin the second section almost as if the Eulogy and Moral had never intervened:

> Then, as mankinde, so is the worlds whole frame
> Quite out of Joynt, almost created lame:
> For, before God had made up all the rest,
> Corruption entred, and deprav'd the best:
> It seis'd the Angels, and then first of all
> The world did in her cradle take a fall. . . .   (191-6)

This second Meditation includes the famous passage beginning "And new Philosophy calls all in doubt," where Donne sardonically turns the optimism of the scientists into proof of pessimism:

> And freely men confesse that this world's spent,
> When in the Planets, and the Firmament
> They seeke so many new; they see that this
> Is crumbled out again to his Atomies.   (209-12)

But this is not related to "the untimely death of Mistris Elizabeth Drury." The passage on the new philosophy is an integral part of a meditation on the effects of sin; the effects of the new philosophy represent the final stages in a long and universal sequence of decay.

The second Eulogy reveals an even further split in the poem. Instead of pursuing the explicitly religious imagery of the first Eulogy, Donne here attempts to secularize the compliments, at the same time using images traditionally associated with Mary:[7]

> She whom wise nature had invented then
> When she observ'd that every sort of men
> Did in their voyage in this worlds Sea stray,
> And needed a new compasse for their way;
> She that was best, and first originall

---

[7] Cf. Southwell's poem on the Virgin's Nativity: "Load-starre of all inclosed in worldly waves, / The car[d] and compasse that from ship-wracke saves." The imagery is based, of course, on the "Ave Maris stella" and the interpretation of the name Mary as meaning "Star of the Sea": cf. Puente, 1. 263: "Shee is the Starre of the sea, for that shee is the light, consolation, and guide of those, that sayle in the sea of this worlde, tossed with the greate waves, and tempestes of temptations. . . ."

Of all faire copies, and the generall
Steward to Fate; she whose rich eyes, and brest
Guilt the West Indies, and perfum'd the East. . . .   (223-30)

The traditional religious feelings which have thus far been growing in
the poem are here balked, particularly by the references to "wise nature"
and "Fate." The poem has broken apart, and the break is not mended
by the blurred imagery one finds in the following Moral and in the
transition to Section III (lines 237-50). Here Donne presents the imagery
of "this worlds generall sickenesse" with an imprecise and damaging
ambiguity. What is the "feaver," the "consuming wound?" Is it that
conventional one described in the Introduction as the result of the girl's
death? Or is it the infection of Original Sin? The vague and general
imagery tries to include both elements, but it will not do. The last words
of the transition—"ages darts"—tell us clearly that the third and fourth
Meditations, on loss of proportion and color, deal with the results of
sin, not with emotions related to the poem's alleged protagonist.

The remaining Eulogies and the Conclusion try desperately to maintain
something of the introductory hyperbole, but it cannot be done. The poem
does not justify the elaborate imagery with which Donne attempts to
transmute the girl into a symbol of virtue's power. The imagery seems
extravagant—even blasphemous—not because of what we know about
the circumstances of the poem's composition, but because the imagery is
not supported by the poem as a whole.

The very fact that the poem is rigidly divided into sections and subsections gives us another aspect of its failure. Nearly all the joints between
sections and subsections are marked by strong pauses or by clumsy transi-
tions; while the Morals are strained in an attempt to bring Meditation
and Eulogy into some sort of unity. The parts will not fuse into an
imaginative organism. One can omit all the rest of the poem and simply
read through the Meditations consecutively; the sequence is consistent
and, with a brief conclusion, would form a complete—and a rather good
—poem.

We should not leave the *Anatomy* without noticing in some detail the
richness with which Donne develops these strictly religious aspects of the
work. Let us look for a moment at the third Meditation, as complex a
passage as Donne ever wrote. It works by a fusion of two main ideas.
Astronomical observations seem to prove that the universe is decaying as
a result of sin, for it seems to have lost its spherical, circular nature, the
sign of immutable perfection. At the same time the passage mocks the
vanity and presumption of man in attempting to understand and control
God's mysterious universe. The irony of such attempts is that they only
reveal—in two ways—the corruption of all things. Nevertheless man
persists in the intellectual, Abelardian effort to comprehend the un-

knowable or inessential, persists in the *curiositas* which St. Bernard denounced as the father of pride.

Donne begins 251ff.):

> We thinke the heavens enjoy their Sphericall,
> Their round proportion embracing all.
> But yet their various and perplexed course,
> Observ'd in divers ages, doth enforce
> Men to finde out so many Eccentrique parts,
> Such divers downe-right lines, such overthwarts,
> As disproportion that pure forme:

"Perplexed" is the central word here. The course of the heavenly bodies is so involved, so tangled, that man cannot follow it and is "enforced" to discover, or to invent ("finde out"),[8] a fantastically complicated scheme of the universe which serves to "disproportion that pure forme," but never surely hits the truth of things. We may also take "perplexed" in another sense: the heavenly bodies themselves seemed to be confused about their course.

> It teares
> The Firmament in eight and forty sheires,
> And in these Constellations then arise
> New starres, and old doe vanish from our eyes:
> As though heav'n suffered earthquakes, peace or war,
> When new Towers rise, and old demolish't are.

"It," grammatically, seems to refer to the heavens' "perplexed course." But in this context "It" may also refer by implication to the science of Astronomy which invented the forty-eight constellations; thus, when man's "knowledge" has settled things by violence ("teares"), erratic heaven refuses to conform. Nevertheless, presumptuous men

> have impal'd within a Zodiake
> The free-borne Sun, and keepe twelve Signes awake
> To watch his steps; the Goat and Crab controule,
> And fright him backe, who else to either Pole
> (Did not these Tropiques fetter him) might runne:

The Goat and Crab are ugly symbols of sensuality, and will the Sun obey such commanders? Apparently so; yet the Sun is full of guile that may deceive us:

[8] See OED, "find," v., 2, 15; 4, 20. Charles Monroe Coffin gives an interesting discussion of this whole Meditation in a different context: *John Donne and the New Philosophy* (New York: Columbia University Press, 1937), pp. 181-2.

> For his course is not round; nor can the Sunne
> Perfit a Circle, or maintaine his way
> One inch direct; but where he rose to-day
> He comes no more, but with a couzening line,
> Steales by that point, and so is Serpentine:
> And seeming weary with his reeling thus,
> He meanes to sleepe, being now falne nearer us.

The sun is degenerate, having fallen nearer to the sphere of corruption
—serpentine in his winding and in his wiliness, and, like a drunken man,
reeling toward a "lethargy" like that which has overtaken earth.

> So, of the Starres which boast that they doe runne
> In Circle still, none ends where he begun.
> All their proportion's lame, it sinkes, it swels.
> For of Meridians, and Parallels,
> Man hath weav'd out a net, and this net throwne
> Upon the Heavens, and now they are his owne.
> Loth to goe up the hill, or labour thus
> To goe to heaven, we make heaven come to us.
> We spur, we reine the starres, and in their race
> They're diversly content t'obey our pace.

Here the complex feelings of the Meditation reach a climax. All man's
hubristic attempts have resulted only in a deceptive "mastery" of corruption. Man's claims to worldly power and knowledge mean only that he
refuses to undergo the spiritual discipline necessary for his salvation.

The remainder of this third Meditation is not of such sustained power,
and indeed goes to pieces in its last ten lines. A discussion of the earth's
solidity interrupts the theme of proportion, and a shift to abstract morality
at the close is too abrupt. The best of the poem is over.

The full title of Donne's *Second Anniversary* itself suggests the pos-
sibilities of a unity not achieved in the earlier poem: *Of the Progresse of
the Soule. Wherein, by occasion of the Religious death of Mistris Elizabeth Drury, the incommodities of the Soule in this life, and her exaltation
in the next, are contemplated.* Here, clearly, is an "occasion" to use
Mistress Drury as a symbol naturally integrated with the traditional
matter of religious meditation: a "Religious death" (not the "untimely
death" of the *Anatomy*'s title) is the ultimate aim in this life for all the
devout. The poem's structure indicates that Donne is indeed moving
throughout with the imaginative ease that marks the management of a
truly unified conception.

The *Progress* consists of an Introduction, only half as long as the Introduction to the preceding poem; a Conclusion, less than half as long; and
even sections which constitute the body of the work. These proportions,

in a poem over fifty lines longer, indicate an important shift in emphasis. The Introduction and Conclusion to the *Anatomy*, with their emphasis on hyperbolic praise of the dead girl, make up a quarter of that poem; whereas these portions make up only about an eighth of the *Progress*. Each section of the *Progress* is subdivided in a manner reminiscent of the *Anatomy*. The first section contains (1) a Meditation on contempt of the world and one's self; (2) a Eulogy of the girl as the pattern of Virtue; (3) a Moral, introduced by lines which recall the refrain of the preceding poem:

> Shee, shee is gone; she is gone; when thou knowest this,
> What fragmentary rubbidge this world is
> Thou knowest, and that it is not worth a thought;
> He honors it too much that thinkes it nought.

But, as the following outline shows, the "refrain" does not appear hereafter, and of the remaining sections, only the second concludes with a distinct Moral; in the rest the moral is absorbed into the Eulogy:

Introduction, 1-44.

Section I, 45-84.
1. Meditation, 45-64.
2. Eulogy, 65-80.
3. Refrain and Moral, 81-4

Section II, 85-156.
1. Meditation, 85-120.
2. Eulogy, 121-46.
3. Moral, 147-56.

Section III, 157-250.
1. Meditation, 157-219.
2. Eulogy, 220-50.

Section IV, 251-320.
1. Meditation, 251-300.
2. Eulogy, 301-20.

Section V, 321-82.
1. Meditation, 321-55.
2. Eulogy, 356-82.

Section VI, 383-470.
1. Meditation, 383-446.
2. Eulogy, 447-70.

Section VII, 471-510.
 1. Meditation, 471-96.
 2. Eulogy, 497-510.

Conclusion, 511-28.

This gradual modification of the strict mold which marked the sections of the *Anatomy* suggests a creative freedom that absorbs and transcends formal divisions. The first striking indication that this is true is found in the ease of the reader's movement from part to part. We are freed from the heavy pauses that marked the close of each section in the *Anatomy:* omission of the refrain and, above all, omission of the flat, prosy Morals, makes possible an easy transition from section to section; the only heavy pause occurs at the close of the long Moral in Section II. We are always aware that a new sequence is beginning: it is essential that we feel the form of the poem beneath us. But each new sequence, with the above exception, follows inevitably from the close of the preceding one, as at the close of the first section, where the words of the very brief Moral, "thought" and "thinkes," lead directly to the dominant command of the second Meditation: "Thinke then, my soule, that death is but a Groome . . . Thinke thee laid on thy death-bed . . . Thinke . . . Thinke . . . "; the traditional self-address of religious meditation.

The transition within each section from Meditation to Eulogy is even more fluent; we do not find here the sharp division of meaning which marked these two elements in the *Anatomy*. In the previous poem every Meditation was strictly a scourging of the world and of man, every Eulogy the picture of a lost hope. But in the *Progress* every Meditation, together with this scourging, includes the hope of salvation which is imaged in the Eulogy, and in every Meditation except the first, this hope, this upward look, is stressed in the latter part of the Meditation, with the result that the reader is carried easily into the realm where the symbol of perfect virtue now lives.

In Sections III and V the distinction between Meditation and Eulogy is even further modified, for the Meditation itself falls into two contrasting parts. In Section III we have first (157-78) a meditation on the loathsomeness of the body, which "could, beyond escape or helpe," infect the soul with Original Sin. But Donne does not dwell long on this; he lifts his eyes from these "ordures" to meditate, in a passage twice as long (179-219), his soul's flight to heaven after death—a flight that leads directly to the Eulogy. Likewise, in Section V, after meditating the corrupt company kept on earth (321-38), Donne lifts his eyes to meditate (339-55) the soul's "conversation" with the inhabitants of Heaven—a theme which leads naturally into the Eulogy of Heaven's new inhabitant.

Fundamentally, the union of Meditation with Eulogy is due to a difference in Donne's treatment of the Eulogies in this poem. Here he has avoided a clash between eulogy and religious meditation by giving up, except in the brief Introduction and first Eulogy, the Petrarchan hyperbole which in parts of the *Anatomy* attributed the decay of the world to the girl's death. This hyperbole, together with the single reminder of the refrain, appears to be brought in at the beginning of the *Progress* to link this poem with its predecessor, in line with Donne's original plan of writing a poem in the girl's memory every year for an indefinite period. The labored Introduction to the *Progress* is certainly a blemish on the poem; yet it may be said that the reminiscences of the *Anatomy* are functional: they suggest that the negative "anatomizing" of the other poem may be taken as a preparation for the positive spiritual progress to be imaged in the second poem. At any rate, Donne does not use this hyperbole in the six later Eulogies, nor in the brief Conclusion, of the second poem. Instead, he consistently attempts to transmute the girl into a symbol of virtue that may fitly represent the Image and Likeness of God in man, recognition of which is, according to St. Bernard, the chief end and aim of religious meditation.

Thus Juan de Avila's *Audi Filia* begins its section on self-knowledge with a chapter (57) summarizing the command to "know thyself" which St. Bernard found in the famous verse of his beloved *Canticle:* "Si ignoras te, O pulchra inter mulieres, egredere, et abi post greges sodalium tuorum. . . ." [9] If the soul, the intended Bride, does not know herself—that is, does not know whence she comes, where she is, and whither she is going —she will live forever in the "Land of Unlikeness," that land of sin and disorder in which man forgets that he was made in God's Image and Likeness, and thus lives in a state of exile where the Image is defaced and the Likeness lost. As Gilson explains, "Man is made to the image of God in his free-will, and he will never lose it; he was made to the likeness of God in respect of certain virtues, enabling him to choose well, and to do the good thing chosen; now these he has lost" by sin. But the central fact is that the Image—free will—is indestructible; and hence "to know ourselves is essentially," in St. Bernard's view, "to recognize that we are defaced images of God." [10] Take care, says St. Bernard, "now thou art sunk into the slime of the abyss, not to forget that thou art the image of God, and blush to have covered it over with an alien likeness. Remember thy nobility and take shame of such a defection. Forget not thy beauty, to be the more confounded at thy hideous aspect." [11]

In accordance with the twofold aim of meditation implied in the last

---

[9] This quotation from the *Canticle* (1.7) is given in the version cited by St. Bernard in his *Sermones in Cantica Canticorum,* 34. 1; *Patrologiae cursus completus,* clxxxiii. 959; it differs from the modern Vulgate reading.

[10] Etienne Gilson, *The Mystical Theology of Saint Bernard,* trans. A. H. C. Downes (New York: Sheed and Ward, 1940), pp. 225 (n. 45), 70.

[11] St. Bernard, *Sermones de Diversis,* 12. 2; *Patrologiae cursus completus,* clxxxiii. 571. I quote the translation by Downes in Gilson's study mentioned above, p. 71.

sentence, Donne's *Second Anniversary* presents seven Meditations which may be called, for the most part, a description of the "defaced image," the Land of Unlikeness; while the seven Eulogies, for the most part, create a symbol of the original Image and Likeness, the lost beauty and nobility that must not be forgotten. That is not to say that Donne gives up Petrarchan imagery; not at all—but this imagery is now attuned to the religious aims of the poem. The Eulogies are sometimes too ingenious; yet the excessive ingenuity remains a minor flaw: it does not destroy the poem's unity.

The fifth Eulogy is a good example:

> Shee, who being to her selfe a State, injoy'd
> All royalties which any State employ'd;
> For shee made warres, and triumph'd; reason still
> Did not o'rthrow, but rectifie her will:
> And she made peace, for no peace is like this,
> That beauty, and chastity together kisse:
> She did high justice, for she crucified
> Every first motion of rebellious pride:
> And she gave pardons, and was liberall,
> For, onely her selfe except, she pardon'd all. . . .   (359-68)

The hyperbole is here so tempered, so controlled, by interpretation in terms of the virtue essential to a restored Likeness, that the more extravagant images which follow become acceptably symbolic of the importance of such virtue in the world: it is the one thing needful:

> She coy'nd, in this, that her impressions gave
> To all our nations all the worth they have:
> She gave protections; the thoughts of her brest
> Satans rude Officers could ne'er arrest.
> As these prerogatives being met in one,
> Made her a soveraigne State; religion
> Made her a Church; and these two made her all.   (369-75)

Thus throughout the *Progress* Meditation and Eulogy combine to present its central theme: the true end of man.

Let us look now at the whole movement of the poem; we can then see that this central theme is clearly introduced at the beginning of the first Meditation, carried to a climax in the fourth and fifth sections, and resolved in the Eulogy of Section VI. There is no flagging of power in this poem: it is a true progress. After the labored Introduction, Donne strikes at once into the heart of his theme:

> These Hymnes, thy issue, may encrease so long
> As till Gods great *Venite* change the song. [end of Intro.]
> Thirst for that time, O my insatiate soule,
> And serve thy thirst, with Gods safe-sealing Bowle.
> Be thirstie still, and drinke still till thou goe
> To th' only Health, to be Hydroptique so. (43-8)

The "Bowle" is the Eucharist, a "seale of Grace," as Donne calls it in his sermons.[12] One thinks of the "Anima sitiens Deum" in St. Bernard—the Soul, the Bride, which thirsts for God, desiring a union of will between herself and God, that union which at last results in Perfect Likeness after death.[13] This imagery is then supported in Section II by the line, "And trust th' immaculate blood to wash thy score" (106); as well as by the lines of Section III (214-15) where Donne refers to death as the soul's "third birth," with the very significant parenthesis, "Creation gave her one, a second, grace." One needs to recall that at the close of the *Anatomy* Donne has said that he

> Will yearely celebrate thy second birth,
> That is, thy death; for though the soule of man
> Be got when man is made, 'tis borne but than
> When man doth die.

The omission of Grace may be said to indicate the fundamental flaw of the *First Anniversary:* it lacks the firm religious center of the *Progress*.

This promise of salvation is the positive aspect of the soul's progress; but, as Gilson says, "By this thirst for God we must further understand an absolute contempt for all that is not God." [14] This complementary negative aspect is consequently introduced immediately after the above lines on the Eucharist:

> Forget this rotten world; And unto thee
> Let thine owne times as an old storie bee.
> Be not concern'd; studie not why, nor when;
> Doe not so much as not beleeve a man. (49-52)

Donne is taking as his prime example of vanity that curiosity which forms the first downward step in St. Bernard's Twelve Degrees of Pride— curiosity, which occurs, St. Bernard tells us, "when a man allows his sight and other senses to stray after things which do not concern him."

---

[12] See Itrat Husain, *The Dogmatic and Mystical Theology of John Donne* (London: S.P.C.K., 1938), pp. 30-1.
[13] Gilson, *Saint Bernard*, pp. 111-12.
[14] *Idem*, p. 238. n. 161.

So since it [the soul] takes no heed to itself it is sent out of doors to feed the
kids. And as these are the types of sin, I may quite correctly give the title of
"kids" to the eyes and the ears, since as death comes into the world through
sin, so does sin enter the mind through these apertures. The curious man,
therefore, busies himself with feeding them, though he takes no trouble to
ascertain the state in which he has left himself. Yet if, O man, you look
carefully into yourself, it is indeed a wonder that you can ever look at
anything else.[15]

This theme of curiosity remains dormant until Section III of the poem,
where it emerges gradually from Donne's magnificent view of his own
soul's flight to Heaven after death. It is important to note that this is not,
strictly speaking, "the flight of Elizabeth Drury's soul to Heaven," as
most commentators describe it.[16] It is Donne's own soul which here is
made a symbol of release, not only from physical bondage, but also from
that mental bondage which is the deepest agony of the greatest souls:

>   she stayes not in the ayre,
> To looke what Meteors there themselves prepare;
> She carries no desire to know, nor sense,
> Whether th' ayres middle region be intense;
> For th' Element of fire, she doth not know,
> Whether she past by such a place or no;
> She baits not at the Moone, nor cares to trie
> Whether in that new world, men live, and die.
> *Venus* retards her not, to 'enquire, how shee
> Can, (being one starre) *Hesper*, and *Vesper* bee.   (189-98)

In the last two lines Donne is renouncing one of his own witty *Paradoxes
and Problems;* in the earlier part he is renouncing the astronomical
curiosity which had drawn his scorn in the greatest passage of the
Anatomy. Here, however, as Coffin has well shown (pp. 171, 185-92), there
is a much stronger emphasis on problems such as "fire" and the moon
which were being debated in Donne's own day. From all such vain con-
troversies the soul is now freed and

>   ere she can consider how she went,
> At once is at, and through the Firmament.   (205-6)

[15] St. Bernard, *The Twelve Degrees of Humility and Pride,* pp. 6, 55-6. See Gilson,
Saint Bernard, Appendix I, on the importance of *curiositas* in St. Bernard's thought,
where "kids" is shown to be another reference to the *Canticle,* 1. 7: "Si ignoras te. . . ."
[16] Charles Monroe Coffin has made some helpful comments on this passage in a letter
which he kindly allows me to quote: "in the imagined progress of his own soul, he has
implied the felicitous passage of hers. . . . There is, to me at least, a rather certain
ambiguity in the situation, as I think there should be, and the momentary assimilation
of the vision of his own progress into that which has "exalted" E. D. into heaven seems
appropriate and, I should say, inevitable."

It is not until Section IV that this theme reaches its full, explicit development. Turning here from the heavens, Donne scourges the search for physical understanding of earth and its creatures; yet, as before, the very flagellation suggests an almost indomitable curiosity, and shows a mind that has ranged through all the reaches of human learning:

> Wee see in Authors, too stiffe to recant,
> A hundred controversies of an Ant;
> And yet one watches, starves, freeses, and sweats,
> To know but Catechismes and Alphabets
> Of unconcerning things, matters of fact— (281-85)

matters which do not concern the true end of man, as implied in the following lines:

> When wilt thou shake off this Pedantery,
> Of being taught by sense, and Fantasie?
> Thou look'st through spectacles; small things seeme great
> Below; But up into the watch-towre get,
> And see all things despoyl'd of fallacies:[17]
> Thou shalt not peepe through lattices of eyes,
> Nor heare through Labyrinths of eares, nor learne
> By circuit, or collections to discerne.
> In heaven thou straight know'st all, concerning it,
> And what concernes it not, shalt straight forget. (291-300)

All wordly philosophy is vain, for essential truth, says Donne, cannot be learned through sense-impressions of external things, nor through that "Fantasie" which transmits sense-impressions to the intellect. Such philosophy is the way of pride; true knowledge comes only through humility, as Donne, echoing St. Bernard, declares in a significant passage of his *Essays*:

> It is then humility to study God, and a strange miraculous one; for it is an ascending humility, which the Divel, which emulates even Gods excellency in his goodnesse, and labours to be as ill, as he is good, hath corrupted in us by a pride, as much against reason; for he hath fill'd us with a descending pride, to forsake God, for the study and love of things worse then ourselves.
> (pp. 3-4)

True knowledge lies within and leads to virtue, the fourth Eulogy explains:

[17] Cf. Francisco de Osuna, p. 201: "Sion means 'a watchtower,' that is, the grace received by the heart during its recollection, whence much knowledge of God can be discerned."

> Shee who all libraries had throughly read
> At home in her owne thoughts, and practised
> So much good as would make as many more:
> Shee whose example they must all implore,
> Who would or doe, or thinke well . . .
> She who in th' art of knowing Heaven, was growne
> Here upon earth, to such perfection,
> That she hath, ever since to Heaven she came,
> (In a far fairer print) but read the same. . . .   (303-14)

Religious virtue creates, or rather *is*, the restored Likeness which, according to St. Bernard, makes possible some knowledge of God; with St. Bernard, as Gilson says, "the resemblance of subject and object is the indispensable condition of any knowledge of the one by the other." [18] This is made plain in the sixth Eulogy, which provides the resolution of the whole poem by obliterating all traces of Petrarchan compliment and giving explicitly in the terms of St. Bernard a definition of the soul's perfection on earth. The sixth Meditation leads the way into this Eulogy by an abstract definition of "essential joy":

> Double on heaven thy thoughts on earth emploid;
> All will not serve; Only who have enjoy'd
> The sight of God, in fulnesse, can thinke it;
> For it is both the object and the wit.
> This is essential joy, where neither hee
> Can suffer diminution, nor wee.   (439-44)

God is both the object of knowledge and the means of knowing; though this full knowledge and joy can never be achieved on earth, we can, the Eulogy explains, come closest to it by striving to restore the Divine Likeness, as did she,

> Who kept by diligent devotion,
> Gods Image, in such reparation,
> Within her heart, that what decay was growne,
> Was her first Parents fault, and not her owne:
> Who being solicited to any act,
> Still heard God pleading his safe precontract;
> Who by a faithful confidence, was here
> Betroth'd to God, and now is married there . . .
> Who being here fil'd with grace, yet strove to bee,
> Both where more grace, and more capacitie
> At once is given. . . .   (455-67)

---

[18] Gilson, *Saint Bernard*, p. 148.

Compare the words of St. Bernard, speaking of that conformity between the soul's will and God's which leads to mystic ecstasy:

> It is that conformity which makes, as it were, a marriage between the soul and the Word, when, being already like unto Him by its nature, it endeavors to show itself like unto Him by its will, and loves Him as it is loved by Him. And if this love is perfected, the soul is wedded to the Word. What can be more full of happiness and joy than this conformity? what more to be desired than this love? which makes thee, O soul, no longer content with human guidance, to draw near with confidence thyself to the Word, to attach thyself with constancy to Him, to address Him with confidence, and consult Him upon all subjects, to become as receptive in thy intelligence, as fearless in thy desires. This is the contract of a marriage truly spiritual and sacred. And to say this is to say too little; it is more than a contract, it is a communion, an identification with the Beloved, in which the perfect correspondence of will makes of two, one spirit.[19]

The "faithful confidence" of Donne's poem is akin to the "confidence" (*fiducia*) of St. Bernard, an attribute of the soul which has passed beyond fear of divine punishment and stands on the threshold of mystic ecstasy.[20] This recognition of the end of man on earth and in Heaven is the fulfillment of the poem; the brief remainder is summary and epilogue.

In such a poem of religious devotion the sevenfold division of sections assumes a significance beyond that of the fivefold division of the *Anatomy*. Seven is the favorite number for dividing religious meditations: into those *semaines* and *septaines* that were characteristic of the "New Devotion" in the Low Countries;[21] or into the contrasting meditations for each day of the week that formed the basis of popular daily exercises throughout Europe. A glance at the summary of the latter exercises, as presented by Fray Luis,* will show that Donne is following closely their general tenor and development: from thoughts of sin, death, and the miseries of this life, to thought of happy "conversation" with the blessed in Heaven, of "essentiall joy" and "accidentall joyes."[22] But the sevenfold division of

[19] St. Bernard, *Sermons on the Song of Songs*, 83. 3; *Life and Works of Saint Bernard*, trans. Samuel J. Eales (London, 1889-96), iv. 508.

[20] Gilson, *Saint Bernard*, pp. 24, 113, 138n.

[21] See Pierre Debongnie, *Jean Mombaer de Bruxelles* (Louvain, 1927), pp. 168, 170-1, 184-7, 209-11; and H. Watrigant, "La Méditation Méthodique et l'École des Frères de la Vie Commune," *Revue d'Ascétique et de Mystique*, iii (1922), 134-55. See also Puente, i. 43f.

* [Given in chapter 1 of *The Poetry of Meditation*. Ed.]

[22] With the latter part of the *Second Anniversary* compare Loarte, *Exercise*, pp. 92-3:

Secondly, ponder what a comfort and sweete delight it shal-be, to be in that blessed societie of so many Angels, Saintes, Apostles, Martyrs, Confessors, Virgins, al of them being so bright and beautiful? what shal it be to see the sacred humanitie of Christ, and of his blessed mother? howe shal a man be ravished with the hearing of the sweet harmonie and melodious musicke that shal be there, and to enjoye so sweete a conversation everlastingly.

Thirdly consider howe yet besides these, ther shal be another glorye muche more

this poem suggests more than a relation to the practice of methodical meditation. As Donne says in his *Essays*, "Seven is ever used to express infinite." (p. 129) It is the mystic's traditional division of the soul's progress toward ecstasy and union with the Divine. St. Augustine thus divides the progress of the soul into seven stages,[23] and anyone familiar with mystical writings will realize how often the division has been used by later mystics, as in St. Teresa's *Interior Castle*. Thus Donne's *Progress* uses both mystical structure and mystical imagery to express a goal: the Infinite, the One.

This does not mean that Donne's *Progress* is, properly speaking, a mystical poem, even though he uses in his title the mystical term "contemplate," and in the poem cries, "Returne not, my Soule, from this extasie" (321). The next line after this—"And meditation of what thou shalt bee"—indicates that the ecstasy is metaphorical only. "Meditation" is always discursive, always works through the understanding; it is only the preparation for ascent to the truly mystical state now generally understood in the term "contemplation," which St. Bernard defines as "the soul's true unerring intuition," "the unhesitating apprehension of truth." [24] Donne's use of the word "contemplate" in the title of his *Progress* may indicate a higher spiritual aim than the "represent" of the *Anatomy*'s title, but his *Progress* remains a spiritual exercise of the purgative, ascetic life. It represents an attempt to achieve the state of conversion best described by Donne himself in a prayer at the close of his *Essays in Divinity*:

> Begin in us here in this life an angelicall purity, an angelicall chastity, an angelicall integrity to thy service, an Angelical acknowledgment that we alwaies stand in thy presence, and should direct al our actions to thy glory. Rebuke us not, O Lord, in thine anger, that we have not done so till now; but enable us now to begin that great work; and imprint in us an assurance that thou receivest us now graciously, as reconciled, though enemies; and fatherly, as children, though prodigals; and powerfully, as the God of cur salvation, though our own consciences testifie against us.

---

excellent, and surpassinge all humane capacitie: which shal be, to see God face to face, wherein consisteth our essential beatitude. For that al other thinges, what soever may be imagined, be but accidental glorie: which being so exceeding great and incomparable, what shal the essential be?

[23] See St. Augustine, *De Quantitate Animae*, with trans. by F. E. Tourscher (Philadelphia: Peter Reilly, 1933), chaps. 33-5.

[24] St. Bernard, *On Consideration*, trans. George Lewis (Oxford, 1908), p. 41.

New Bearings in Donne: "Air and Angels"

by A. J. Smith

Genius carries its perils, and the genius of Samuel Johnson has proved all but fatal to the true understanding of the poets he called metaphysical. Nothing could be more brilliant, in the circumstances, than that illustrious description of the yoking of heterogeneous things by violence together. Nothing, doubtless by reason of that very brilliance, has set more honest critics in the mire. For the truth is that the circumstances in which Johnson made his judgment were totally unpropitious. He was handling the intimate product of a tradition—almost of a culture—long dispensed with and more than a century out of mind, of preconceptions as different from his own as the qualitative Aristotelian physics differed from the quantitative Newtonian physics which ousted it. And he was unaware that anything had changed but a fashion of writing. He could not avoid the prime critical error of treating the offspring of an alien climate as though it were native to his own soil.

The idea of metaphysical poetry thus begotten had been fertile, as we all know—to our cost, dare one say? In Johnson's analysis lies more than the germ of the Donne-cabbalism of our time, not least that large part of it which derives from Mr. Eliot. Here take their root our familiar notions of radical imagery, baroque tension and doubt, unified sensibility, emotional apprehension of thought, and the like, their lineage apparent in their repetition of the Johnsonian error of violent confusion of periods. We hear of the identity of

> the essential metaphysical process of imagery, and of the process of modern imagery—the secret and invisible welding of the most contradictory elements, combined with the confusion of the senses, or rather fusion of the senses, which is the hallmark of modern suggestive writing.[1]

" New Bearings in Donne: 'Air and Angels.'" Contributed by A. J. Smith to *English*, vol. xiii (1960), published for the English Association by The Oxford University Press. Copyright © 1960 by the author. Reprinted by permission of the author.

[1] J. Isaacs, *Poetry* (London, 1951), p. 26.

It is not too much to say that the issue is bedevilled at the outset for such a critic by his assumption that the modern mystique of the image is generally valid. He quotes as a universal dogma Pound's famous definition in *Poetry*, March 1931: "An *Image* is that which presents an intellectual and emotional complex in an instant of time." [2] But it is presuming on fortune to expect that any theory so steeped in contemporary assumptions could truly describe the intentions, or the writings, of people to whom it would have been unintelligible, who used figures for ends, and produced them by means, alike remote from us. Little of what we mean today when we talk of images is relevant to the figurative writing of men trained in rhetoric. Nor may a fancied resemblance between philosophical perplexities or spiritual crises help us to write like Donne in any but a superficial way. The gulf that separates his age from ours will not close again.

For what, after all, is the ground of the metaphysical style in poetry? It is nothing more occult, or less remote, than the sixteenth century tradition of wit. And that tradition, in its turn, was moulded if not generated by the great Renaissance master-art of rhetoric, which characterized as *ingegnosa*—witty—both the ability to handle brilliantly the stock devices of argument and persuasion, and the subtle quality in the brilliantly handled device that made it persuasive. We still await a full-scale analysis of the part played by rhetoric in the formation of sixteenth century styles; but one may say, in brief, that as far as it concerns English poetry its effects were these. It imbued writers with the notion that their task, as poets, was the witty dressing-up, the vivifying or revivifying, of stock themes—good doctrine, classical or historical subjects, the Petrarchan situations. It inclined them to see all discourse as approximating to the oratorical; that is, as disposed to dispute, to prove, to persuade, to teach.[3] It supplied them with devices for the witty execution of these intentions: of proof, as induction or enthymeme, of argument, as analogy, of praise or dispraise, as the comparison in degree.

These devices or techniques, almost without exception, worked by the detailed comparison of specific properties, and depended upon the existence of a copious supply of commonplace material, serving as so much munition for general rhetorical ends. But the process of comparison of properties, as of the discovery of apt material, was only possible while the Aristotelian doctrine of the nature of matter prevailed and men still

[2] *Ibid.*, p. 34.

[3] The lineage of these ideas is apparent. "In particular, ancient poetry was strongly influenced by rhetoric . . . rhetorical rules of equal elaborateness and complexity were applied by the ancients to poetry also. Much poetry was designed to teach and persuade, and rhetoric clearly assisted in this task. . . . There was a persistent idea that thought was largely common property, that a number of ideas are natually inherent in any situation, and that it is not by abandoning or amending these ideas that the poet must show his skill . . . originality consisted in expressing them in new terms and in the best possible way." Michael Grant, *Literature* (London, 1954), p. 139.

regarded objects as bundles of attributes, analyzing and classifying them in their commonplace books by those attributes in the categories called the "places" of logic. Here, in fact, is the heart of the matter. For the fierce emphasis upon the witty comparison of things by like attributes, and indeed upon the analysis of attributes in general, produced not only such characteristic sixteenth century forms as the emblem, but its close kin, the so-called "metaphysical image." Alike, these throw-ups of the old logic are misleadingly termed "image," for precisely what they do not do is appeal to the visual imagination. Fossilized nuggets of commonplace material, they are to be "read," allegorywise, for meaningful juxtapositions of symbolic and stereotyped attributes. To come to them with more sophisticated views of imagery is to find them monstrous, as Johnson saw them, or indicative of strange psychological states, as more recent critics have proclaimed them.

Yet Donne's sixteenth century predecessors, one need not say, were in no direct sense rhetoricians. Though they used rhetorical devices in a conceited way, they observed in the main the traditional distinction between their art and that of the orator; and even under the ever-growing pressure of the need to excel in wit had not quite abandoned the assumption that poetic embellishment requires the grace of Court before the polemical hurly-burly of the Inns of Court. *The Faerie Queene* and the Court Masque present the serious face of Renaissance English poetics—wit exercised in the intricate task of feigning a protracted and graceful action that yields coherent moral meanings at several levels, that teaches and delights at once as was poetry's office. The sonnet-sequences of the 1590s, with their fantastic remanipulations of the hallowed Petrarchan properties, exemplify the reverse side. Both were modes of revivifying dry bones by wit. What was new about Donne's poetry—and it is new only in a limited sense—was that the poet found his means of witty presentation in a thorough-going application of argumentative techniques. Mock-disputation, defenses of the indefensible or of the egregiously paradoxical, had long been a favorite undergraduate diversion, conducted of course with all possible brilliance of sophistry. Donne simply brought into poetry for quite orthodox ends the manners of a game with which every such frequenter of the Inns of Court would have been intimately familiar. The typical scheme of his poems is the elaboration, the enlivening, of some stock theme by means of a virtuoso play of dialectical fireworks. This is certainly not to deny them serious point or autobiographical relevance. Only Donne chose, like all his contemporaries, to speak through the accepted situations and conversations; which is a way of saying that he treated poetry as a communal and not a private art.

But how thoroughly representative a product of its time that art was, as Donne practiced it! Here coincided at once the dominant literary prepossessions of the age: bravura dialectics; "Imitation," reduced by now to the witty rehandling of stock properties; allegorical or emblematic interpretations; extreme figurative ingenuity. It is not surprising that poems and techniques alike have remained enigmatic, however sensitively handled, to an era which sought their explanation in obscure states of mental tension or lost conditions of sensibility; whose most cherished critical canons, indeed, expressly repudiated the resort of extraneous circumstances. One of the paradoxes of Donne-olatry in an analytic age has been its surrender to the lure of the glittering fragments at the expense of the whole poem; an obliquity which also misfocuses the fragment. For Donne's authentic late Renaissance voice is not to be teased out of bracelets of bright hair, or great princes in prison, or the effects of New Philosophy, or things "extreme and scatt'ring bright"; not, at any rate, when these have suffered the distortion of losing their context. It is a voice we may hear when we are prepared to try to be the contemporary reader for whom Donne wrote—when, in other words, we equip ourselves to unravel the argument of the whole poem as it emerges from a highly intricate process of intellectual maneuvering in the alien manner of mock-rhetoric, which like as not turns on some long-forgotten stock position, situation, or theme. The problem is within the competence of scholarship and nimble wits.

The question of Donne's standing remains. The need for reappraisal was implicit in Miss Tuve's discovery of the relevance of rhetoric, and subsequent inquiry has hinted that disenchantment may be dramatic. It is possible, of course, to call in doubt the final critical value of such findings, as Professor Empson has questioned Miss Tuve: training in rhetoric did not inhibit the admission of the unconscious into poetry or limit the worth of writings to that of their surface intention. But what is quite beyond denial with these Renaissance writers is that it is not much use discussing values, most of all unconscious ones, until you know what they were driving at consciously; and with this critics of the Thirties school have never shown themselves much concerned. Ultimately, however it offends our pieties, we have to ask what "Air and Angels" "means." It is the minimum demand upon our critical premises that they should lead us to a consistent reading, or show us why the poet fails to afford one. Here as in the rest of his work, when we know what Donne thought he was doing we can get down to him in some confidence that we are not grappling with shadows; and it is high time we set ourselves seriously to discover that.

Air and Angels

Twice or thrice had I loved thee,
   Before I knew thy face or name;
   So in a voice, so in a shapelesse flame,
Angells affect us oft, and worship'd bee;
   Still when, to where thou wert, I came,
Some lovely glorious nothing I did see.

But since my soule, whose child love is,
Takes limmes of flesh, and else could nothing doe,
    More subtile then the parent is,
Love must not be, but take a body too,   10
    And therefore what thou wert, and who,
        I bid Love aske, and now
That it assume thy body, I allow,
And fixe it selfe in thy lip, eye, and brow.

Whilst thus to ballast love, I thought,   15
    And so more steddily to have gone,
    With wares which would sinke admiration,
I saw, I had loves pinnace overfraught,
    Ev'ry thy haire for love to worke upon
Is much too much, some fitter must be sought;   20
    For, nor in nothing, nor in things
Extreme, and scatt'ring bright, can love inhere;
    Then as an Angell, face, and wings
Of aire, not pure as it, yet pure doth weare,
    So thy love may be my loves spheare;   25
        Just such disparitie
As is twixt Aire and Angells puritie,
'Twixt womens love, and mens will ever bee.

The real source of difficulty in this poem is that Donne's first concern is wit, and the relatively slight point emerges almost incidentally
from a marvellously complex and consistent play of figure. But it opens
simply enough, with an exploitation—one of a number in Donne's love-
verse—of the stock Petrarchan excuse, and compliment, that all the
poet's past affairs were only an anticipation of the present one:

If ever any beauty I did see
Which I desired, and got 'twas but a dreame of thee.[4]

In the present piece the compliment is deftly turned to further complimentary effect with an analogy from angel-lore, which also quietly
motivates the whole ensuing play—evidence not only of brilliance of wit,
but of meticulous planning. A typically high-flown inference from the
initial conceit, that if the poet has loved his mistress before, in others,
she must have existed as a kind of bodiless Universal, closes the initial
section and prepares the next move. It is entirely characteristic of this
witty manner of writing, and of Donne's in particular, that every chance
is seized to stuff in extra effect—as here with the by-play of paradox,
"lovely glorious nothing."

[4] "The Good-morrow."

The development opens obliquely with a cunningly contrived analogy, particularly clever, rhetorically, in the way it is integrated with the point it supports. It becomes, in fact, a concealed but pointed mock-syllogism; or technically, "example," the form of reasoning rhetoricians assigned to the poet.[5] A soul cannot act without a body; but Love is a child of the soul; therefore, since the child's subtlety cannot exceed the parent's, Love must also seek a body before it can be effective. Now the move is easily completed. The poet has allowed Love to find its body, and his mistress has materialized for him as that child of his soul has fixed itself in her various admirable parts. Here again conceited reasoning and compliment go neatly together. But indeed, it is not the least of this poem's felicities that they develop so throughout.

The counter-movement initiated at line 15 sets up a dialectical tension, whose resolution will of course be the final effect of the piece. It is carried in an impeccably neat maritime figure. Seeking ballast in physical beauty to keep his love's light craft on a steady course, he has been all but submerged by the excess of it his mistress has provided. Love is overwhelmed in admiration, and hardly more satisfactorily lodged now than at first, when it lacked a vehicle. Accordingly "some fitter must be sought." Here one may remark how cleverly Donne is maintaining together the several levels, as it were, of his play—the simulacrum of consistent logical inquiry, with its impersonal probing of alternatives, and the slight complimentary love-plot on which the poem is threaded. The two intentions coincide, quite wonderfully, in such a phrase as "extreme and scatt'ring bright."

The resolution of the self-set problem is at once the crux of the poem and of our difficulty. It is presented in an analogy so exceedingly fine-spun that its distinctions at first appear meaningless; whose whole appeal, moreover, is to popular points that we cannot now hope to take spontaneously. But we know the intention. The analogy aims to show how the poet's love can still find a body although it can use neither the "nothings" he has previously loved, nor the too-great beauty of the form in which his mistress, the consummation of those old loves, now appears to him. And this, at least, it evidently does, for its conclusion is confidently stated however it is arrived at:

> So thy love may be my loves spheare;

[5] "So that as the logician uses for his means the most noble instrument, that is the Demonstration, or Demonstrative Syllogism, so the dialectician uses the Topical Syllogism, the sophist the Sophistical—that is the seeming and deceitful—the rhetorician the Enthymeme, and the poet the Example, which is less worthy than all the others." B. Varchi, *Lezioni* (Florence, 1590), p. 573. Wilson defines Example as "a manner of Argumentation, where one thyng is proved by an other, for the likeness, that is found to be in them both." *The Rule of Reason* (1551), H. vii[v].

Donne is saying that neither the philandering love of shadows nor the mere admiration of physical beauty is in keeping with the propriety of love; that the only proper vehicle for his love is her love. An unreturned love is no love, as he says elsewhere:

> It cannot bee
> Love, till I love her, that loves mee.[6]

He is, in short, demanding that she love him in return.

But the analogy which has ingeniously put that demand in correct metaphysical terms has a further relevance. Pointing a distinction between the purity of angels and of the air which they take to give them substance, its claim is that this parallels the defining distinction between men's and women's love. Its specific intention is thus the indication of the difference in degree of purity; and yet this is clearly declared to be little, for both are pure, though air is less pure than the angel which assumes it. But the poet has hinted that he is actually showing the difference between the particular loves in question, his and hers. Given this, the rest of the poem provides the meaning. It is simply that his love came first and compels her love by its ardor—he loves unprompted, but she loves only in return for love. And this is in the analogy also, for the angel wears the air, takes it up, and moulds it to his purpose, whereas the air is just passive, waiting to be used, though perfectly responsive to the user when he comes. Here, presumably, in this mere passivity or initial neutrality, lies woman's inferiority as a minion of love. The distinction between the purity of air and of angels is closely analogous to that between the love of a sex which will love only in return for love, though well enough then, and one which conceives love for a specific object and works to compel an answering love. Love's office is "indulgently to fit Actives to passives," [7] and though both sorts have their worth, the actives, working spontaneously, are the purer devotees.

The outcome is tenuous; though it may have seemed less so to Donne's audience. What we are likely to ask is whether Donne wrote his poem to set it out as a discovery; if, in fact, the value of the piece lies, as that of "The Ecstasy" has been said to lie, in the acuteness of its psychological insight, its contribution to the "metaphysic of love." It would be a pity to think so, for not only are the metaphysics, such as they are, evidently for show, in a brilliant simulacrum of analogical illustration or "proof," but the argument they elaborate was not new when Donne used it. The crucial distinction, like the matter of "The Ecstasy," was a debating issue of the Renaissance theorists of love, and had long come into the rhetorical market-place. Some fifty years before Donne, Sperone Speroni answered the question whether man's or woman's love is the

---

[6] "Love's Deity."   [7] "Love's Deity."

worthier by affirming "the condition of things" to be such that "the lover in loving his beloved, moves her to love him":

> Our love, in respect of that of women, as it is greater and more ardent so is it more quick to kindle: for which reason with justice we term them beloved and ourselves lovers. And the reason for this is that although Love may be present in a woman's heart, it cannot operate there directly; but returning to her from her lover in the manner of a victorious captain it achieves its effect with redoubled force.[8]

It is not, then, the novelty of its attitudes or insights that makes the poem worth while. They are stock—there is no direct enlargement of perception or addition to knowledge. But is the piece in any useful sense the expression of an emotion? It carries an obvious complimentary intention, and a much less obvious implication that the poet wishes his mistress to love him in return for his love. Yet these, far from being central impulses, are only pegs of plot on which the various plays are hung: they are likely to have generated less feeling than did the sheer pleasure of writing well. The question of autobiographical relevance is manifestly immaterial. We are offered here only the flimsy minimal element of the common love-situation; again a given, not an end. As for more occult sources of value, "metaphysical," or "radical," or "baroque" imagery, there seems no need to endow "Air and Angel" with them, however beguiling its rhetorical features.

Yet finally, however vulnerable the fashionable defenses, it would certainly be contrary to inner convictions to deny "Air and Angels" the name of poetry, and perhaps as fine poetry as anything Donne offers. It is, to say no more, superbly written. The clean precision and intermittent splendor of the diction; the subtle modulations of its rhythms and phrasing, ripe for musical setting; its controlled mastery of expression, so complete that the intricate stanza-pattern appears to reproduce the exact structure of the complex idea—there is a fineness, a pungent elegance about all this, that holds the imagination like good fugue. Nor is an age conscious of its own hysteria likely to undervalue Donne's adult detachment, the cool forensic sanity of his tone. But we have also the criterion which we were all along compelled to use in order to make sense of the poem: wit. And as the sixteenth century understood the term, "Air and Angels" is superbly witty, all the more so because of its tone and its stylistic felicity. Of course, it is open to us to find the unconscious here; as in some sense we may find it in any human expression. But it would be less devious to acknowledge that until we are ready to make case-book testimony of literature in general these are the only values that matter,

---

[8] "Dialogo di Amore," in *Opere* (Venice, 1740), i. 33.

all that can help us to understand or appreciate such poetry. There was a poetry of wit, as there has been a poetry of the passions, or of vision, or of the unconscious, or what you will; and to that poetry the assumptions of our own day tend to make frail guides.

Chronology of Important Dates

1572	Born in London
1576	John Donne (father) died
1584, 23 October	Matriculated Hart Hall, Oxford
1587-1591	At Cambridge (?) or abroad (?)
1591, by May	Law Student at Thavies' Inn
1592, 6 May	Admitted to Lincoln's Inn
1593	Henry Donne (only brother) died in prison, having been committed for sheltering a priest
1596, June	Sailed with Essex on the Cadiz Expedition
1597, August	Sailed on Azores Expedition (The Islands' Voyage)
1598	Secretary to Sir Thomas Egerton, the Lord Keeper
1601, December	Secretly married Anne More, niece of Egerton's wife
1602, February	Imprisoned, and dismissed from Egerton's service
1602, April	Released and marriage ratified
1602-06	Lived with Sir Francis Wooley, his wife's cousin, at Pyrford, Surrey
1606-11	Lived at Mitcham, with (later) a room in the Strand
1605-07	Assisted Thomas Morton in controversy with Catholics
1610	*Pseudo-Martyr*
1610, 17 April	Hon. M.A., Oxford
1611	*Conclave Ignati* and *Ignatius His Conclave*
1611	*An Anatomy of the World (The First Anniversary)*
1611, November-December 1612	Abroad with Sir Robert and Lady Drury
1612	*The Second Anniversary*, with reprint of *The First* . . .
1612-1621	Lived in house in Drury Lane
1615, 23 January	Ordained priest
1615, April	Doctor of Divinity, Cambridge
1616, October-February 1622	Reader in Divinity at Lincoln's Inn
1617, 15 August	Anne Donne (wife) died
1619, May-December 1620	Abroad with Doncaster on Embassy to Germany
1621, 19 November	Dean of St. Paul's: moved to Deanery
1623, Winter	Seriously ill: composed *Devotions* (published 1624)
1624, March	Appointed Vicar of St. Dunstan's in the West
1631, 31 March	Died at Deanery
1633	*Poems*
1640	*LXXX Sermons*, with first version of Walton's *Life of Donne* prefixed
[1646]	*Biathanatos*
1649	*Fifty Sermons*

Notes on the Editor and the Authors

HELEN GARDNER. Reader in Renaissance English Literature, Oxford. Editor of *The Divine Poems of John Donne* (Oxford, 1952) and *The Metaphysical Poets* (London, 1957); author of *The Art of T. S. Eliot* (London, 1949) and *The Business of Criticism* (Oxford, 1959).

CLEANTH BROOKS. Professor of English at Yale University. Author of *The Well Wrought Urn* (New York, 1947); (with R. P. Warren) *Understanding Poetry* (New York, 1938); *Modern Poetry and the Tradition* (Chapel Hill, 1939); and (with W. K. Wimsatt, Jr.) *Literary Criticism: A Short History* (New York, 1957).

J. E. V. CROFTS. Formerly Professor of English, Bristol University.

WILLIAM EMPSON. Poet, and Professor of English at Sheffield University. Author of *Seven Types of Ambiguity* (London, 1930); *Some Versions of Pastoral* (London, 1935); *The Structure of Complex Words* (London, 1951); and *Milton's God* (London, 1961).

SIR HERBERT GRIERSON (1866-1960). Professor of English, Aberdeen University 1894-1915; Regius Professor of Rhetoric and English Literature, Edinburgh University 1915-35. Editor of Donne's *Poems* (London, 1912) and of *Metaphysical Poetry, Donne to Butler* (Oxford, 1921); author of *The First Half of the Seventeenth Century* (London, 1906), *Cross Currents in English Literature of the XVIIth Century* (London, 1929), and numerous other works.

PIERRE LEGOUIS. Professor of English, Lyons University. Author of *Donne the Craftsman* (Paris, 1928) and *André Marvell, poète, puritain, patriote* (Paris, 1928). Editor and translator of *Donne: poèmes choisis* (Paris, 1955).

J. B. LEISHMAN. Senior Lecturer in English, Oxford. Author of *The Metaphysical Poets* (London, 1934), *The Monarch of Wit* (London, 1951), *Themes and Variations in Shakespeare's Sonnets* (London, 1961). Translator of Rilke, Hölderlin, and Horace.

C. S. LEWIS. Professor of Mediaeval and Renaissance Literature, Cambridge. Author of *The Allegory of Love* (Oxford, 1936), *A Preface to Paradise Lost* (Oxford, 1942), *English Literature in the Sixteenth Century* (Oxford, 1954), *Studies in Words* (Cambridge, 1959), and *An Experiment in Criticism* (Cambridge, 1961).

LOUIS L. MARTZ. Professor of English, Yale University. Author of *The Poetry of Meditation* (Yale University Press, 1954).

MARIO PRAZ. Professor of English Literature, Rome University. Author of *Secentismo e Marinismo in Inghilterra* (Florence, 1925); *Studies in Seventeenth-Century Imagery*, vol. i (London, 1939), vol. ii (London, 1948); *The Romantic Agony*, translated Davidson (2nd edition, Oxford, 1951); *The Hero in Eclipse*, translated Davidson (Oxford, 1956); *The Flaming Heart* (New York: Doubleday Anchor Books, 1958).

GEORGE SAINTSBURY (1845-1933). Regius Professor of Rhetoric and English Literature, Edinburgh University 1895-1915. Journalist and Scholar. Saintsbury's works are too numerous to list. Relevant are his histories of criticism, English prosody, and English prose rhythms and his edition of *Minor Caroline Poets*, 3 vols. (Oxford, 1905, 1906, and 1921).

EVELYN M. SIMPSON. Fellow of Newham College, Cambridge. Editor (with G. R. Potter) of *The Sermons of John Donne*, 10 vols. (University of California Press, 1953-62), and of *Essays in Divinity* (Oxford, 1952), and (with Percy Simpson) of *The Works of Ben Jonson* vols. vi-xi (Oxford, 1938-52). Author of *A Study of the Prose Works of John Donne* (2nd edition, revised, 1948).

A. J. SMITH. Lecturer in Renaissance Literature, University College of Swansea, University of Wales.

Selected Bibliography

EDITIONS

The Poems of John Donne, ed. H. J. C. Grierson, 2 vols. (London, 1912); *The Divine Poems of John Donne*, ed. Helen Gardner (Oxford, 1952). Both these are critical editions with introductions and commentaries.

John Donne: Complete Poetry and Selected Prose, ed. John Hayward (London: Nonesuch Press, 1929); *The Complete Poetry and Selected Prose of John Donne*, ed. Charles M. Coffin (New York: Random House Modern Library, 1952). Both these contain generous and judicious selections from the prose works.

The Sermons of John Donne, ed. C. R. Potter and Evelyn M. Simpson, 10 vols. (University of California Press, 1953-62).

Devotions upon Emergent Occasions, ed. John Sparrow (London, 1923).

Essays in Divinity, ed. Evelyn M. Simpson (Oxford, 1952).

BIOGRAPHY

Walton's *Life of Donne* in its final (1675) version is available in the World's Classics edition of Walton's *Lives* (Oxford, 1927). For a discussion of Walton's methods and his reliability as a biographer, see David Novarr, *The Making of Walton's Lives* (Cornell University Press, 1958). Gosse's *Life and Letters of John Donne*, 2 vols. (London, 1899), though highly unsatisfactory, has not yet been replaced by a full scholarly life. There is an excellent short life in Evelyn M. Simpson, *A Study of the Prose Works of John Donne* (2nd edition, Oxford, 1948). See also K. W. Gransden, *John Donne* (Longmans, "Men and Books," London, 1954), and Frank Kermode, *John Donne* (British Council, "Writers and their Work," London, 1957). Both these attempt a summary "life and works."

CRITICISM

In addition to works excerpted from in this volume and those mentioned in the introduction, the following may be consulted:

Clay Hunt, *Donne's Poetry, Essays in Literary Analysis* (Yale University Press, 1954) and Donaphan Louthan, *The Poetry of John Donne* (New York, 1951). Both these, particularly the latter, exemplify what Mr. Eliot has called the "lemon-squeezer" school of criticism and contain a number of analyses that seem more ingenious than convincing.

Leonard Unger, *Donne's Poetry and Modern Criticism* (Chicago, 1950) is the clearest and most consistent attempt to criticize and analyze the concept "metaphysical" poetry as it developed in the Twenties and Thirties and to discuss Donne's love-poetry in terms of "complexity of attitudes."

The most important recent study is Robert Ellrodt, *Les Poètes métaphysiques anglais*, 2 vols. (Paris, 1960).

Geoffrey Keynes, *Bibliography of John Donne* (3rd edition, Cambridge, 1958) contains a very full list of "Books and Articles."